SAFETY AND SURVIVAL AT SEA

By the same authors:

SURVIVAL AT SEA   (Centro Internazionale Radio-Medico)
EXPOSURE AT SEA   (Centro Internazionale Radio-Medico)

Safety
and
Survival
at
Sea

E. C. B. Lee, OBE, C.Eng., FRINA
and
Kenneth Lee, MBBS, LRCP, MRCS, DIH

A Giniger Book
published in association with
W. W. Norton & Company Inc. New York

Printed in Great Britain

DEDICATED TO THE MEMORY OF
GUIDO GUIDA
FRIEND OF SEAMEN
FOUNDER OF THE CENTRO INTERNAZIONALE
RADIO-MEDICO, ROME, 1935

Contents

Foreword

This book is an extension of the studies *Survival at Sea* and *Exposure at Sea*, which were written at the request of the late Professor Guido Guida and presented to the Studies Section of the International Radio Medical Centre, Rome, in 1965 and 1968. The help received from various sources in the preparation of those studies is again acknowledged with thanks.

Numerous colleagues and associates in the Ministry of Defence and other governmental Departments and Agencies, the professions and industry have been consulted in the present work and some of them have critically examined whole sections of the text, in particular Lieutenant Commander T. O. Bevir, G. P. Botha, Captain H. H. Brown, J. F. Coates, J. Cox, Lieutenant Commander P. M. Dullingham, Commander C. G. Forsberg, Professor Perry Gilbert, J. A. Grant, A. G. Hall, Miss Doris M. Hawkins, J. V. Houghton, D. P. Howell, A. Kennedy, Dr David Lewis, Captain J. H. Linggard, Commander W. B. Luard, W. Lupton, Captain N. R. McLeod, Captain C. W. Mitchell, F. T. Morris, S. C. Newman, W. Oldham, Professor J. E. Smith, Senior Captain N. E. M. Smith, P. H. Warne, and F. West. Valuable assistance has been received from the United States Coast Guard and from survivors, some of whom wish to remain anonymous. Copyright holders have been generous in granting permission for the reproduction of selected passages—a full list is given at the end of the book. Members of the Naval Lifesaving Committee and personnel who have tested equipment and participated in survival trials have all made a contribution to the work. D. Eager has given help with the illustrations. Kenneth Parker and Giles Wright have given welcome guidance in preparing the book for publication. We express our gratitude to all concerned.

My son Kenneth, who has collaborated in the work, is responsible for all the medical aspects.

The sea is capricious and the action to be taken in an emergency must depend on the prevailing circumstances, which can only be assessed on the spot. Nevertheless, there is much to be learnt from the past. We have attempted to draw conclusions from reports of disaster at sea and offer them for guidance when danger threatens.

Bath   *Eric Lee*
1970

1

Shipwreck

Shipwrecks still occur despite improvements in the design and construction of ships, in navigational aids, in the maintenance of high degrees of professional skills afloat and the increasing vigilance of international and governmental administrations, classification societies and maritime authorities. Capsizing, collision, explosion, fire, heavy weather and stranding all take their toll of ships and men each year. In time of war, when ships become the target for destruction by enemy forces, the losses are consequently greater.

The action taken when disaster occurs depends on the prevailing circumstances. There is the natural desire to save the ship and its cargo, but this is of no avail if the ship sinks quickly. There is also the desire to safeguard the lives of all the people on board, and this usually becomes more difficult the longer the order to abandon ship is deferred. Some ships remain afloat in whole or in part for a long time and in such cases it may be more hazardous to take to the boats if far from land than to remain on board and await rescue; this advice is summed up in the old saying, 'Never leave the ship until the ship leaves you'.

In this chapter are reported examples of shipwreck, their causes and effects and the activities they promote. The lessons learnt are brought out and advice is given on how to safeguard life on a wrecked ship and how to get safely away.

CAPSIZED SHIPS

Ships which turn upside down are said to capsize or 'turn turtle'. The capsizing is due to inadequate operational stability. A stability satisfactory for steady steaming in calm water may be quite inadequate in heavy weather, when ice accumulates on the upper works, or when damage and flooding occur. Even the inclination of a ship when in a sharp turn may be sufficient to cause cargo to shift and so start a capsize.

Masters are provided with information about the stability of their ships and aids are available for assessing the stability.

Supply Vessel Borie. *North Atlantic*

The *Borie*, 135 feet long, 199 gross tons, with cargo on deck (none below), was proceeding in clear weather, light wind and seas of 3 to 4 feet from the south. When changing course from 345° to 295° she took a list of 4° to 5°. The list increased dangerously within a minute or two, the deck cargo was heard to shift and the vessel capsized. 'The mate and a deckhand climbed on to the overturned hull and after a few minutes heard the engineer hammering on the hull from within. A short time later the master's body was seen floating near the bow of the vessel and was hauled aboard. Both the mate and deckhand attempted to resuscitate him but without success. Approximately 3½ hours later . . . the MV *Halliburton* 212 arrived on the scene and rescued the two men from the hull. . . . A diver was dispatched by helicopter and with the aid of self-contained breathing apparatus the engineer was rescued.'

The US Coast Guard considered that the principal cause of the disaster was the inadequate operational stability of the vessel in the loaded condition.

Fishing Trawler Arctic Viking. *North Sea. October*

Arctic Viking ran at full speed before a very heavy sea and lost stability when on the crest of a wave. The skipper, Philip Gardner: 'It was all over in less than a couple of minutes. Suddenly we were hit by a very big sea and the ship heeled over. Immediately we were hit by another sea and the ship was laid right over. We had no chance to save those who were below deck.' She remained with her starboard side uppermost and horizontal for about thirty seconds and then capsized. The starboard raft was released and the fourteen survivors from the crew managed to get into it. The *Arctic Viking* stayed afloat upside down for about two hours, then she pointed her bows in the air, stayed in that position for about eight minutes and then slid stern first under the surface. Five men lost their lives.

Tanker Toyo Maru. *Sea of Japan. March*

'Two crewmen were rescued from inside the overturned tanker *Toyo Maru* after drifting for thirty-three hours in the Sea of Japan. The tanker capsized in rough seas. Coastguard patrol boats found the floating hull and knocked on it. The men inside knocked back. A hole was cut in the hull and the two survivors were pulled out.'

Design Precautions

Ensure that the ship's stability characteristics are suitable for all anticipated conditions of loading and weather. Consult the Inter-Governmental Maritime Consultative Organization

(IMCO) documents 'Recommendation on Intact Stability of Fishing Vessels' or 'Recommendation on Intact Stability for Passenger and Cargo Ships under 100 metres in length' as appropriate. Incorporate a stabilization system if necessary, to provide a comfortable roll combined with high initial stability. Check calculated stability by an inclining test, and add permanent ballast if necessary.

Operating Precautions

Take special care with the stowage of cargo, and follow the IMCO 'Code of Safety Practice for Cargoes'. Pay particular attention to ore concentrates, which flow like a liquid when they are wet—fit strong subdivisions well secured at the ends, to reduce the 'free surface' effect.

After loading, correct by transfer of fuel or water any initial list and maintain zero list throughout the voyage. Secure all items liable to movement. Allow for any loss of metacentric height during the voyage.

Action

If bad weather threatens, close and secure all doors, hatches, air escapes, etc., opening to the weather. Close watertight doors and hatches in the ship.

Adjust course and speed to minimize the effects of the weather. Rig lifelines.

Improve stability by jettisoning any deck cargo; dump unwanted 'top weight'; lower derricks; empty fresh water and sanitary gravity tanks; remove ice accretion; reduce all liquid free surfaces; flood empty double-bottom tanks if this can be done quickly and without creating large free surfaces.

Survivors trapped in air pockets of capsized ships should strike the structure with something hard—the heel of a boot will do—listen for sounds of rescuers, and answer the signals.

Rescuers should have equipment for opening the ship's structure, breathing apparatus, lifelines and waterproof torches. Harness, heaving-line and rescue stretcher should be available as the casualty may be unable to help himself.

CAPSIZED BOATS AND CRAFT

A common cause of boats capsizing is the loss of stability due to the free surface effect of loose water in the boat. Other causes are unbalanced loading and rough weather.

(In sailing-boat work the word 'capsize' is sometimes used to denote the condition where wind or sea knocks the boat on to its beam ends with the mast horizontal or even below the horizontal; this is more properly described as a 'knock-down', and 'capsize' should be reserved to mean 'turn upside down'.)

Sailing boats have also been known to turn end-over-end, or somersault (an effect sometimes known as 'pitch-poling') in steep seas. High-speed planing boats at a steep angle are also liable to somersault due to the air pressure on the underside of the hull.

There are many reports of lifeboats capsizing when launched from ships at sea.

Lifeboat from MV Ross. South Atlantic. October
Captain John Dodds: 'Another huge wave capsized the boat, leaving the nine of us struggling in the water. We tried to right it but she turned over five times. Finally we put five men in the boat, to bail her out, while the rest of us hung on to the outside.'

Inflatable Boat L'Hérétique. Mediterranean. June
A tow was accepted from the fishing-boat in a high wind and rough sea. Dr Alain Bombard: 'Conditions were by no means good; with each wave the tow slackened and then tightened again with a violent twang. . . . The tow tightened just as we were on the crest of a wave, which then broke on us. In a flash *L'Hérétique* had turned turtle and we were in the water . . . gone for good were the camera and cine-camera, the radio set, the compass and the binoculars.'

Carley Float from the Yacht Reliance. English Channel. June
Ann Davison and her husband abandoned their wrecked yacht in the Portland Race and took to a Carley float. They were repeatedly thrown from the float owing to the action of the waves. Ann Davison: 'Then we were flung into the sea again, and this time we saw how it happened. Saw with slow-motion clarity how the float was sucked up under a great overhanging crest, and thrown over backwards in the boiling tumult as the wave broke. This time it was very hard to get back on the float. . . . We got right inside the float,

4

crouching on the wooden box with water up to our armpits. He shouted "LOOK OUT." Instinctively I leant forward, head down on the ring to meet what was coming. And we did not turn over. I found myself shouting: "That's it. That's it. Lean forward. Head down. That foxes them."'

Inflatable Raft from FV Helgi. *North Atlantic. September*
During a drift of forty-five miles in twenty-two hours, in wind force 12–13 and extremely heavy seas, a ten-man inflatable raft capsized five times and was righted by the occupants walking or crawling inside the canopy.

Lifeboat from MV Richmond Castle. *North Atlantic. August*
Chief Officer Walter Gibb: 'As the Captain's boat drew near several men jumped into her simultaneously from the same side of my boat with the result that the boat capsized and lay keel up for a period until we could right it again. We righted the boat by means of the keel grab rails. We got as many men as possible on to the bottom of the upturned boat and by putting our feet against the keel and by putting our full weight on the keel grab lines we eventually righted the boat.'

Lifeboat from SS Arletta. *North Atlantic. August*
Chief Officer W. M. Duncan: 'We remained on this upturned lifeboat for two and a half days, being unable to right it with only three men. The weather abated, so we rigged a line through the grab lines and got over to the lee side and waited a suitable chance: we eventually turned her over.'

Collapsible Lifeboat from the Titanic. *North Atlantic. April*
The *Titanic*'s collapsible lifeboat B was upside down. The water temperature was $-\frac{1}{2}$°C (31°F). 'By now Hurst and three or four others were crouching on the keel. Lightholler and Thayer scrambled aboard too. Bride was still under the boat, lying on his back, bumping his head against the seats. . . . Then came A. M. Barkworth. . . . Colonel Gracie arrived later. . . . When he drew alongside more than a dozen men were lying and kneeling on the bottom. No one offered a helping hand. With each new man, the collapsible sagged lower in the sea. . . . Next Assistant Cook John Collins swam up and managed to get on too. Then Bride dived out from underneath and scrambled on to the stern. By the time Steward Thomas Whiteley arrived, collapsible B wallowed under the weight of thirty men. As he tried to climb aboard, someone swatted him with an oar, but he made it anyhow. Fireman Harry Senior was beaten off by an oar, but he swam around to the other side and finally persuaded them to let him on too.'

5

Sailing Yacht Tzu Hang. *Southern Ocean. February*
Miles Smeeton reported of the 46-foot ketch: 'A wave passed under *Tzu Hang* and she slewed slightly. Beryl corrected her easily, and when she was down in the hollow she looked aft to check her alignment. Close behind her a great wall of water was towering above her, so wide that she couldn't see its flanks, so high and steep that she knew *Tzu Hang* could not ride over it. It didn't seem to be breaking as the other waves had broken, but water cascading down its front, like a waterfall. She thought, "I can't do anything. I'm absolutely straight." This was her last visual picture, so nearly truly her last, and it has remained with her. The next moment she seemed to be falling out of the cockpit, but she remembers nothing of this sensation. Then she found herself floating in the sea, unaware whether she had been underwater or not.'

The yacht had turned stern-over-bow, turned over on to beam ends, rolled away facing the sea and then fell off broadside to sea; she was dismasted in the process.

Power Boat. Lake Windermere. October
'Mr Robert Spalding, aged twenty-nine, escaped with bruises when his power boat somersaulted at 105 m.p.h. on Windermere. Mr Spalding, who was trying to break the world speed record for 1,650 c.c. craft, was hurled from his boat.'

Design Precautions

As a precaution against pooping, that is, a sea coming over the stern, each end of the boat is given ample buoyancy above the waterline, so that the stern lifts when a wave overtakes the boat and the bow does not dig in.

Open boats are fitted with buoyancy tanks or inherently buoyant material of sufficient amount to ensure safe flotation in the event of the boat being swamped or open to the sea. British Merchant ships' lifeboats have a reserve of buoyancy calculated on volume; it is in excess of one-tenth of the cubic capacity of the boat. British Naval practice is to calculate the reserve of buoyancy on weight; namely, when the fully equipped boat is open to the sea, a weight of not less than 10% of the weight of the boat is required to be added in order to put the gunwale under water. The buoyancy items are secured to ensure that they do not break away and float free in the event of the boat being damaged. They are also sited as high as possible in the boat so as to reduce the chance of capsize and to facilitate

6

the lights, shapes and sound signals which ships should carry,
the conduct to be followed under conditions of restricted
visibility,
the rules for steering and sailing,
the signals for requesting assistance when in distress;

and make recommendations on the use of radar information.
Some authorities have local rules, such as the Great Lakes
Rules, which have to be followed when navigating in their area.
Collisions between ships are usually the result of failing to
observe the regulations and to interpret accurately radar
information.

Many collisions occur in the head-on meeting or close-passing
situations in confined waters or crowded approaches. To obviate
such collisions the International Chamber of Shipping recom-
mends the use of one-way routing in the Straits of Dover and
other areas. Safety sea-lanes, consisting of a series of two-way
lanes with a safety buffer zone separating the inward and outward bound traffic, are used in the approaches to New York
harbour and other seaports.

The loss of SS *Titanic* in 1912, as a result of colliding with an
iceberg, is probably the greatest sea tragedy of all time. This
disaster led the maritime nations to meet together in London
in the winter of 1913–14 for the first International Conference
on the Safety of Life at Sea (SOLAS). The requirements for
British merchant ships were made more stringent by the Merchant Shipping Act 1914, and a North Atlantic Track Lane
Agreement and an International Ice Patrol were established.
Weather routing has now superseded Track Lanes. The ice
patrol is undertaken by the United States Coast Guard; it
commences in late February or early March, depending on
ice conditions, and continues to the end of June or thereabouts.
Timely information and advance warning to shipping is given
of the extent and limits of icebergs and sea ice in the North
Atlantic tracks in the vicinity of the Grand Banks. The observed
and forecast ice conditions are disseminated by means of US
Coast Guard Radio Argentia (NIK) and further disseminated
via US Naval Radio Station Washington (NSS) and Canadian
Forces Station Mill Cove (CFH). The International Ice Patrol
also has a search and rescue responsibility.

the lights, shapes and sound signals which ships should carry,
the conduct to be followed under conditions of restricted
visibility,
the rules for steering and sailing,
the signals for requesting assistance when in distress;

and make recommendations on the use of radar information.

Some authorities have local rules, such as the Great Lakes
Rules, which have to be followed when navigating in their area.

Collisions between ships are usually the result of failing to
observe the regulations and to interpret accurately radar
information.

Many collisions occur in the head-on meeting or close-passing
situations in confined waters or crowded approaches. To obviate
such collisions the International Chamber of Shipping recom-
mends the use of one-way routing in the Straits of Dover and
other areas. Safety sea-lanes, consisting of a series of two-way
lanes with a safety buffer zone separating the inward and outward bound traffic, are used in the approaches to New York
harbour and other seaports.

The loss of SS *Titanic* in 1912, as a result of colliding with an
iceberg, is probably the greatest sea tragedy of all time. This
disaster led the maritime nations to meet together in London
in the winter of 1913–14 for the first International Conference
on the Safety of Life at Sea (SOLAS). The requirements for
British merchant ships were made more stringent by the Merchant Shipping Act 1914, and a North Atlantic Track Lane
Agreement and an International Ice Patrol were established.
Weather routing has now superseded Track Lanes. The ice
patrol is undertaken by the United States Coast Guard; it
commences in late February or early March, depending on
ice conditions, and continues to the end of June or thereabouts.
Timely information and advance warning to shipping is given
of the extent and limits of icebergs and sea ice in the North
Atlantic tracks in the vicinity of the Grand Banks. The observed
and forecast ice conditions are disseminated by means of US
Coast Guard Radio Argentia (NIK) and further disseminated
via US Naval Radio Station Washington (NSS) and Canadian
Forces Station Mill Cove (CFH). The International Ice Patrol
also has a search and rescue responsibility.

righting should a capsize occur—the 20-foot dory *English Rose III*, which was rowed safely across the North Atlantic in 1966, was so fitted. Seating arrangements usually interfere with the siting of buoyancy to best advantage.

Bulkheads are fitted to limit the extent and effect of loose water, which must be bailed or pumped away as quickly as possible as its free surface effect on stability is very serious. Decking greatly improves the safety of the boat by reducing the possibility of swamping.

Grab lines at gunwales and handholds at keel and bilge rails are fitted for use in righting.

Action

Secure all essential equipment with lanyards so that none is lost in a capsize.

When launching a ship's boat, lead a slip painter [boat rope] forward and secure it so that when the boat is lowered into the water it is held under the falls. Unless it is fitted with a quick-release gear, do not put the boat in the water until all way has been taken off the ship. If unavoidable, tow by the painter (if towed by the falls it would be impossible to unhook) and use helm to sheer the boat off. Where there is a special risk of fire, as in tankers, use a wire painter. Have a knife available to cut the painter if necessary.

For seaboats fitted with Robinson's or similar disengaging gear, bear off hard from ship's side immediately the gear is released. Adjust the painter and stop the tiller with light cordage so that the boat will steer away from the ship's side when slipped.

To right a capsized boat, secure lines to the bilge rails, reeve them right round the boat, brace the feet against the side of the boat, and haul on the lines.

If the boat cannot be righted, remain with it and await rescue. Do not attempt to swim to a safer refuge unless the distance is short and easy and well within your competence.

COLLISION

Safe navigation in the presence of other ships is assured by following the International Regulations for Preventing Collisions at Sea. These regulations prescribe:

The German Hydrographic Institute provides ice reporting and forecasting services for the Baltic and the USSR for the North Siberian shipping route. Charts showing average monthly ice conditions for the Arctic and Antarctic regions are available from the UK Meteorological Office and the Hydrographic Department, Ministry of Defence (Navy) and from the US Naval Oceanographic Office.

Navigational warnings concerning derelicts and wrecks dangerous to shipping, lights which are temporarily extinguished, displacement of buoyage, beacons and other navigational aids, drifting mines, sea ice, firing practice and exercise areas, are broadcast by radio. Details are given in the *Admiralty List of Radio Signals*, Volume V, and in similar publications by other maritime countries.

Sir Joseph Rawlinson–Danube VIII–Black Deep. *Thames Estuary. September*

The sludge vessel *Sir Joseph Rawlinson* sank in about four minutes after collision with the tug *Danube VIII* and hopper barge *Black Deep* in fog on 28 September 1965. There were nineteen crew; ten were rescued and nine perished.

Second Officer Claude Knight: 'The tug collided with our port bow, glanced off, and then the hopper hit us near the engine room. The engine stopped and power failed.'

The Court of Inquiry found that 'very large floodable spaces aft, as were the whole undivided machinery spaces . . . [were] somewhat dangerous as designed . . .' and 'strongly recommend the Board of Trade . . . seriously and firmly to expedite at international level recommendations in order to avoid a similar disaster'.

Cedarville–Topdalsfjord. *Straits of Mackinac. May*

US Coast Guard: 'At approximately 09.45R on 7 May 1965 the American SS *Cedarville* and the Norwegian MV *Topdalsfjord* collided in fog in the Straits of Mackinac, Michigan. As a result the SS *Cedarville* sank at approximately 10.25R on the same day with the loss of seven lives thereon. In addition there are three more crew members still missing. Sixteen other crew members of SS *Cedarville* were injured, while nine were rescued uninjured. . . .

'The number 1 lifeboat was never released and sank with the *Cedarville*. The number 2 lifeboat with several crew members aboard was released from the falls as the *Cedarville* sank beneath it. Both liferafts floated free. The majority of the crew were thrown into the water (estimated temperature 36°F).

'The *Cedarville* sank as a direct result of the large ingress of water through the damaged portion of the hull sustained in the collision. Progressive flooding of the cargo holds and tunnel space could not be controlled due to the design of the vessel and the capability of bilge and ballast system.'

Andrea Doria–Stockholm. *North Atlantic. January*
The Italian liner *Andrea Doria* and the Swedish-American liner *Stockholm* were in collision near the Nantucket lightship at about 23.10 on 26 January 1956.

The bow of the *Stockholm* struck the starboard side of the *Andrea Doria* abreast the bridge. The bow penetrated about thirty feet at upper-deck level and seven feet at the level of the lowest deck. The *Stockholm* then slipped and bounced alongside the *Andrea Doria* as the latter ship went ahead.

The *Andrea Doria* took an immediate list of 18–19 degrees to starboard, continued listing until the side dipped under, and finally sank by the bows eleven hours after the collision.

The force of the collision temporarily jammed two of the lifeboats on the starboard side, but they were got free later. The boats on the port side were unusable because of the heavy list. The boats on the starboard side were swung outboard a long way when lowered, owing to the list, and could not be boarded in the normal way. Many of the crew, mostly waiters and stewards, got away in three of the lifeboats and these were only half full. Lifesaving capacity had therefore to be supplied by other ships.

Of the 1,706 persons on the *Andrea Doria* (572 crew and 1,134 passengers) 1,662 were rescued. Forty-three persons went down with the ship, some having been killed at the time of the collision. One child was fatally injured when thrown by her father into a lifeboat.

Damage to the bow of the *Stockholm* caused the anchor chains to fall out of the ship, become tangled and moor the ship to the sea bed; this caused the death of three seamen. A girl from the *Andrea Doria* was found on the *Stockholm* after it had disengaged.

Passenger Liner Titanic. *North Atlantic. April*
The British Atlantic liner *Titanic*, on her maiden voyage, collided with an iceberg at about 2340 on 14 April 1912 in latitude 41° 46′ N, longitude 50° 14′ W. She sank at 0220 the following day. The temperature of the water was $-\frac{1}{2}$°C (31°F). There were not sufficient boats for all who were aboard, the boat capacity being 1,178 and the total complement 2,207. The losses totalled 1,502.

The *Titanic* first listed to port and then tilted by the bow. 'As the tilt grew steeper the forward funnel toppled over. . . . The *Titanic* was now absolutely perpendicular. . . . The *Titanic* settled back slightly by the stern. . . . As she glided down, she seemed to pick up speed.'

Abadesa–Miraflores. *Westerschelde. February*
'The fire in the forecastle of the British tanker *Abadesa* followed a collision with the Panamanian tanker *Miraflores*, on 25 February 1963. . . . The crew of a Dutch tug said that they saw five people from the *Miraflores* burn to death in the blazing oil which spread over the river. Another seven or eight of the Panamanian's crew were reported missing.'

Design Precautions

A raked bow will minimize the effects of collision by tending to limit damage to structure above the waterline. A 'soft-bow' construction also reduces collision damage. Protruding bulbous bows should be of soft construction and well compartmented.

Fit a collision or fore-peak bulkhead within the foremost one-twentieth length of the ship on the waterline so as to restrict flooding in the event of an end-on collision; a second collision bulkhead is recommended for ships over one hundred metres long. Other watertight bulkheads should also be fitted, and so far as passenger ships are concerned international regulations on watertight subdivision have to be met.

Fit quick counterflooding arrangements with automatic cross-flooding pipes or remote valve control in ships where asymmetrical flooding is possible.

All pipes connecting to holes in the underwater shell must be kept accessible so as to permit speedy damage repair and be fitted with screw-down non-return valves.

Sliding watertight doors should be fitted in preference to hinged doors, as they can be operated against a rush of water and a list; moreover they have no clips to go awry.

Pumps serving a bilge main for removing water from a ship are required by the regulations issued by the International Convention on Safety of Life at Sea in 1960.

Carry collision mats, tarpaulins, timber, cement and other stores for blanking holes and supporting structure where there is a special risk of damage, as in wartime.

Ships intended for navigating in ice should have their hulls specially strengthened and their machinery parts increased in strength and protected against shock. Sea inlets and overboard discharge valves should be provided with means for keeping them free of ice, and special arrangements made for releasing deck water.

Nuclear ships must have special structural arrangements forming a collision barrier to prevent the leakage of radiation from the reactor compartment in the event of a collision. It is also a recommendation of SOLAS 1960 that a nuclear ship should remain afloat and have sufficient stability when not less than two adjacent main watertight compartments are flooded in all anticipated conditions of loading.

Operating Precautions

Hold a drill on operating watertight doors, valves, closing scuttles, scuppers, air escapes, etc., before leaving port and at weekly intervals during the voyage.

Adhere to the International Regulations for Preventing Collisions at Sea. As far as is practical give other shipping a wide berth. If it is necessary to 'give way' to another ship, ensure that any alteration of course is both early and substantial.

In restricted visibility:
Proceed at a safe speed having regard to existing circumstances and conditions. Maintain a particularly good lookout, bearing in mind that this means not only a good visual lookout for possible dangers but also means that all available navigational aids must also be used in a seamanlike way.

In ships fitted with radar, a continuous and efficient radar watch is to be maintained. The position, course and speed of all targets approaching the ship must be ascertained by plotting or other efficient means. Early and substantial action must be taken to avoid a 'close quarters' situation.

Sound the appropriate fog signal. In the event of a 'close quarters' situation developing, ring alarm bells; crew to emergency stations. Close watertight doors, etc. Get way off the ship, go astern if advisable.
Note: The Admiralty Court has expressed the opinion that coasters should consider visibility 'restricted' when the range of visibility is two miles or less. The distance would be greater for bigger or faster ships.

Action

If a collision cannot be avoided:
Reduce speed. Stop and go astern. Use anchor if appropriate. Manœuvre to lessen the impact. It is safer to make contact end-on or near the end of a ship, rather than amidships.

After Collision

Transmit radio message, giving name, position of ship and details. Render assistance to other ship if necessary, or possible. Ascertain extent of damage, sound tanks, start pumps if appropriate, list or trim vessel to bring damaged part out of water as far as possible and make temporary repairs.

Use collision mat on shell damage below the waterline, plug and shore from inside, and make a cement box. Counterflood to correct heel and trim if necessary, but avoid large free surfaces and undue reduction in metacentric height.

Take a roll call.

If it is decided to beach the vessel, select a firm, smooth, gently sloping beach free from strong currents. Beach just after high tide. Approach beach slowly and ground gradually. Flood tanks to bed the vessel down. Use ground tackle to secure the vessel's seaward end and, if necessary, take lines ashore to secure the landward end.

EXPLOSION

Explosions arise from heating a certain proportion of air and flammable vapour in a confined space, for example from:

introducing ignition in a boiler furnace where fuel or fuel vapour is present in the furnace, furnace brickwork or gas passages;

overheating and vaporization of lubricating oil and condensation into a mist in a crank-case, gear case or other enclosed and lubricated mechanism, forming an explosive mixture with the air, and ignition by a hot spot; this type of explosion can also occur when opening the crank-case, etc., after shut down;

overheating of gas given off during battery charging;

overheating or ignition of petrol fumes in the bilge or

closed engine or fuel-tank compartment of a motor boat;
overheating of ammunition or other dangerous goods;
enemy attack and sabotage;
flooding of boiler room, as when a ship sinks.

Explosions can cause serious injury and death, put machinery out of action and cause structural damage leading to shipwreck.

Underwater explosions as from depth-charges are felt over distances of two miles or more. They cause damage to boats and injury to people in the water, in particular to lungs, intestines, eardrums and sinuses.

Tanker Alva Cape. *New York Harbour. June*
The British tanker *Alva Cape*, carrying light virgin naphtha, and the American tanker SS *Texaco Massachusetts* collided in New York harbour on 19 June 1966. The *Alva Cape* was holed in Number 1 starboard tank, extensive fire damage was sustained and the vessel grounded. There was loss of life.

During salvaging operations on *Alva Cape* on 28 June 1966 an explosion occurred. Flame and smoke were emitted from the collision hole and there were two further explosions. Four persons were killed and seven others injured. The US Coast Guard investigator found: 'That the cause of the casualty was the ignition of an explosive mixture of naphtha vapours in Number 2 center tank. The probable cause of the ignition of the first explosion was static electricity generated by the carbon dioxide being discharged into Number 2 center tank. The force of the explosion ruptured the bulkhead between Number 2 center and Number 1 starboard tanks with resulting fire at the collision hole where an adequate supply of oxygen was available. That the subsequent explosions were caused by the heating of naphtha vapours in the adjacent cargo tanks. . . . That the recommended inerting procedures as set out in the National Fire Protection Association publication relating to control of gas hazards on vessels to be repaired were not adhered to in that a marine chemist did not approve or supervise this inerting procedure.'

Cargo Ship Kyung In. *Korea Strait. July*
'South Korean cargo vessel Number 15 *Kyung In*, 412 tons gross, exploded and sank. . . . One of the vessel's crew of fifteen died of his injuries, four were seriously injured and three are missing. . . . The vessel was carrying a cargo of ammonium nitrate and nitric acid.'

Fishing Vessel Jack Tar. *Gulf of Mexico. June*
'The 38-foot charter fishing vessel *Jack Tar* had just finished loading
140 gallons of petrol at . . . Pelican Island, Galveston . . . when
Captain Paul V. Marvel, the only person on board, pressed the
starter button and there was an explosion below deck. . . . The
Jack Tar subsequently burned and sank. The 400-foot loading arm
of the L-shaped pier on Pelican Island was destroyed after burning
for three hours. . . . Captain Marvel suffered burns on his arms,
hands and face.'

Survivors in Water. Doldrums (Atlantic). September
Nursing Sister Doris M. Hawkins, who had abandoned the torpedoed SS *Laconia*: 'Squadron Leader Wells swam towards me. At
that moment there was a loud explosion which I was later told must
have been the bursting of the submerged boilers; whatever the
cause, the explosion through the water was terrific. I felt a sickening
pain in my back, while Squadron Leader Wells, who had been
facing the explosion, seemed to curl up just as we reached his and
Lieutenant Tillie's raft. His condition gradually improved as the
night wore on; but he never lost his abdominal pain. My own back
had been injured, as revealed in an X-ray photograph many weeks
later.' Squadron Leader H. R. K. Wells died fourteen days later.

Survivors in Water. Mediterranean
'A few seconds after the vessel had disappeared there was a loud
underwater explosion in the vicinity, and a column of water was
thrown up in a kind of mushroom effect. Fifteen of the survivors who
were in the water at this time were taken to hospital at Malta
suffering from stomach injuries caused by the explosion, although
several of them were as much as one hundred yards away.'

Lifeboat from SS Kelso. *North Atlantic. August*
Captain A. Hinchcliff: 'About twenty minutes after taking to the
boat there was a terrific underwater explosion, so violent that it
cracked some of the planks in the boat, which started to leak badly.
. . . Although we were a mile away then the effect was terrific.'

MV Reina Del Pacifico. *Irish Sea. September*
The ship was on sea trials following reconditioning. 'Full-speed
trials were commenced at noon, and concluded at 1.40 p.m. The
ship continued at full speed. At about 4.30 p.m. over-heating was
observed in the No. 2 port outer cylinder. The fuel was cut off this
cylinder, and the engine speed began to fall. A few minutes later
fuel was cut off from the entire engine, which slowed to well below
trailing speed, and either stopped altogether or almost stopped. At,

15

or just before, the instant of stopping, starting air was applied in an attempt to prevent seizure. The engine turned for a few revolutions, and then the explosion took place (at 4.46). It spread to all four engines. The severity of the resultant damage was least at the point of origin, and increased to a maximum at the starboard after corner of the engine room. Fifty-seven crank-case doors were blown off, seven were partially blown off, fourteen were bulged outwards, and floorboards and other fittings were damaged. Subsequent examination revealed a partially seized piston and an overheated gudgeon pin bush on No. 2 port outer cylinder.' Twenty-eight men were killed and twenty-one injured.

Submarine Auriga. *Mediterranean. February*
'One man was badly hurt and six others suffered minor burns, cuts and superficial injury in an explosion in the submarine *Auriga*. . . . The accident occurred in the forward accommodation space as the submarine was charging her batteries. . . . The deck of the crew's forward living accommodation was blown up. Extensive damage was done to the space, which is 35 feet wide.'

Design Precautions

Minimize the risk of explosions in machinery spaces by the use of safety techniques, explosimeters or flammable-gas detectors, safety doors, explosion-relief flame-trap devices, crank-case oil-mist detectors, and an automatic spray system; lead oil-engine crank-case breathing pipes direct to atmosphere. Use instruments to monitor essential data, display readings in the machinery control room and on the Bridge, and supplement with visual and aural alarms.

Lead vent pipes from tanks containing flammable liquids well into the open air, distant from possible sources of ignition, and terminate with flame-proof gauzes.

Exclude electrical equipment from dangerous areas, or make it flameproof or intrinsically safe. Carry electric light and power cable in conduit or otherwise suitably protect. British practice on this subject is described in the *Regulations for the Electrical Equipment of Ships* published by the Institution of Electrical Engineers. This sets out, on the first page, the Statutory Requirements regarding electrical equipment of ships.

Meet the electrical installation requirements of the classification authority. Lloyd's Register of Shipping set out their code of practice in a book entitled *Extracts from the Rules for the*

Construction and Classification of Steel Ships, No. 6: Electrical Equipment and Electrical Propelling Machinery.

Certain classes of electrical equipment are certified by a Government service known as BASEEFA (British Approvals Service for Electrical Equipment in Flammable Atmospheres). The types of protection which can be approved in this way are as follows:

Flameproof: complying with BS 229 (similar to US 'explosion proof' equipment)
Intrinsically Safe: complying with BS 1259
Type N Lighting Fittings: complying with BS 4533
Increased Safety Equipment: complying with BASEEFA Certification Standard SFA 3008
Specially Protected Equipment: complying with BASEEFA Certification Standard SFA 3009

British practice is to designate approved equipment as BASEEFA certified, the former 'BUXTON' certificate now being restricted to mining equipment.

Regulations concerning the carriage of dangerous goods are laid down in the Inter-Governmental Maritime Dangerous Goods Code, Vols. 1 to 9, and so far as the UK is concerned in the Merchant Shipping (Dangerous Goods) Rules 1967 and the Merchant Shipping (Fire Appliances) Rules 1965, Part II. The Regulations and Rules govern the packing, marking and labelling, documentation and stowage of the goods and are particularly stringent for passenger ships. The ships are fitted with safety devices and procedures are laid down for eliminating the risk of explosion.

The procedure recommended for safe practice on tankers engaged in the carriage of petroleum and similar commodities is set out in the Tanker Safety Code published by the Chamber of Shipping of the United Kingdom. It provides for the display of notices concerning naked lights and entry to compartments; special fire-prevention arrangements including restriction on the use of the galley; prohibition of smoking in certain spaces; precautions during loading and discharging; restrictions on the use of aluminium paint and aluminium and light-alloy portable equipment; and avoidance of generating electrostatic charges.

In warships where there is a special risk of explosions above and below water, the use of brittle materials is avoided and the following features are incorporated:

Hull

Double bottom and extensive watertight subdivision; overhanging masses supported; portable fittings secured; magazines and ammunition routes as necessary, made flashtight; spraying and venting arrangements to magazines.

Machinery

Machinery feet mounted on rafts or on rigid/resilient mountings; earthing strips fitted; flexible pipes.

Electrical Equipment

Stiff shafts and high loading bearings for machines; special latching arrangements for switchgear; switchboards mounted so that flexing of adjacent structure does not crush them; control gear designed to withstand high accelerations and mounted on yielding straps.

Motor boats with closed engine or fuel compartments have at least one inlet vent extending from the open air to about mid-depth of the compartment, and at least one vent extending from the bottom of the compartment to the open air. Both the inlet and the outlet vents have a cowl or equivalent fitting at the upper end. The filler cap to fuel tank is on the open deck, proud of the deck and clear of openings into the hull; it is marked 'Petrol only' or 'Diesel only' as appropriate. Fuel tanks in metal boats should not be of plastic material. Metal tanks in wood and GRP boats are permanently earthed to the engine. All boats fitted with W/T have their stays earthed to the hull.

Operating Precautions

Maintain safety devices in good order and check safety procedure at frequent intervals.

Station a watchkeeper at the end of an engine and not at the side.

When lighting, relighting or shutting down a boiler fired with a residual fuel (e.g. FFO), sight that the furnace floor is free of fuel and purge the furnace and gas passages with air for at least five minutes. Where distillate fuel (e.g. Dieso) is used, purge throughout the sighting period and provide continuous air flow through furnace and gas passages from purging to ignition. Shut off fuel automatically if all flame goes out; this is monitored by flame detectors.

In all dangerous spaces remove any accumulation of gases by extractor fan. 'Gas free' before undertaking any work in the space. Eliminate all means of ignition and keep the compartment ventilated. Obtain permission from the responsible officer before entering the compartment and have a responsible person in constant attendance outside the compartment. Wear a lifeline and breathing apparatus or have them immediately available. Use only portable tools (pneumatic, not electric) and lamps approved for the purpose. Pass the tools in a canvas bag. Use wooden or suitable plastic utensils, not metal ones, for removing debris.

When stowing dangerous goods comply strictly with the rules.

Do not stow explosives or oxidizing substances like ammonium nitrate and sodium chlorate in a compartment fitted with steam smothering arrangements unless the steam pipes have been blanked off.

Do not, when in the presence of volatile fuels or electrically initiated explosives, put on or remove clothing which generates an electrostatic charge—do it when in a safe place and carry out earthing procedure before entering a danger area, e.g. place one hand on exposed metal work of ship's structure and at the same time the other hand on the exposed metal work of the explosive item.

Do not open hot crank-case or inspection doors until the specified time after shut-down.

Do not, when working in a dangerous space, make sparks as by dropping a steel tool on to the structure, or striking the structure with steel-protected footwear.

Do not use a tank-cleaning method which creates a dangerous gas mixture. Take precautions, such as almost filling the tank with water, skimming off the oil and emptying the tank, before starting to clean it.

Do not use metal plates on tank-cleaning apertures. Use reinforced plastic plates (e.g. Crow Brand Tufnol) because of their anti-spark and anti-corrosion properties.

Tankers fly flag 'B' of the International Signal Code during the transfer of bulk petroleum cargo.

When refuelling petrol tank of a motor boat, wet the hands before holding the petrol hose and nozzle, make mechanical contact between the nozzle and the metal round the filling hole. No one should embark or disembark during refuelling.

Action

In the event of a significant rise in temperature in the crankcase, etc., shut down the element and correct. Keep heat away from explosive materials, cool by spraying the structure in way, use water spray in magazines or, if necessary, flood.

When there is no chance of avoiding a serious explosion transmit distress signal, scuttle the ship, abandon and move well clear to a distance of one mile or more.

FIRE

Fires occur at sea from a number of causes, a common one being carelessness in accommodation spaces.

Burning Ship SS City of Guildford. *Mediterranean. March*
The Purser, Mr E. R. Robinson: 'I told them to take off their lifejackets to enable them to swim faster through the flames. . . . I came across two soldiers, so pulling off their lifejackets I just pushed them overboard. Both these men managed to swim clear of the flames and were rescued. . . . The flames spread over the after part of the ship and the surrounding waters. There was no alternative, other than dive through the blazing water, so I dived from the poop, the impetus carrying me a considerable distance under water. I continued swimming under water until I thought my lungs would burst but on coming to the surface I realized that the effort had been worth while, as I was just on the outside of the blazing water, about seventy feet away from the ship.'

Exploding Ship SS Portsea. *Mediterranean. July*
Able Seaman H. W. T. Woods: 'I was blown high into the air. . . . I regained consciousness and found myself swimming under water. I continued to swim until I came to the surface, only to find myself in the middle of a mass of burning oil with nothing to be seen of the ship but her two masts which were sticking up out of the water. I dived under the water again, and although I am not a good swimmer,

managed to keep going until I saw that I was clear of the burning oil which appeared as a dark shadow above me.'

Wartime Convoy. Mediterranean
Captain R. D. Macfarlane: 'The sea was one sheet of fire and as we were so close we had to steam through it. I put the helm hard-a-port and had to come down from where I was on monkey island to the bridge to save myself from being burned. It seemed as though we had been enveloped in flame and smoke for years, although it was only a matter of minutes, otherwise the ship could never had survived. The flames were leaping mast high—indeed, air pilots reported that at time they reached 2,000 feet. The heat was terrific. The air was becoming drier every minute, as though the oxygen was being sucked out of it, as in fact, it was. When we inspected the damage afterwards, we found that nearly all the paint on the ship's sides had been burnt away and the bottoms of the lifeboats reduced to charcoal.'

SS Lakonia. *North Atlantic. December*
The Greek cruise ship *Lakonia* caught fire on 23 December 1963 when near Madeira. 125 lives were lost.

The fire began in a deserted hairdresser's saloon.

The Greek Supreme Council on Maritime Accidents: 'Both during the firefighting endeavours and during the abandonment of the vessel the actions of the crew were uncoordinated, each one acting spasmodically and not on the basis of a pre-existing and well laid-out plan.' At the passengers' abandonment drill no instructions had been given to all the passengers on the manner of wearing and attaching lifejackets and the precautions to be taken when springing into the sea with a lifejacket on. 'This was the cause of the death of quite a number of them, who sprang into the sea from the upper decks at the last phase of the abandonment of the ship.' The provision master was at fault in breaking open the door of the hairdressers' saloon, and then not attempting to close it again 'be it even temporarily by means of a tarpaulin, blanket or some other means'. The fireproof doors were not completely closed. 'This also caused a draught feeding the Barbershop-hairdressers' saloon area (which could have been isolated), the main forward staircase acting as a funnel and contributing to the speedier spreading of the fire. Another result of this error was the reduction to ashes, within the first minutes of the outbreak of the fire, of four lifeboats.' No attempt was made to strip down flammable materials. Too many fire hydrants were opened at the same time, causing ineffective pressure. Spray nozzles, which should have been used in fighting such a smoky fire, were not used. 'Also, it does not seem that the firefighters ever attempted to approach the centre of the fire by crawling, so as not to be choked by the smoke, although, as testified, there was no smoke up to a height of about 50 centimetres from the floor.'

The loss of the vessel and the death of the passengers and crew was reported to be due to the gross negligence of the Master and seven other officers.

SS Yarmouth Castle. *North Atlantic. November*
'At or about 0045 (EST), 13th November 1965, the Panamanian [cruise ship] SS *Yarmouth Castle* (with 376 passengers and 176 crew) was *en route* Miami, Florida to Nassau, Bahamas. A fire was discovered in the forward staircase area, which rapidly spread and enveloped the amidship passenger section and the bridge area. The vessel subsequently capsized and sank at 0603 the same morning. . . . As a result eighty-five passengers and two crew are missing (presumed dead) and three passengers are known dead.

'Survivors said that there had been no fire drill, that they were short of lifejackets, that fire alarms and sprinklers did not function, that lifeboats stuck in their davits, and hoses were not used. But the crew, led by Captain Byron Boulslinas, were praised by several passengers. Officers and men, they said, implored passengers to keep calm, gave up their own lifejackets and warned frightened people not to jump into the sea in case of sharks. One survivor said that some lifeboats jammed because the ropes had been painted. Rescue ships found one lifeboat capsized in the water near the debris left by the sinking ship.'

The United States Coast Guard Marine Board of Investigation found that 'the source of the ignition . . . could be attributed to any one or a combination of the following—malfunctioning of lighting circuit in room 610, sparks entering room 610 through the natural ventilation ducts during blowing of boiler tubes, acts of persons entering room 610. . . .' There was 'inadequate control of the security patrol . . . failure of early use of the general alarm or the public address system and failure of windows and shutters on outside staterooms to be maintained in a condition so that they could be easily opened . . . the general alarm did not ring during the casualty . . . lack of pressure on fire hydrants forward. . . . Master and ship's officers failed to take firm and positive action. . . . A progressive list developed to port as the result of the accumulation of water on the several decks from the sprinkler system, open fire hydrants and probably sanitary lines damaged during progression of the fire. As this list progressed the open side ports became awash and, as the testimony indicated that there were no watertight doors other than the three doors in the machinery and boiler spaces closed, the sea flooded the vessel amplifying the list and the vessel rolled over and sank.'

Tanker. North Atlantic. August
'The first torpedo appeared to strike deep down, splitting the ship open and covering the decks with gasoline, while the second one set fire to the ship and within half a minute the ship was a blazing inferno from the bridge aft; the crew abaft the bridge had no hope of surviving. . . . I saw Number 2 forward lifeboat was undamaged and the Wireless Officer volunteered to release this boat. This man crawled on his hands and knees through the flames and released the falls, jumping into the boat as she fell upright into the water. Seven of us bundled into this boat which was still made fast to the ship by the forward painter. I was unable to release the painter but managed to swing the boat off from the ship. Actually it was lucky for me that the painter had jammed, as the ship still had way on her, on releasing the painter we should have drifted into the flames.'

Design Precautions

Avoid the use of combustible materials. Separate the accommodation spaces from the remainder of the ship by thermal and structural boundaries. Arrange for the detection, containment and extinction of any fire in the space of origin. Arrange for the containment and control of smoke. Prepare fire-control plans showing all necessary information for the guidance of ship's officers, and exhibit them permanently at prominent positions in the ship.

Protect the means of escape. Provide fire-resistant lifeboats in ships which are at high risk, e.g. oil tankers.

Fire Precaution and Prevention

The following are the more important precautions to be observed on board ship:

Acetylene Bottles
Keep the cylinder upright, with valve end uppermost. Keep the valve on the bottle closed when the torch is not in use. Keep the regulating valve clean and free from oil, grease and grit.

Burners
Do not light from a hot furnace wall.

c

Boat Engines
Do not use an open bucket and funnel, or a syphon, when refuelling. Use the approved safety-can equipped with a flexible hose spout only.

Cigarettes and Tobacco
Do not smoke in bed or leave a lighted cigarette unattended. Extinguish when finished with.

Cleaning Materials
Do not leave fuel oil, or other substances for cleaning burners, in open buckets.

Combustible Stores and Equipment
Do not stow against bulkheads, but allow a space so that water can be played on the structure.

Dock
Keep the firemain charged when in dock, or connect the firemain to the shore supply. Have a direct telephone link with the local Fire Station. Have someone on the bridge to receive a fire-alarm signal and to close watertight doors and fire doors.

Drill
Hold regular fire drills.

Electrical Work
Restrict to authorized and qualified personnel only.

Emergency Fire Pump
Use for regular wash-down services; deck personnel will thus become familiar with it; in a serious fire engine-room staff may not be able to get to the emergency fire pump.

Fire Alarms
Test at regular intervals and maintain in good order.

Fire Appliances
Maintain in good order; inspect, test, repair and recharge as appropriate.

Fire Patrol
Carry a fire extinguisher when on duty in hazardous spaces, e.g. car decks of ferries.

Galley
Keep clean, especially the sides of pans and the grease filters in the exhaust trunking. Check temperature safety arrangements for deep friers. Do not leave unattended when power or fuel is switched on.

Gas Bottles
Stow in a container with drain led overboard.

Gas Cooker (Propane or Butane)
Fit the cooker in a tray with a drain led overboard. Fit safety taps and carry a gas detector in the bilge. Do not use in an enclosed space. Do not use hose connexions or rubber piping.

Light Bulbs
Keep clean of dirt and grease.

Linoleum Deck Coverings
Lay in rectangles, clear of bulkheads and fittings.

Lockers
Inspect. Remove oily clothes and combustible material.

'No Smoking' Notices
Display in Paint Store and other hazardous spaces.

Oil
Keep out of bilges, off tank tops and floor plates. Attend to oil leaks and clean up oil spills immediately. Arrange a separate oily-bilge system.

Oxygen Bottles
Do not lubricate fittings on oxygen bottles with oil or grease.

Paper, Packing Material
Dispose as soon as stores are broken out.

Petrol-driven Craft
Carry an explosimeter. Keep bilges clean and well ventilated. Fit a flame-trap to carburettor. Cover the drip tray with gauze.

Radio Equipment
When the radio is switched on and is unattended, leave the door wide open (shut off self-contained air-conditioning unit) and inspect the compartment at intervals of not more than thirty minutes.

Rags, Cotton Waste
If clean, keep in covered bins. If soiled, oily or paint-soaked, keep in covered metal containers and empty them daily.

Sawdust
Sweep up and put into covered metal containers as soon as possible. Empty the containers daily.

Spontaneous Combustibles
Take special care with stowage of coal, copra, cotton, fish meal, kapok, seedcake, toe puff, etc. Keep free from oil and moisture. Take care that fuel and lubricating oils do not fall or splash on to hot surfaces.

Steam Smothering
Do *not* use in presence of explosives and other self-oxidizing materials which react dangerously with water.

Ventilation Trunks
Keep clean of lint and grease; maintain closure arrangements.

Wood Chips and Shavings
Sweep up and dispose at end of day's work.

Firefighting
Fire cannot exist without the presence of combustible material, heat and oxygen; firefighting is therefore the process of eliminating one or more of these three ingredients, by

removing combustible material or preventing more of it becoming ignited,
cooling of combustible material and the surrounding air to a temperature below ignition point,
excluding oxygen, by smothering the fire or shutting off the ventilation.

Training courses in fire-fighting are available.
The types of portable extinguisher, appliances and fixed systems for dealing with typical fires are as follows:

Boiler-room Oil Fire
Portable extinguisher—foam. Appliance or fixed system—spray nozzles, foam, steam smothering. Keep fan running to drive smoke up funnel. If the space is evacuated, close it down,

shut off fan or drench with steam or pour foam through foam inlet tubes.

Cold-weather Fires
Portable extinguisher—carbon tetrachloride.

Electrical Apparatus
Switch off current. Use extinguishers appropriate to the material on fire. If current cannot be switched off, use CO_2 or fresh-water spray on items of normal ship's voltage and CO_2 on radar, W/T and similar high-voltage equipment. Do *not* use salt water on an electrical fire.

Explosive Stores
Spray the compartment, flood if necessary. Cool the surroundings. Do *not* use steam smothering.

Flammable Liquids
Use foam hand extinguisher or system. Play the foam on vertical surfaces (*not* directly on to the surface of the burning liquid) for it to run down and cover the fire. Spray is effective if the whole area is reached.

Machinery-room Oil Fire
Portable extinguisher—foam. Appliance or fixed system—spray nozzles, foam, steam smothering. Shut off ventilation and close all openings.

Structural and General Fires
Portable extinguisher—gas/water. Appliance—jet/spray nozzle. Break down all smouldering solids and drench the pieces. Cool the surrounding structure and spaces and keep a watch for re-ignition. Shut off ventilation and close fire-resistant doors and shutters.

To pass through a smoke-filled area bend low or crawl as the carbon monoxide concentration is less at lower levels. If carbon dioxide has been used for extinguishing the fire, walk upright, for the concentration of CO_2 is greater near the deck. If the clothes are alight do not run further than necessary, but roll on the deck as soon as possible. Use a smoke mask if available.

27

Action by Discoverer

If the fire is a small one, shout for help, press the fire alarm-push if one is near, shut off ventilation and fight the fire with the appropriate type of portable fire-extinguisher or other means.

If the fire is out of hand and help is not readily available, close the door and go for help. Get word to the Bridge.

Do not attempt to rescue a person overcome by smoke or fumes without first raising the alarm and putting on breathing apparatus and lifeline.

Action by Bridge

Sound the Fire Alarm (continuous blast of the ship's whistle for a period of at least 10 seconds supplemented by the continuous ringing of the general alarm bells for not less than 10 seconds).

Use the appropriate fire-fighting technique. Shut off all mechanical ventilation near the fire; cut off natural ventilation unless fire-parties are present. Stop the ship, or manoeuvre so that the wind blows the fire overboard by the shortest route; go astern if necessary. Close fire-resistant doors near the fire.

Inform the engine room and request extra pressure on the fire main. If the fire is near the engine room, start the emergency pump.

If the radio officer is not on duty, call him to the radio room. If the fire is serious, transmit an emergency signal to alert other vessels and coastal stations. Follow with a distress signal if necessary. Report the ship's position. Clear and swing out the lifeboats ready for use.

If it is not possible to prevent a calamity, scuttle and abandon the ship: move well clear if there is a danger of an explosion.

STRANDING

Stranding is the commonest form of total loss of ship.

Information about the sea bed, reefs, coasts, etc., is given on British Admiralty charts and changes to the charts are published in *Admiralty Notices to Mariners*. Other publications aimed at the avoidance of stranding are the *Admiralty List of Lights*, *Admiralty List of Radio Signals*, *Admiralty Tide Tables* and the *Admiralty Sailing Directions*, which are also known as *Pilots*.

Publications dealing with special danger areas are NEMREDI (North Sea and Baltic) and CHINPAC (China Sea and Pacific). The Hydrographic authorities of other countries issue similar publications. Masters are obliged to report any damage or destruction of aids to navigation.

Cargo Ship Sinergasia. *Gulf of Bothnia. December*
The Greek ship *Sinergasia* ran aground in a snowstorm outside Holmund after engine breakdown on 18 December 1966. She broke in two. There were thirteen crew, some of whom attempted to swim ashore. All perished. It was thought that the lifeboats were iced up.

Cargo Ship Clan Keith. *Mediterranean. November*
The British cargo ship *Clan Keith* struck rocks off the Tunisian coast at about 1910 on 5 November 1961, broke in half and sank. Six men survived and sixty-two were lost.

Captain L. Pitts reported that with five others he launched a life-raft which seemed to be in perfect order. He sat in the raft near an entrance. 'The next thing I remember was a severe jolt and I was thrown out through the opening.' When he surfaced the liferaft had disappeared. He swam around and took off all his clothing, although there were thirty-foot waves, and he took off his life-jacket because he had more freedom of movement. He saw a red flare which lit up the lifeboat and liferaft and he swam to them. When he reached the raft the Third Officer said, 'It's no use coming on board, sir, we are sinking.' Captain Pitts then swam to the lifeboat and with the help of a ship's officer tried to pull the lifeboat towards the raft. 'It slowly disappeared from us and their voices died away. It was the last we ever saw of them.'

Design Precautions

Ships are usually designed with a stern trim on account of propeller immersion and overall performance. This trim lessens the effect of stranding.

A compartmented double bottom and appropriate pumping system are fitted to lessen the effect of flooding in the event of damage to the bottom of a ship. Ideally, the inner bottom should extend throughout the length of the ship between the fore-peak and after-peak bulkheads and across the ship to the turn of bilge.

In nuclear-propelled ships the nuclear containment vessel is kept clear of the double bottom so that in the event of bottom damage the containment vessel remains intact.

An echo sounder is fitted to give a continuous record of the depth of water and a special type is available which gives the depth at some distance ahead of the vessel.

Operating Precautions

Make a plan for the voyage, and ensure a sufficient supply of fuel to complete the voyage.

Obtain fixes of the ship's position at regular intervals by all known methods and pay due attention to weather forecasts. Keep the charts corrected; refer to Tide Tables and Sailing Directions. Do not steer too close to known hazards. Do not place undue reliance on radar; this has led to the stranding of many vessels in recent years.

Ensure that the pumping equipment is in good order.

Action

In the event of stranding stop the engines, sound the general alarm, close watertight doors and swing out the boats. Sound bilges and tanks to assess the amount of any damage.

Subsequent action depends on the nature of the bottom. If of sand or similar substance, short bursts of the engines at full-astern power may get the vessel off; failing this, work the engines ahead with the rudder hard over, then put the engines astern. Alternatively, flood the tanks to sink the vessel, thus making a hole, then pump out, and the vessel may float free.

If the bottom is of rock do not use the engines for fear of increasing the damage. Minimize the movement of the ship by taking on ballast and laying ground tackle.

Lighten the vessel by discharging ballast and fresh water, lowering boats and anchors, jettisoning cargo, etc.

Refloat by use of ground tackle (two bower anchors in tandem, heavy wire and purchase, use of winch), or by tug.

Try to stop the vessel swinging broadside to the beach or reef.

WEATHER CASUALTIES

Heavy weather and high seas may produce structural damage, resulting in flooding, and shift of cargo leading to instability. Lightning may cause fires. Ice accretion on superstructure, masts and rigging may cause a capsize.

Bad weather may cause men to be washed overboard from ships and boats, and pitched out of some types of inflatable liferaft.

Ship design has been directed to improvements in seakeeping qualities and in protection of personnel. Standards for the freeboard of ships and regular surveys to ensure that the standards are maintained are given in the International Load Line Convention 1966, implemented in the UK by the Merchant Shipping (Load Line) Rules 1968. The failure of ships' structure may arise from bad design, such as square corners to openings in highly stressed structure, unsuitable material or workmanship, especially welding. A computer is now available for fitting on shipboard, whereby safe loading arrangements are quickly determined.

Typhoon shelters formed by large breakwaters are provided for the protection of small craft where there is special risk, as at Hong Kong.

Warnings of gale, storm or hurricane, weather bulletins and forecast messages are broadcast in plain language; synoptic and analysis messages in a code drawn up by the World Meteorological Organization. The British Meteorological Office broadcasts synoptic weather reports for the North Atlantic from Portishead Radio Station every day. Special shipping forecasts are available from Coast Radio Stations. Details of these facilities are given in the *Admiralty List of Radio Signals*, Vol. III, details of fog warnings and ice reports are given in Vol. V. Other maritime countries have similar publications.

Ships fitted with radiofax equipment now produce their own up-to-date synoptic weather charts. Weather facsimile transmitting stations under the auspices of the World Meteorological Organization are established all over the world. The ship's equipment automatically receives and records the transmission. The radiofax equipment is also used by some shipping lines for the production of a daily newspaper.

Weather bulletins for shipping in UK coastal waters are broadcast by the British Broadcasting Corporation each day on 1,500 metres at 0202, 0640, 1155 (Sunday only), 1355 (Monday to Saturday) and 1757 hours BST. The bulletin at 0202 is also broadcast on VHF. The bulletins are originated by the

31

Meteorological Office; the words 'wind', 'force', 'millibar' and 'visibility' are omitted so as to economize on broadcast time.

Forecasts for coastal waters giving wind, weather and visibility are broadcast by BBC Radio 4 at the end of its programme each day, at about 2345 hours BST. The forecast is for the period up to 1800 hours on the following day. The BBC also broadcasts gale warnings on Radio 2 as soon as possible after receipt of the warning. Of special value to yachtsmen before setting out is the weather forecast which can be obtained by telephoning the local Meteorological Office; the number is given in the Post Office telephone directory.

Ocean Station Vessels, usually known as Ocean Weather Ships, are stationed in the North Atlantic. They supplement the weather data received from observers in ships and aircraft and by the automatic tracking of radiosonde meteorological balloons provide information about the upper air. The positions of Ocean Weather Stations are given in the *Admiralty List of Radio Signals*, Vol. II.

In addition to reporting meteorological data, the Ocean Station Vessels provide services for search and rescue, navigational aid (direction finding, radar and beacon) communications and oceanographic research. Some of the ships provide medical assistance and some accept AMVER [Automated Merchant Vessel Report] messages for retransmission to US Coast Guard, New York.

Weather routing has been long established in the North Atlantic. Precise weather-routing of ships under shoreside supervision is now available. The main object is to keep ships clear of high waves.

Britain provides a special ship from 1 December to 30 April for the support of her fishing fleet. She is stationed in waters north of Iceland and her primary function is to advise trawler skippers about weather conditions; she also carries a doctor. Other European countries provide similar facilities, including technical help with the repair of machinery and electronic equipment, and some carry spare parts for supply to fishing vessels.

Sailing Ship. Mediterranean

St Paul's ship was carried before the wind and managed to anchor close to shore. 'And when they had taken up the anchors, they committed themselves unto the sea, and loosed the rudder bands, and hoisted up the mainsail to the wind, and made toward shore. And falling into a place where two seas met, they ran the ship aground; and the forepart stuck fast, and remained unmoveable, but the hinder part was broken with the violence of the waves. And the soldiers' counsel was to kill the prisoners, lest any of them should swim out, and escape. But the centurion, willing to save Paul, kept them from their purpose; and commanded that they which could swim should cast themselves first into the sea, and get to land: And the rest, some on boards, and some on broken pieces of the ship. And so it came to pass, that they escaped all safe to land.'

Persian Fleet. Aegean Sea
Herodotus reported in the *Histories*, Book Six: 'From Thaos the fleet stood across to the mainland and proceeded along the coast to Acanthus, and from there attempted to double Athos; but before they were around this promontory, they were caught by a violent northerly gale, which proved too much for the ships to cope with. A great many of them were driven ashore on Athos and smashed up—indeed, report says that something like three hundred were wrecked, and over twenty thousand men lost their lives. The sea in the neighbourhood of Athos is full of man-eating monsters, so that those of the ships' companies who were not dashed to pieces on the rocks, were seized and devoured. Others unable to swim, were drowned; others, again, died of cold.'

Cargo Ship Lampsis. *North Atlantic. January*
The Greek cargo ship *Lampsis* (EC-2 Liberty type), loaded with manganese ore, was on passage from Casablanca, Morocco to Philadelphia, Pennsylvania.
    United States Coast Guard:
    'At 2019 (10th January 1966) RCC New York received word from CGC *Androscoggin* (34° 33' N 51° 15' W) that *Lampsis* in position 34° 34' N 51° 30' W reported she had a cracked main deck. . . . *Lampsis* reported taking on water. Weather on scene wind NW 31 knots, seas NW 25 ft, cloudy, visibility 6 miles. *Androscoggin* reported further that *Lampsis* had damaged boilers due to separation of the bulkhead between the fireroom and Number 3 hold and that the Master anticipated abandoning ship at daybreak, if not sooner.
    'At 2355 *Androscoggin* arrived on scene at *Lampsis*, position 34° 20' N 51° 05' W. On-scene weather: wind NNW 26 knots, seas NW 20–25 feet, cloudy, visibility 8 miles. *Androscoggin* reported difficulty in finding out status of *Lampsis* due to the language barrier.
    'At 0215 (11th January) . . . the Master of *Lampsis* reported that

33

his main deck was cracked from the sheer strake at the accommodation ladder over the fireroom to the coaming of Number 3 hatch. Number 3 hold was flooded, and they were unable to pump it due to strainers clogged with manganese ore. They had no portable pumps. The bulkhead between the fireroom and Number 3 hold was flexing due to the free surface of water in the hold. One boiler was still in operation. On-scene weather; wind NW 18 knots, seas NW 15–20 ft, cloudy, visibility 8 miles.

'At 1515 *Androscoggin* reported she had put a repair party aboard *Lampsis*. They reported about 8 feet of water in Number 3 hold; both boilers operational; a 12-foot crack extending from the port after corner of Number 3 hatch diagonally to the sheer strake; a crack extending intermittently from the starboard after corner of Number 3 hatch to the sheer strake; three loose rivets in the port hull strap; a continuous crack athwartships across the boat deck, and an intermittent crack athwartships across the main deck aft at Number 4 hatch. Weather: wind NNW 13 knots, seas NW 10 ft, cloudy, visibility 8 miles. . . . The repair party reported that they had repaired *Lampsis*'s main and emergency radios, but were unable to pump out Number 3 hold due to the clogging of strainers. A crack was found in the double bottom of Number 4 hold and all feed water was contaminated. The *Lampsis* reported insufficient fuel or feed water on board now to make Bermuda. The Master requested a tow from the tug *Albatross* and made all preparations to abandon ship. On-scene weather: wind NNW 5 knots, seas NW 3–4 ft, swell NW 8–10 ft, partly cloudy, visibility 9 miles.

'At 0617 (12th January) Master and crew of *Lampsis* abandoned ship. The entire crew (thirty persons) was rescued by *Androscoggin* without mishap. The Master reported that the water in the engine room had risen from the floor plates to 15 feet in 30 minutes, and that a crack appeared in the hull at Number 3 hatch from the main deck to below the waterline. On-scene weather: wind SW 10 knots, swell NW 6 ft, cloudy, visibility 6 miles. At noon *Lampsis* was still afloat on an even keel, but had lost freeboard aft and swells were breaking over the stern.

'At 0219 (13th January) *Androscoggin* lost radar contact with *Lampsis* at 6,500 yards. At 0522 she reported search for debris unsuccessful due to heavy rain squalls. At 1120 *Androscoggin* reported that a large oil slick and numerous empty oil drums had been sighted. The sinking of *Lampsis* was considered confirmed.'

Car Ferry Heraklion. *Aegean Sea. December*
The Greek car ferry *Heraklion*, on passage from Canea to Piraeus, met heavy seas and a gale and was lost with 241 lives on 8 December

1966. The chief mate, one of the 47 survivors, attributed the disaster to the heavy seas and to the shifting of cars and a huge refrigerated vehicle. He saw the seas surging into the vessel. 'The ship was listing badly. We could not even walk. We had no time to get into the lifeboats. We jumped into the sea.'

Another survivor, a Navy non-commissioned officer: 'It was a scene out of hell. People were screaming, women were crying, cars, tables, chairs were crashing about the decks.' The alarm bell was given too late and he alleged that no officers organized rescue work and that after embarkation there had been no drill for abandoning ship.

A third survivor, a seaman, said that when the ship began listing in rough seas he grabbed a lifejacket. But it had no strings and when he was swept overboard by a wave he lost it.

Car Ferry Skagerak. *North Sea. September*
The Norwegian car ferry *Skagerak* was on passage from Kristiansand to Hirthals in a strong gale on 7 September 1966 when she was struck on the car-loading port by a large wave and foundered.

Captain Anstein Dvergsnes, the Master: 'At 1100 I heard a peculiar "thunder" from the stern. We tried desperately to get the ship into the wind's eye. I was thinking about the railway wagons whose weight might capsize her.'

Mr Kenneth Thompson: 'We were having a cuppa when the most awful crash went up. . . . Within a matter of minutes the ship began to list. . . . My wife and I went to the starboard side where rubber rafts were being launched. . . . There were about seventeen in my raft, which was tossed about like a toy duck. People were pitched out and twice my wife had to swim back for it. Everybody was seasick.'

Trawler Poulbot. *North Atlantic. March*
'The skipper and two crew members of the 90-ft French trawler *Poulbot* died when they were swept overboard in high seas off the south coast of Ireland.'

Wooden Steam Ship Dumaru. *North Pacific. October*
The *Dumaru*, with a cargo of gasoline in drums and ammunition, ran into a severe tropical storm, was struck by lightning and caught fire. She was abandoned and soon afterwards there was an explosion which wrecked the ship.

Motor Boat. Venice Lagoon. September
A tornado swept along the lagoon at 2134 hours. A motor boat (*motoscafo*) with fifty passengers was lifted clear of the water,

35

overturned and sank with the loss of twenty-two lives. Adolfo Sottile: 'I was in there in the centre [after cabin] when it began to rain. Everyone hurried to close the windows to keep the water out. Many people who were in the bow cabin had run there in order to shelter from the rain and they gathered round the doorway. Women were crying out and were frightened. When the motor boat underwent the first list everyone was thrown to one side and I think that this is how they made the boat less stable. Two or three thuds, then the motor boat overturned. All were near the doorway leading to the pilot's cabin and it was difficult to get out. I filled my lungs with air and tried to reach the other exit, towards the poop. I was reaching it when I used up my strength. . . . Suddenly the motor boat sank by the bows and in the poop, where I was, a little air bubble gathered, I breathed in twice and regathered my strength. I seized the door, I went up and reached the rail. In those moments I collided with chairs and the cabin superstructure but at last I found myself outside and swam upwards. I took an eternity to reach the surface, but I managed it. While I looked around me I saw the shape of the motor boat turn and sink swiftly. There were high waves that tossed me about. I saw near me a woman who was floating, I grabbed her and reached the landing stage. Then someone helped me get on to it.'

Cargo Ship Ambassador. *North Atlantic. February*
The British freighter *Ambassador* was loaded at Philadelphia with 9,516 tons of wheat and corn in bulk. All hatches were tightly secured and all, except No. 3 hatch, were fitted with locking bars; a heavy gangway and turntable were placed on No. 3 hatch. On leaving Philadelphia for the UK on 12 February she had a meta-centric height of 2 ft 4 in. and a list to port of 2°; the list was due to the disposition of fuel and could have been corrected.

At first there was moderate following wind, on 16 February it backed and increased to force 8, on the 17th it was WNW and force 9; the engines were slowed down. One of the two port lifeboats was smashed. Water was found in No. 6 and No. 5 port fuel tanks and the cofferdam abaft No. 4 tank. A heavy sea caused the gangway on No. 3 hatch to shift and tore two of the three tarpaulins. The gangway was resecured and battens were nailed over the tarpaulins. The wind increased to force 10, the vessel rolled heavily, her port rail going under, and the list to port increased to 10°. She was hove-to at 1950.

At about 0100 on 18 February a heavy sea broke the gangway on No. 3 hatch, tore the tarpaulins and dislodged some of the hatch boards. Water entered the hatch, flowed to the 'tween deck, deep tank and after port of No. 2 hold. The hatch cover was replaced and a new tarpaulin fitted, but the tarpaulin was soon washed over to the starboard side and the port side hatch boards were lost. It was difficult to draw fuel from the settling tanks by gravity feed because of the increasing list, and the engines were stopped at 0330. The second port lifeboat was lost. The list increased to 20° and the starboard lifeboats could not be used. A radio telegraphy urgency message was sent and was followed by an SOS. The water rose in the engine room, steam was lost at 0800 and the engine room was abandoned at 0930. The decision to abandon ship was apparently taken during the afternoon and attempts at rescue were made on 18 and 19 February; these are reported in Chapter 6, page 208.

The ship was taken in tow at about 2200 on the 19th, the hawser parted at 0400 on the 21st and the ship was lost from the tug's radar screen at 1930.

The Court of Formal Investigation found that the principal cause of the sinking was the breaching in heavy weather, whilst the ship's list was increasing, of one of her hatches with portable covers which had not been fitted with locking bars.

The Court found that the water in No. 6 and No. 5 port fuel tanks and the cofferdam abaft No. 4 tank had gained access through the air pipes leading to the upper deck which had not been closed.

Design Precautions for Normal Weather

Eliminate flat surfaces of shell plating likely to suffer impact in bad weather. Eliminate stress concentrations; all openings in highly stressed members to be well rounded; use notch-tough steel.

Fit lightning-conductors to each mast of all wood, composite and steel ships having wooden masts or top-masts. Details of British practice are given in the IEE *Regulations for the Electrical Equipment of Ships* (section 22).

If pooping is likely to occur, fit freeing ports or scuttles of adequate area in a safe place (not near the waterline).

Maintain adequate height of bulwarks and guard-rails and provide fittings for rigging life-lines.

Provide a safe-load computer in ships subject to high longitudinal bending stresses, e.g. tankers, bulk carriers and general cargo vessels.

Design Precautions for Cold-weather Service

If ice accretion is likely to occur ensure that stability characteristics are adequate: e.g. fishing vessels should have the metacentric height, righting lever and righting lever curve as recommended by the Inter-Governmental Maritime Consultative Organization publication mentioned on page 3.

Inside the vessel

Precautions concerning hull structure and machinery are given on page 11. The following internal equipment should be fitted:

thermal insulation to weather boundaries of all accommodation and working spaces;

heaters in ventilation system, supplemented with space heaters;

thermal insulation to pipes carrying cold liquids and fresh-air trunks passing through accommodation spaces;

draught screens and air locks, particularly near doors opening to the weather;

valves in salt-water branch supply to exposed hydrants; valve and screwed-hose connexion to one main condenser outlet or its associated evaporator pump suction, for connecting to suction of fire and bilge pumps;

heaters under deck gratings, and near essential equipment (e.g. steering gear);

low-temperature CTC fire extinguishers.

Surfaces exposed to weather and openings therein

Restrict all openings forward of superstructure to an absolute minimum and site all other openings in sheltered positions; fit the following:

recessed access doors, with flexible watertight cover (e.g. PVC-coated nylon) to form an air lock; shallow baffle on foreside of doorway;

electrically heated fan panels, control units, wipers and heated spray nozzles to all selected windows;

steam-heated coils to air-escape and ventilation openings which are fitted with wire gauze; alternatively two gauzes in opposite directions to one another, or a gauze inside the hull where it can be serviced;

steam heating to all supply inlets exposed to spray;

watertight covers to all supply and exhaust openings exposed to weather;

adequate drains and scuppers to prevent water accumulating on deck.

Structure, equipment, etc. in exposed positions

Reduce top hamper to a minimum and streamline it; eliminate all projectives on which ice may form;

eliminate as much rigging as possible by fitting tubular bipod or tripod masts and pass exhaust gases up them, or if used for access aloft, fit internal ladders with integral hot-water supply;

any necessary rigging to have low ice-adhering properties, such as ICI Parafil, a twistless rope with smooth Alkathene sheath;

eliminate spurnwaters or make them removable; protect equipment with watertight flexible covers and provide heating where necessary;

site radar and other aerials as high and as far aft as possible to avoid contact with spray;

fit pneumatic de-icing device to radar scanner, masts, bridge front as considered necessary;

site fire hydrants in sheltered positions, insulate and provide with heating if necessary;

fit leak-offs in water-mains that are wholly or partly exposed to provide continuous movement of water;

pass steam through handrails and bind handrails with light insulating material;

fit switch sockets for portable electric heaters at essential positions, e.g. look-out and signalling positions;

prevent ingress of water on to equipment, pack with grease and cover with de-icing compound;

arrange steam-driven deck machinery for continuous steam heating; insulate exposed steam supply and drain pumping together;

fit flexible watertight covers over electrically driven machinery, use low-temperature greases and de-icing compound;

fit heating, if necessary, to hydraulic deck machinery; provide stowage for de-icing compound, liquid, hand and ice picks;

insulate foam-type and gas/water-type fire extinguishers

D

and foam compound stowage at hydrant position and fit with steam heating;

coil sirenette drains round horn and insulate the whole; arrange to by-pass steam trap when required; alternatively fit air-operated siren with integral heating arrangements and associated power supply;

heat exposed gravity tanks with external steam coil and insulate the whole;

heat ready-use tanks containing liquid with internal steam coil and insulate;

fit waterproof cover to all boats, extending to well below the gunwale; fit fabric sleeve to upper block, long enough to cover the lower block when boat is stowed close home; keep exposed length of falls as short as possible and protect associated cordage rack with a flexible cover;

fit drain cocks for draining engine circulating system completely, and to sump for draining hot lubricants immediately after running the engine; fit portable electric heater for starting the engine.

Operating Precautions

Watch the weather and study the meteorological reports. If possible, dodge any bad weather. If this is not possible, take the following precautions:

check that the hatches are securely battened down, and set up locking bars; unship, plug, or cover weather-deck ventilators where these are not fitted with automatic closing devices; fasten deadlights over port holes where vulnerable; press up or drain slack tanks where stability would be improved; check security of boats and derricks; check lashings, etc., of cargo; rig life-lines on exposed decks;

prepare for spreading oil: e.g., use a 20 ft-length of canvas hose, with one end sewed up, holes pierced at about 3 ft intervals, secured to leeside of forecastle head and stoppered at deck level. Fill with vegetable oil and allow to trickle down ship's side;

prepare for removing ice accretion;

adjust speed and course of ship to minimize the effects of bad weather.

Heaving-to

Heave to in rough seas, i.e. put the ship on the heading which enables her to ride the storm best. Select one of the following methods, depending on the characteristics and condition of the ship and the prevailing circumstances:

Heading the ship with wind and seas fine on the bow, keeping the engines slow ahead so as to maintain steerage way. With this method drifting to leeward and rolling are minimized, but pitching, panting, slamming and vibration may become so serious as to necessitate a different heading.

Lying-a-hull, with ship stopped and beam to wind and sea. This produces heavy rolling which may result in the cargo shifting. The rate of drift is likely to be high, so plenty of sea room is required.

Running with the sea on the quarter, with engines slow ahead so that the waves overtake the ship. Plenty of sea room to leeward is required. Steering is usually difficult and small ships may be in danger of being pooped or broaching to.

Disabled Ships

If the ship is disabled and in shallow water, secure anchor in hawse pipe and pay out the cable to trail on the sea bed. If in deep water lower one or two anchors until about three shackles of cable have been walked out. Alternatively, stream a sea-anchor, weighted if necessary, or a bight of mooring rope from the weather bow. Call for a tug if necessary. If the ship has a tendency to come stern up to wind, stream the sea anchor or mooring rope from the weather quarter. Spread some canvas, e.g. hatch covers, as a sail to best advantage. To prevent seas breaking on board, spread oil from the weather side. Fill a canvas bag with cotton waste or oakum soaked with oil, weight the bag, puncture it and trail it from the weather side; alternatively fill an old canvas hose with oil, seal the hose at both ends, puncture it and put it over the weather side, or flush oil from the water closets.

Damaged Ships

Head the ship so that the damaged part is sheltered, and repair the damage. If stability is lost: reduce 'free surfaces'; clear loose water from ship; jettison deck cargo; dump inessential 'top weight' items; lower derricks; slip anchor; empty fresh-water and sanitary gravity water tanks; flood double-bottom tanks, if this can be done quickly.

Navigating in Ice Waters

Keep watch against underwater spurs of ice. If collision is imminent, take it square on the stem. Use the weak spots in the icefield but take care to make all turns very slowly. Keep special watch when going astern and have good communications with the Bridge. If taking a run at the ice, do it square on to stem and before vessel comes to a stop put engines full astern.

Release from Ice

Various methods are available, depending on circumstances; the following have proved efficient:

Go full astern. If this fails, stop engines, put helm over and go full ahead. Put helm from side to side, with engines full ahead.

Strike ice at point of contact with crow bars.

Saw ice if practicable.

Move vessel transversely by transferring water ballast.

Move vessel longitudinally by alternately flooding and pumping fore and aft peak tanks.

Lay ice anchor, or attach warp to ice astern, lead to windlass and use windlass when engines are full astern.

Lay ice anchor abreast of strong high point and lead to windlass.

Lay ice anchor on each beam, heave on them alternately, with engines full astern.

Use explosive charges about 50 feet away from ship's structure. Commence with a small charge laid in a small hole in ice and increase charge as necessary.

Navigating under Icing Conditions

Operational precautions

Keep scuppers and drains clear. Apply grease or de-icing

compound as appropriate to exposed mechanisms, e.g. bottle-screw, freeing ports, anchor and cable gear. Pack all joints, crevices, etc., with grease and cover with de-icing compound. Lay coir matting on the deck where a good foothold is required. Wear cold-weather clothing. Keep weather watch and request weather reports and forecasts. Limit the time look-outs, etc., are exposed.

Action
Remove ice accretion manually by mallet, pick, etc. Play steam jet or heated salt water (e.g. by pumping from a cooling water discharge line and thence through the fire main at pressure). Play sea-water jet at maximum pressure. Use exhaust gas from gas turbines. Adjust course and speed to minimize amount of spray coming aboard and to eliminate asymmetrical accretion of ice. Run for shelter.

If the ship has to be abandoned, do it before the capsize takes place.

WAR CASUALTIES

Maritime countries suffer their greatest casualties at sea when at war.

Out of about 27,000 persons involved in shipwreck in the British Merchant Marine from 1940 to 1944, 32% died—26% in the water and 6% in lifeboats. During the period 1939–45 between 30,000 and 40,000 men in the British Navy (or 66% of the total Naval casualties for the war) probably lost their lives due to drowning; the number of men who died after reaching some temporary lodgement in the water was very large and next to drowning, cold from immersion and exposure were the most frequent causes of death.

War damage to ships frequently results in fuel oil spreading over the surface of the sea, and sometimes the oil catches on fire. Extensive damage causes ships to sink very quickly with greater likelihood of suction being created in the water.

The convoy system is used for merchant ships in wartime. Convoy escort vessels and aircraft protect the merchantmen, and convoy rescue ships, astern of the convoy, pick up survivors from ships which have been attacked and abandoned.

Troopship SS Lancastria. *English Channel. June*
Wing Commander Martin '. . . saw a soldier jump overboard from
the deck below. A steel helmet was on the man's head, its strap
beneath his chin. On hitting the sea the head jerked back, snapping
the neck like a brittle twig. The body turned face down and drifted
sluggishly away.'

Merchant Ship President Sergeant. *North Atlantic. November*
The ship was under enemy attack. 'A Chinaman from the *President
Sergeant* had dived from the ship's bridge and had landed head first
in the bottom of one of the lifeboats. He was suffering from a compound and depressed fracture of the skull, a broken wrist and
complete left-sided paralysis.'

Ship drifting. SS Penoliver. *North Atlantic. October*
Captain N. G. Naish: 'The ship sank in two minutes, stern first; I
had just time to run on deck, then walked over the ship's side into
the sea. When I came to the surface the ship had completely disappeared. A number of the crew jumped over the starboard (leeward) side and owing to the strong wind, rough sea and set of the
current, the ship drifted over them and they were drowned. Those
who jumped over the port (windward) side were saved.'

Ship drifting. SS Waroonga. *North Atlantic. April*
Captain C. C. Taylor: 'In spite of the heavy sea the boats on the
weather side were lowered more easily than I expected, although
the ship was drifting away the whole time. . . . The ship was drifting
on the boats on the leeside, and we had great difficulty in pushing
ourselves clear of the ship's side. We broke five oars in the attempt.'

Oil on Water. MV Tricula. *North Atlantic. August*
Chief Officer Mr K. J. Morris. 'I was again taken down by the
suction (of the sinking tanker) and on coming to the surface once
more saw a raft and managed to swim to it with great difficulty as
the sea was covered with fuel oil.' [The survivor was rescued twelve
hours later.] 'The doctor on board took us into his care and gave us
treatment, first of all removing the fuel oil with kerosene. Our eyes
were affected by the oil. The doctor gave us only forty-eight hours
to live, as we were so smothered in oil that the pores of our skin were
unable to breathe. However, we all recovered eventually.'

Ship Sinking. MV Gatinais. *English Channel. December*
Able Seaman F. W. Morris: 'About three minutes after the torpedo
struck, the ship turned over and sank. I took a deep dive to get clear
of the ship. . . . As I was swimming a large piece of wood hit me on
the back of the head, knocking me unconscious. When I came to I

found that a piece of rope had very fortunately become entangled round my arm, which lashed me to the piece of wood and this kept me afloat.'

Ship Sinking. North Sea. Winter
Commander [later Vice-Admiral Sir] Peter Gretton and six other men were on the foc's'le head arranging a tow. 'The bulkheads aft had given way, and the stern was slowly but surely sinking below the water, while, to our discomfiture, the bows rose higher and higher. There was nothing to do but jump for it. . . . Eventually, one brave man was persuaded to lead, and we all quickly followed him into the water. . . . I came off best because . . . I had discarded my lifejacket. . . . The others omitted to grasp the top of their cork jackets and were all given a sharp blow under the chin as they hit the icy water, one man being knocked right out.'

Suction. SS Ben Albanach. *Mediterranean. January*
Three men in water, clinging to a wheel with tyre. First Officer Mr A. P. Paterson: 'The destroyer hit us a glancing blow with her starboard bow and swept us along her starboard side, where the wash of her propellers, now going astern, capsized our support and dragged us under the water. When I came to the surface again the Master was missing.'

Suction. SS Glendalough. *North Sea. March*
Captain J. T. Kinch: 'The ship sank beneath me. I let go of the rail but was carried under by the suction. As I had my lifejacket on I quickly came to the surface.'

Suction from Holed Ship. MV San Ernesto. *Indian Ocean. July*
'Number 3 boat was drawn into the hole made by the torpedo and smashed.'

Tanker Sourabaya. *North Atlantic. October*
The SS *Sourabaya* was torpedoed. Captain W. T. Dawson: 'One AB and the Second Steward refused to jump into the sea and went down in the ship.'

Cargo Ship Andalucia Star. *South Atlantic. October*
The SS *Andalucia Star* was torpedoed three times, and oil covered the sea round the forward part of the ship. Captain J. B. Hall: 'I saw a passenger standing looking over the side and asked him why he had not gone into his boat, but he made no reply whatsoever, so I requested him to help me launch a raft. He did so without uttering a word, and on being told to jump into the water and get on to the raft with the others he just stood still and made no attempt to do so,

neither did the Carpenter, so I pushed both of them into the sea and followed them.'

Design Precautions

Make the shell and upper deck strong enough to withstand as much enemy attack as practicable. Protect with armour any vital part such as the Bridge. Take special precaution as for warships, as listed on page 18. Fit defensive equipment as appropriate, and duplicate essential services as far as practicable.

Keep inside surface of shell and surfaces of bulkheads clear of all impedimenta so as to facilitate damage repairs. Provide damage-control stores as stated on page 11. Provide life-saving equipment of the highest standard and in adequate numbers to allow for possible damage by enemy action.

Operating Precautions

Establish a damage-control organization, damage-control parties, positions, stores and communications.

Maintain strict watertight integrity and state of preparedness when standing into danger.

Action

Ascertain the extent of the damage.

Minimize the spread of flooding, establish a flooding boundary, build temporary cofferdams, subdivide free surfaces longitudinally.

Stop leaks, pump out flooded compartments, check that no debris chokes pump suctions or scuppers, plug any damaged air-escape pipes. Shore damaged structure. Jettison top weight if necessary to improve stability. Correct heel and trim by counterflooding and transfer of liquids, if this can be done quickly without creating dangerous free surfaces.

ABANDONING SHIP

Design Precautions

Site the survival craft at easily accessible positions close to the exits from the ship, clear of the propellers, if possible at a wall-sided part of the ship, clear of masts, funnels and other structures which might strike the craft alongside should the ship capsize quickly, and clear of discharges on the ship's side. In warships, where enemy damage may occur, spread the stowages over as much of the length of the ship as possible. In tankers and other ships which carry a large amount of oil, site boxes of sand near the survival craft to provide a foothold in the event of oil spillage.

Muster List

A Muster List is drawn up before the ship sails and copies are posted in the crew's quarters and other parts of the ship. It gives the duties assigned to various members of the crew in an emergency. The Master will arrange regular practice musters and boat drills.

Passengers' Drill

Attend the drills and make sure you understand them. Study the instructions posted in your cabin. Know where your life-jacket is stowed and familiarize yourself with it so that you can put it on and fasten it in the dark. Know your lifeboat station and assembly point and memorize your route so that you can find them in the dark even with debris in the way.

Have warm clothing readily available, also a small personal bag including electric torch.

General Emergency Signal

This signal consists of more than six short blasts followed by a long blast on the whistle or siren supplemented by the same signal on the general alarm bells.

'Lifeboat Stations'

If time permits before abandoning ship, drink as much water as possible, the warmer the better, and put on plenty of cloth-ing—thick underwear and waterproof top wear if possible.

The Master will endeavour to place extra provisions, especi-ally water, and thick clothing in the lifeboats. The boats' covers and strongbacks (the detachable beams running fore and aft, over which the covers are stretched) will be retained if possible. A distress signal will be sent, giving the ship's position, and sextants and chronometers will be put in the boats.

'Abandon Ship'

The Master will endeavour to take way off the ship and give the order to abandon at the best time. Obey the order promptly and in accordance with previous drill and training. The signal to lower boats is one short blast on the whistle. The Master will have the ship searched to ensure that no one is left behind and he will detail a crew member to assist a passenger if necessary.

Boarding Survival Craft

If the survival craft cannot be boarded from the deck of the ship, endeavour to get into it without getting wet, by descending side ladder, scrambling net, man rope or canvas hose improvised for the purpose. The chances of survival are increased if the body is kept dry.

Jumping into Water

When it is necessary to jump into the water, loosen tight clothing, especially neckwear, and select an area where the sea is free of oil, fire or wreckage. Jump feet first to prevent injury to the head when striking flotsam; have the legs together and slightly flexed at the knee, mouth closed, one arm across the lifejacket holding it close to the body and the thumb and forefinger of the other hand closing the nostrils after taking a deep breath and before impact with the water. If the lifejacket is made of cork or other hard substance likely to cause injury, both hands should be used for pulling it down from the chin.

It is better to abandon ship from the windward side as the ship may drift faster than the survivor can swim. It is also better to abandon from the high side if there is any chance of the ship capsizing before the survivor can swim clear; there is also probably less oil on the high side. If a choice has to be made between the windward side and the high side, choose the windward side.

Swim smartly clear of the ship so as to avoid suction as the ship sinks.

If the ship is badly holed on one side, abandon from the other side, or you may be sucked into the hole. Keep away from revolving propellers. If there is any danger from suction, keep the body vertical so as to minimize the suction force.

If the body is completely immersed, underwater explosion may tear the lungs and intestines and damage eardrums and sinuses.

Lifeboats and rafts should be taken well clear from ships which are likely to explode.

Oil Fire on Water

If you cannot get to the boats and have to take to the water, proceed as follows: Wear as much clothing as possible to give protection from the flames. If the lifejacket is of the bulky, inherently buoyant type, discard it; you would not be able to swim underwater with it; it is best to have an inflatable life-jacket kept tightly packed in its pouch. Go to the windward side of the ship, take a deep breath, grasp the nose and cover the mouth with one hand and cover the eyes with the other hand, and jump feet first. Swim away from the ship, keeping under water as long as possible.

When coming up for breath, look up, extend your arms over your head and pull them in a wide vigorous sweep, forcing the body above water. Protect the eyes, mouth and nose by the hands when breaking the surface. Turning the back to the wind, make wide sweeping movements with your hands and arms across the surface to splash the surface and drive the flames away. Take a deep breath, protect your face with your hands, and submerge by a feet-foremost surface dive, then swim under water. Repeat for further breaths until clear of the flames.

Mental Reactions

Attend the drills and familiarize yourself with the equipment to prepare yourself for an emergency. Most people react passively to the orders given them; the orders should be simple and in a language which is easily understood. The principle of 'follow my leader' should be used if necessary. One or two people may be immobilized by fear and some may even prefer to remain in the comfort of their cabins and go down with the ship rather than take to the boats. These people must be pushed into activity.

Anyone who becomes hysterical should be dealt with firmly, e.g. slapped on the face, immobilized or isolated in order to prevent a panic situation arising. Some people may become utterly selfish and rush the boats; these should be firmly dealt with, even to the extent of the lifeboat officers being armed.

Muster

The Master or senior surviving officer will:

endeavour to marshal all the survival craft (inflatable rafts to windward take the drogue inboard and trip the water-pockets, the rescue quoit and line is thrown from raft to raft and is hauled in);

take a roll-call to ascertain if anyone is missing; search for survivors in the water; put officers in charge of survival craft; transfer personnel to best advantage; take provisions from redundant craft; and lay near the scene of disaster until dawn.

It is best for survival craft, especially rafts, to remain near the scene of disaster and await rescue, particularly if a distress message and position have been sent. By remaining close together they are more easily detected by search forces.

Lifeboats may seek a landfall, distance and circumstances permitting. The Master will check the compasses and determine the course, taking into consideration wind, temperature, possibility of rain *en route* and of joining shipping tracks. Where a chart wallet is provided in the lifeboat it is usual to plot the ship's noon position each day to facilitate navigation in the event of abandoning ship. If the wallet is sealed in polythene, make some other record of the noon position.

First Action

The leader of a survival craft will:

check for leaks or other damage and make repairs as necessary; rig protection from the weather; put the emergency transmitter into operation; give first aid to those who need it; make the injured comfortable without aggravating the injuries; collect any flotsam likely to be useful; order a short rest, then get organized; allocate routine duties.

2

Man in the water

Man is not adapted to life in the water. His resistance to immersion depends on physique, being greater with fat, short-limbed men than with the thin and long-limbed. Prolonged immersion in all waters except the very warmest is lethal to even the fittest of men.

The major hazards to life are drowning and chilling, resulting in marked lowering of body temperature below 35°C, 95°F (*hypothermia*). Death can be accelerated by choking (following vomiting), by excessively rapid and deep breathing (*hyper-ventilation*—see page 76), by exhaustion and by giving up the struggle to remain alive.

Sudden death may arise from the impact of cold water on the pharynx, which can irritate a nerve which also affects the maintenance of blood pressure and the speed of heart action. Blood pressure drops, the victim faints (*syncope*) and the heart is slowed, stopped (*reflex inhibition of heart action*), or caused to beat irregularly (*reflexly induced cardiac arrhythmia*).

Other causes of death are attacks by sharks, barracuda and other sea creatures. Underwater explosions and oil fires on the surface of the sea, which frequently occur in wartime, add to the hazards, and direct enemy attack on men in the water is not unknown.

To prolong life in the water the wearing of lifejackets and protective clothing is essential.

DROWNING

Drowning results in death within a few seconds and is thus the preferred cause of death when all hope of survival is lost.

In the absence of an effective lifejacket, drowning is the most common immediate cause of death in the water.

North Atlantic. May
'A jolly boat was lowered, with five men in it; it capsized on becoming waterborne, throwing its occupants into the sea. Two of

51

these were drowned, but the remaining three men managed to swim to a raft.'

HYPOTHERMIA

The naked or lightly clad body cools rapidly when immersed in cold water. The following changes take place as the deep body, or core temperature, drops:

	°Centigrade	°Fahrenheit
temperature regulation of body fails	33	91·4
shivering response ceases, muscular rigidity commences, speech becomes difficult	32·2	90
drowsiness occurs	31–29	88–83
unconsciousness occurs	29	83
death occurs	25	77

These temperatures are much greater than that of most waters of the world; immersion is therefore a very serious hazard.

The core temperature continues to fall for about twenty minutes after removal from the water and this 'after-drop' has been the cause of the many delayed or collapse-deaths of men following rescue from shipwreck.

The extremities of the limbs are the first parts of the body to be affected. Numbness of the fingers and cold paralysis of the hands, known as 'hand-lock', are serious in the survival situation. Clothing and equipment are designed to minimize the amount of manipulation required: e.g. toggles are used instead of buttons and buckles, push buttons instead of turn knobs.

The onset of unconsciousness causes the head to droop. An efficient lifejacket is therefore necessary to support the head and keep the mouth and nostrils above the water; without it death from drowning would occur. In all probability, drowning arising from hypothermia has hitherto been the greatest cause of death at sea. The protection which the lifejacket gives to the occiput delays the fall in core temperature.

Hypothermia is delayed by remaining still in the water, which also necessitates a lifejacket, and by wearing protective clothing, particularly if the outer layer is waterproof. It is accelerated by physical activity and by drinking alcohol.

The rate of cooling depends on the thickness of the sub-cutaneous fat and its initial heat content. Fat people survive longer than thin people, women longer than men. The white races survive longer than the black but not so long as the yellow.

The following table, based on casualty reports, gives the expected time for survival at various temperatures. Search and recovery should continue beyond the times given to allow for exceptional circumstances.

| Sea Surface Temperature | | Maximum time of immersion |
°Centigrade	°Fahrenheit	for survival
0	32	$\frac{1}{4}$ hour
2·5	36·5	$\frac{1}{2}$ hour
5	41	1 hour
10	50	3 hours
15	59	7 hours
20	68	16 hours
25	77	3 days or more

SS Empire Howard. *Arctic Ocean. April*
Water temperature –2°C (29°F). Captain H. J. M. Downie: 'I was the last man to be picked up at 1400. Everyone was conscious when taken out of the water but many of the men lost consciousness when taken into the warmth of the trawlers. Nine of the men died on board soon after being picked up. We were all given a small mouthful of spirits on board the trawlers and this made us sleep, and these unfortunate men went to sleep and did not wake up again.'

Arctic Ocean
Dr MacBain was immersed in water at 0°C (32°F). 'I was fifteen minutes in the water before being able to get on board a raft which floated up from the wreck. On boarding the raft skin anaesthesia was complete to the neck. Joint sense was impaired and there was a well-marked ischaemia [white, dead fingers or toes] of both hands and feet. Massage and work at an oar restored sensation rapidly and painlessly, except in the fingers where sensation returned slowly, still showing traces after eight weeks.' Dr MacBain attributed the fact that those who like himself were obliged to jump into the freezing water did not succumb because they went in fully clothed.

SS Gogra. *North Atlantic. April*
The Chief Officer, Mr G. R. Mudford: 'I think that the force of the explosives, in addition to the extremely cold water which was only 47°F, caused the deaths of many of the men in the water (who were mostly Lascars), for after a short time the whistling and shouting ceased, and I appeared to be the only one alive. In addition to my ordinary clothes I had my bridge coat on. . . . I kicked off my boots and continued to tread water.

'After about three hours in the water I was very weary, and felt I could not go on much longer. I was also beginning to get cramp and was shivering violently. . . . [A ship] lowered a boat and picked me up after I had been in the water three hours and twenty minutes. Although I could not move owing to the cramp, my brain was quite active, and I asked my rescuers to look for other men, but they were all dead. When we eventually drew alongside the boat was hauled up by which time I was quite exhausted so I was put to bed in the sick bay.'

SS Manchester Merchant. *North Atlantic. February*
Captain F. D. Struss: 'I was pulled out of the water into the boat. . . . I had by this time been in the water about $2\frac{1}{2}$ hours, the temperature of which was 47°F, and my body was completely numb when rescued.'

MV Athelsultan. *North Atlantic. November*
'I was in the water about $1\frac{1}{2}$ hours before being rescued, with the temperature 49°F, and I was dressed in uniform coat, sweater and muffler. During the time I was floating round I heard many of the men calling to one another. . . . Gradually the voices died away as they became weaker and when later a corvette came up and dropped lines she got no response; the men's heads were down.'

Carley Float from SS Springbank. *North Atlantic. October*
Able Seaman Peter Kennion Calder: 'There were forty of us on or clinging to a fifteen-man Carley float. Rescue came after seven hours. There was only one casualty, an able seaman who had drunk rum just before abandoning ship. He died after about three hours' immersion.'

Jade Bay, September
'A master's wife drifted off Bremerhaven for fourteen hours today with her lifejacket fastened to her husband's dead body and her eight-month-old baby dead in her arms.'

Arctic Ocean. June
Two kayaks lashed beam to beam broke from their mooring on the ice and drifted away. They were the only means which Dr Fridjtof

Nansen and Hjalmar Johansen had of reaching land, and they contained all the explorers' possessions. Dr Nansen handed his watch to Johansen 'and as quickly as possible I threw off some clothing, so as to be able to swim more easily; I did not dare to take everything off, as I might so easily get cramp. I sprang into the water, but the wind was off the ice, and the light kayaks, with their high rigging, gave it a good hold. They were already well out and drifting rapidly. The water was icy cold and it was hard work swimming with clothes on. . . . When I got tired I turned over, and swam on my back . . . I felt, however, that my limbs were gradually stiffening, and losing all feeling. . . . I pulled myself into the edge of the kayak. . . . I tried to pull myself up, but the whole of my body was so stiff with cold that this was an impossibility. . . . After a little, however, I managed to swing one leg up onto the edge of the sledge which lay on the deck, and in this way managed to tumble up. There I sat, but so stiff with cold, that I had difficulty in paddling. The cold had robbed my whole body of feeling, but when the gusts of wind came they seemed to go right through me. . . . I shivered, my teeth chattered, and I was numb almost all over; but I could still use the paddle.'

McMurdo Sound. January
Two Americans, J. Thorne and D. H. Johnson, swam in darkness below 8 ft of bay ice in McMurdo Sound to photograph results of an ice-melting device. They remained submerged for 28 minutes despite a water temperature of $-2\frac{1}{2}°C$ ($27\frac{3}{4}°F$). So chilled were they when they emerged that their arms had to be supported while they drank hot coffee. The men wore two suits of special underwear and several pairs of socks beneath constant volume diving suits of rubber and fabric. The headpiece was clamped on to a metal ring and sealed.

North Atlantic. March
MV *Staffordshire* was south of Iceland when she was attacked from the air by enemy aircraft and had to be abandoned. Some of the boats were destroyed before they could be launched. A passenger, G. S. Ferris: 'Some people who attempted to board the boat fell from the Jacob's ladder into the water—they included women and children and some of them were scantily clad. None of them on surfacing made any movement whatever and they appeared to be lifeless. A Chinese girl who was within reach was dragged by her hair into the boat and she regained consciousness after a few minutes. The boat was over-crowded and we all had to stand. I stood in water in the boat until we were rescued ten hours later. The bones from my knees downwards, bones which previously I did not know existed, felt frozen for several weeks afterwards.'

E

CHOKING

Death to man in the water may arise from asphyxia caused by food particles or vomit blocking the air passages.

River Casualty. July
'An Oxford boy, aged fifteen, who lost his life in the river Cherwell at Oxford went swimming too soon after a meal. . . . Dr H. D. Leggatt said that death was not caused by drowning, but because food had got stuck in the boy's throat.'

River Casualty. March
An undergraduate was thrown into the river after a rowing-club dinner. 'Dr John Rack, a pathologist, who performed the *post mortem* examination . . . said that the air passages were blocked with food particles. There was no river water in the lungs or air passages. The cause of death was choking.'

EXPOSURE TO DEPTH

Men in or close to sinking ships are sometimes carried down with the ship and they may not all regain the surface in safety. The increase of pressure with depth, nearly 15 pounds per square inch for every 33 feet, reduces the volume of air in the lungs and trapped in the clothing, with the result that buoyancy is lost and the body may be more likely to sink than rise to the surface. A lifejacket with the necessary buoyancy should therefore always be worn when standing into danger.

Special arrangements are made to enable personnel to escape from a sunken submarine; early arrangements included the McCann Rescue Bell for multiple escape, and the Davis Submarine Escape Apparatus, and the Momsen Lung for individual escape. The rescue bell is a large structure, containing two chambers one above the other, which is lowered over the submarine's escape hatch. The DSEA and Momsen Lung are based on a closed-circuit breathing set. Currently two methods are in use. One is the chamber method indicated above or modern variations of it which employ a vessel or chamber which is connected to the stricken vessel. The other method involves a buoyant ascent technique which requires a compartment or chamber to be flooded in order to 'lock out' escapers, who then ascend with the aid of buoyancy only, breathing out throughout the ascent to relieve the pressure which would otherwise build up in their lungs. This second method is in use in the Royal Navy and has the advantage that no outside assistance is required in order to make the escape. It involves exposing each escaper to pressure, the effects of which are minimized by a fast flooding rate; hence the use of a 'one man' tower is preferred to flooding an entire compartment, which would involve exposing larger numbers of escapers to pressure for a longer period. The high speeds demanded by this method are achieved by retaining a small air lock in the chamber on flooding; this results in the escaper being almost entirely submerged during the later stages of pressurization. A hood is therefore incorporated in the equipment worn by the escaper into which respirable air is fed automatically. Thermal protection and additional buoyancy on the surface is provided by an inflatable overall suit of which the hood is a part, designated the 'submarine escape and immersion suit'.

Divers and underwater swimmers experience a number of problems not met with on the surface. At depth, nitrogen from their breathing gas goes into solution in the body tissues. If they return to the surface slowly, in carefully calculated stages, the gas comes out of solution and is exhaled in the normal way. Too rapid an ascent causes the nitrogen in the tissues to form bubbles which produce pain and other disabilities known as 'decompression sickness' or 'the bends'.

Nitrogen also has a narcotic effect when inhaled under pressure, and when a diver is deeper than about 150 feet there is increasing difficulty in overcoming the mental effects, which are somewhat similar to drunkenness. It is a dangerous condition which can only be overcome by replacing the nitrogen in the breathing gas with a less dense inert gas such as helium.

Oxygen becomes toxic when breathed at partial pressures greater than twice atmospheric pressure. Pure oxygen breathed at depths greater than 25 feet has been known to cause convulsions and death.

Carbon dioxide poisoning is another hazard to which divers are prone if there is inadequate ventilation of the apparatus.

Other hazards exist. Like those described above they are

unlikely to endanger a diver who has gained a good understanding of the subject. Therefore, underwater activities should not be undertaken without first having received professional instruction; the first few exercises away from the swimming-bath should be made in company with a trained person and the safety precautions of organizations such as the British Sub Aqua Club should be followed at all times.

SS Gogra. *North Atlantic. April*
The Chief Officer, Mr G. R. Mudford: 'She sank within twenty seconds of being hit. I went many fathoms down with the ship, inside the Bridge—I heard many noises and was surrounded with concrete and several dead men: I cannot even now understand how it was that I was the only one from the Bridge who managed to float to the surface alive.'

Sunken Submarine Poseidon. *China Sea. June*
HM Submarine *Poseidon* sank, following collision, to a depth of 125 feet. Six men were trapped in the forepart of the vessel. 'Willis first said prayers for himself and his companions and ordered them to put on their escape apparatus. . . . He then explained that he was going to flood the compartment to equalize the pressure with that outside the submarine. . . . He also rigged a wire hawser across the hatchway to form a support for the men to stand on while the compartment was flooding. . . . After two hours and ten minutes the water was about up to the men's knees, and Willis considered the pressure might be sufficient to open the hatch. With considerable difficulty the hatch opened sufficiently for two men to shoot up, but the pressure then reclosed the hatch, and it was necessary to await further flooding to make the pressure more equal before a second attempt could be made.' The first man came to the surface unconscious and died immediately, but his body was supported by the second man, himself in a state of great exhaustion. 'After a further hour, by which time the men in the compartment were nearly up to their necks in water and the air-lock was becoming very small, a second effort was made. This was successful and the hatch opened and four other men came to the surface.'

ATTACK BY SEA CREATURES

Sea creatures show curiosity about a man in the water, and some of them attack him.

Birds

Man-overboard. British Monarch. *North Pacific. June*
Second Mate Douglas Wardrop, who was in the water for nine
hours, reported: 'Two birds had arrived to inspect me. Suddenly
one of them peeled off and drove right for my head. I raised my
hand and the bird zoomed away. The second bird peeled off and
bore down on me. . . . Just when my eyes and arms were beginning
to feel a real sense of strain, the birds gave me up and flew off.'

Ditched Airman. North Sea. July
Surgeon Lieutenant J. E. Owen RN: 'I had to retrieve the body of an
airman who had come down in the North Sea. His lifejacket was
inflated and he had been floating with his face above water. Both
eyes had been enucleated by sea-birds.'

Fish

Man-overboard. North Atlantic. September
Franz Maria Streycharczyk, who fell overboard in mid-Atlantic,
wearing white undershorts only, was in the water for sixteen hours.
'Pilot fish begin to snap on underwear, so I take off. I am afraid
pilot fish bring sharks.'

Survivors from USS Indianapolis. *North Pacific. July*
Men who had been in the water for four days following the sinking
of their ship were reported to be suffering from fish bites.

Survivors from SS San Gaspar. *North Atlantic. July*
Captain Donald Blyth: 'Whilst swimming [away from a burning
tanker] we were attacked by barracuda which tried to bite us, and
as I had no clothes on and the others were wearing very little, we
made an attractive bait for them. Shoals of small dogfish also
attacked us, but we swam through the night. Tiger sharks appeared
and joined in the attack; I took off my lifebelt, which was chafing
me, and rested my chin on it, and by kicking my feet vigorously was
able to keep the sharks away temporarily, but they became bolder
as time went on. Towards noon we were nearly exhausted, when
fortunately at 11.30 two bombers dropped a rubber dinghy within
twenty feet of us. I got into the dinghy with the First Radio Officer
and the Third Officer and we managed to haul the Third Radio
Officer in, but he was badly bitten about the feet and unconscious
and terribly burned. . . . When we were in the dinghy the sharks
became much bolder and we had to stab at them with the aluminium
paddles to keep them away.'

Survivors from SS Nova Scotia. *Indian Ocean. November*
The Second Officer, Mr N. Robertson: 'There were many sharks
about but I kept in the oil patches as much as possible which
appeared to keep them away. I later learned that about one
hundred and eighteen bodies were washed ashore on the Durban
beach in a mutilated condition.'

Casualties. North Atlantic
J. M. Waters, Captain USCG: 'Shortly after noon, I sighted a
naked body. . . . I had also sighted something else—a huge fifteen-
foot shark only a few feet away from the body. On the second pass
the shark was tugging the corpse around and on the third pass two
sharks were fighting over it. Two minutes later nothing remained.
. . . Only one hundred yards away was another body clothed and
wearing an orange lifejacket. It was not molested. Only a year
before, we had been at this same spot of the Ocean when an un-
clothed survivor of an aircraft ditching was killed by a shark. I
firmly resolved to keep my clothes on should I ever be unfortunate
enough to be adrift in shark-infested waters.'

Underwater Swimmers. Caribbean. February
Bernard Gorsky, who was circumnavigating in the 40-foot Bermuda
Cutter *Moana*: '. . . the warning signal we have agreed to use when
threatened by a shark: a high-pitched "too-too-too", which travels
quite well through the water when given into the breathing-tube. I
have had occasion to use it. A triangular-gulf came down to me at
fifteen feet, I gave the signal—and at once the shark stopped dead,
turned aside, then fled. A little later, another appeared. So I
calmly went up to it and cried: "too-too-too". Yes, there was no
question, the shark found that sound most uncomfortable, and made
off at once.'

Underwater Swimmers. South Pacific
Bernard Gorsky: 'A surgeon-fish cut one of my fingers to the bone. I
did not feel anything of this, but immediately lost so much blood
that I was enveloped in a red cloud. And suddenly, there was that
female shark! She came straight at me and so quickly that . . . I
experienced real terror. And sometimes there would be a shark that
followed our stumbling advance from a distance, wary of coming too
close and making off at top speed the moment we slapped the water
with our hands.'

Survivor. South Pacific. October
Lieutenant Commander Kabat USN floated at night without
clothing or shoes in a kapok lifejacket off Guadalcanal. At dawn he

felt a scratching, tickling sensation in his left foot. He reported, 'Slightly startled, I . . . held it up. It was gushing blood. . . . I peered into the water . . . not ten feet away was the glistening, brown back of a great fish . . . swimming away. The real fear did not hit me until I saw him turn and head back toward me. He didn't rush . . . but breaking the surface of the water came in a steady direct line. I kicked and splashed tremendously, and this time he veered off me . . . went off about twenty feet and swam back and forth. Then he turned . . . and came from the same angle toward my left. . . . When he was almost upon me I thrashed out . . . brought my fist down on his nose . . . again and again. He was thrust down about two feet . . . swam off and waited. I discovered that he had torn off a piece of my left hand. Then . . . again at the same angle to my left. . . . I managed to hit him on the eyes, the nose. The flesh was torn from my left arm. . . . At intervals of ten or fifteen minutes he would ease off from his slow swimming and bear directly toward me, coming in at my left. Only twice did he go beneath me. Helpless against this type of attack I feared it most but because I was so nearly flat on top of the water, he seemed unable to get at me from below. . . . The big toe on my left foot was dangling. A piece of my right heel was gone. My left elbow, hand, and calf were torn. If he did not actually sink his teeth into me, his rough hide would scrape great pieces off my skin. The salt water stanched the flow of blood somewhat and I was not conscious of great pain.' In the excitement of trying to attract the attention of a ship going by, he forgot about the shark, which struck again and bit into his thigh, exposing the bone. At this point he was seen, and several sailors with rifles on the ship began firing at the shark. 'A terrible fear of being shot to death in the water when rescue was so near swept over me. I screamed and pleaded and cried for them to stop. The shark was too close. They would hit me first.'

Men-overboard. Caribbean. December
Fourteen-year-old Jeppsen fell overboard from the Danish ship *Grete Maersk*. Thirteen-year-old Tony Latona threw him a lifebelt and jumped over to help him. Their shouts were not heard. They had been in the water for two hours when they saw sharks coming in to the attack. One struck Jeppsen and ripped two great gashes in his left foot. Jeppsen yelled. Tony reported, 'We kicked and kicked and drove the sharks away. I told Jeppsen that the blood in the water would drive the sharks crazy. I told him to take off his trousers and bind them around his gashed foot to help stop the bleeding. We did not see the sharks then but they must have been hanging around, because an hour later when Jeppsen's trousers fell off, the sharks

61

were back after us in a few minutes. They just swam past me and tried to get at Jeppsen. We kept driving them off but they came back every fifteen minutes. Jeppsen was losing blood and getting weak. Then a shark struck him on the same foot again. He said it hurt. The sharks kept coming back more often, paying less attention to our efforts to drive them off. Pretty soon one struck Jeppsen under the arm. He cried when it gashed him. Another shark came in and tore his knee. He yelled and started going under. He went down screaming, 'My foot'. He came up fighting and screaming, and then went down again. That is the last I saw of him. I saw the blood in the water.'

Canoeists. Peru. February
'Seven children, whose canoe capsized in a river in the east Peruvian jungle province of Madre de Dios, have been eaten alive by a shoal of piranha fish. A fisherman who went to their aid suffered the same fate.'

Man-overboard. North Pacific. June
Douglas Wardrop: 'Ouch! A sharp needle-like pain shot through my left leg. An electric eel moved away and began to circle around me. He was about a foot and a half long with small, pale blue suckers. . . . The eel continued to circle, ugly and sinister in the murky water. . . . After a while the eel disappeared.'

Divers. Mediterranean
Shark, moray eels, barracuda, sea snakes, rays, turtles, porpoise were seen. 'The only attack was carried out by a moray eel which had made its home in an ammunition box which was required for raising. Even then, it first swam away, then appeared to alter its mind and came back with teeth snapping.'

Tuna Fisherman. North Pacific
A fisherman on a tuna clipper off Baja, California, hooked a sword-fish, fell overboard and was run completely through by the 'sword'. The sword entered just below the navel and three inches to the right and missed the spine. Captain J. M. Waters: 'Being fairly blunt, it penetrated no organs or gut, but pushed them aside without damage. If it had been a bullet or a sharp point, it would have been goodbye, Joe.'

Underwater Swimmers. Caribbean. January
Bernard Gorsky harpooned a sting ray. 'François . . . paid out more nylon. Thus liberated, the ray struggled and landed on top of me. I felt its soft, slimy belly and leapt backwards. The lashing tail just

62

touched my visor, and I clearly saw the sting, raised ready for the thrust, but it missed me.'

Underwater Swimmers. South Pacific. January
Bernard Gorsky: 'We were free diving and the water was very clear. There was a coral slope, with a cliff of about nine fathoms below it and here a very large snub-nosed loach suddenly came shooting up at an angle. At eighteen inches Roger turned, the creature halted at the same instant. Roger held the camera against the open mouth and took a picture. There followed a backwards catapult action. The whole took no more than three rather unreal seconds. The thunderbolt speed of the attack and the straightness of the course of that enormous speckled body were worth seeing. . . . Our experience suggests that this would be the most dangerous fish, after the tiger shark.'

Waders. Raroia Reef. South Pacific. August
Two members of the crew of the *Kon-Tiki* waded between the reef and an island. Thor Heyerdahl: 'They were suddenly attacked by no fewer than eight large eels. They saw them coming in the clear water and jumped up on to a large coral block, round and under which the eels writhed. The slimy brutes were as thick as a man's calf and speckled green and black like poisonous snakes, with small heads, malignant snake's eyes, and teeth an inch long and sharp as an awl. The men hacked with their machete knives at the little swaying heads which came writhing towards them; they cut the head off one and another was injured. The blood in the sea attracted a whole flock of young blue sharks which attacked the dead and injured eels, while Erik and Herman were able to jump over to another block of coral and get away.'

Jelly-fish

Underwater Swimmer. Caribbean. December
Bernard Gorsky: 'Suddenly, an invisible thread wrapped round my throat, and I felt a fierce burning. At the same instant I saw Pierre beating something back. "A shoal of Man-of-War, come on, out of this!" They were physalias—"Portuguese men-of-war", poisonous jelly-fish. The burns brought out a violent rash which was painful, but only lasted half an hour.'

Long-distance Swimmer
Commander C. G. Forsberg: 'Jellyfish are encountered on almost every long-distance sea swim. I dread their appearance—always clearly visible through one's goggles. One just has to grit the teeth and bash on. I have had weals on most parts of my body; the lips

63

are most painful. Several swimmers I know have had to be hospitalized but I have escaped lightly—so far!'

Mammals

Fishermen. Galapagos Islands
Bernard Gorsky: 'Adriano . . . had a long furrow on his left hip. . . . He had been linefishing in three feet of water, when a seal attacked and bit him. It is worth remarking that the teeth of an adult seal are as large as those of a tiger, and we were not surprised that Adriano "lost quite a lot of blood". The wound cost him three months hospital. We now learned that at the Galapagos men are quite as afraid of the seal as of the shark.'

Molluscs

Diver. Macassar Strait
It is reported of Victor Berge, pearl fishing in the East Indies, 'I felt something touch me quite lightly on the left arm. Instinct and underwater training saved my life. Quick as a flash, before I had the least notion of what it was, I whirled about, grabbing the razor-sharp knife from my belt sheath, and slashed three or four times with a full sweep of my arm in the direction of this touch. By luck I severed two of the lassooing arms that were gripping me. . . . As I slashed and felt the blade cut through a mass of soft flesh, two more arms laid hold of me, one around each ankle. I felt a vicious jerk at my legs which almost upset me. . . . I was fighting automatically. Each time I would bend to try to cut my ankles free, the creature would jerk me so violently that I seemed to be a little child pulled about at will by a strong man; it was with the greatest difficulty I kept my footing. The helmet and breastplate banged against my head and chest with punishing force. One jerk dashed me against a rock and left me breathless. The force of the beast was terrific and produced a deathly sense of fear. . . . I was using all my strength to resist the creature's pulls, while striving to cut more of these living fetters which bound me. To add to my difficulties I found my weights, where I was getting hit, were swinging the wrong way. . . . The instant my hand would stretch down with the big knife he'd give a terrific jerk, sometimes dragging me ten or fifteen feet, jamming the heavy helmet against my jaws and skull, bruising me against the rough, crusted rock wall. All this in a pool blackened and turbid with the ink the beast had squirted out. . . . I stretched up to give the danger signal (four pulls, meaning "Pull until the line breaks"). Instantly the octopus yanked me a dozen feet, and I had all I could manage just not to topple over. . . . All at once I knew I was going. Just before the wave of fear-freighted unconsciousness swept over me

I threw up my arms, caught both lines, gave four frantic pulls. There was an instant when I had the sensation of being pulled in two lengthways. Then I knew nothing. . . .

'I shot suddenly up to within ten or fifteen feet of the surface. . . . It was at this moment that I regained consciousness with a jerk. I woke to the same dream of being pulled in two: looking down, I could see the sea-demon's suckered arms were still fast about my ankles; the loathsome mass of his body was suspended below. There was nothing I could do. Impossible to stretch down and free my legs with the pull on them and the lines pulling up. The octopus was pulling with all its force, siphoning violently. . . . Ro yelled to the men to pull hard. Deftly he got a stouter line about my body. Two more men caught this and hauled me upward. Ro slipped into the water, his big knife ready. In two sure slashes he had cut off those horrible arms.

'The two men hauled me to the surface, more dead than alive, with pieces of suckered feelers still coiled about my legs. They got me on deck and took off the helmet. . . . Blood all over my face and neck and shoulders, hands and arms and legs torn from the action of the suckers, bruised from head to foot by the banging about. I was pretty well all in. . . .

'We finally agreed the length of each arm must have been eighteen feet; the body not quite the size of a flour barrel.'

Wader. Raroia Reef. South Pacific
Thor Heyerdahl: 'I was wading towards the island when something, with a lightning movement, caught hold of my ankle on both sides and held on tight. It was a cuttle-fish. I jerked my foot as hard as I could, and the squid, which was barely three feet long, followed it without letting go. It must have been the bandage on my foot which attracted it. I dragged myself in jerks towards the beach with the disgusting carcase hanging on to my foot. Only when I reached the edge of the dry sand did it let go and retreat slowly through the shallow water, with arms outstretched and eyes directed shoreward, as though ready for a new attack if I wanted one.'

Shellfish
Submerged Liferaft. Timor Sea. March
Captain Bourdens: 'The raft was two feet beneath the surface and I knew we could not last much longer. I was exhausted and my wife was worse, for now crabs were eating her sore legs.' Madam Bourdens: 'I was crying with pain for two days but I could not see anything on my legs. Then we found these small crabs inside the ulcers.'

65

OTHER PHYSICAL EFFECTS OF IMMERSION

In addition to the major hazards described above, many disabilities arise as a result of immersion. The effects on eyes, ears, nose, throat, stomach and muscles all figure in the reports of survivors and long-distance swimmers.

Burns

Survivor from SS Irene Maria. *English Channel. July*
A trimmer was burnt about the head and chest. He was swept out of a swamped lifeboat; he did not have a lifejacket and was supported by a seaman wearing a lifejacket. The Chief Officer, S. Ostergaard, reported that the trimmer 'became delirious when the salt water began to affect his burns. He had struggled and fought and the seaman had been forced to let him sink.'

Survivor. Mediterranean. April
Third Officer, Mr S. W. Taylor: 'Ten of the crew beside myself saw this small clear channel through the flames and made for it. We had to swim four hundred yards through the flames and everyone of us received severe burns. The ship's carpenter had his eyes severely burned and became hysterical and started swimming madly round towards the flames, but Able Seaman Shearer went to his rescue, towed him clear of the flames and kept him afloat for one and a half hours [when they were rescued]. . . . I remained in hospital ten days. I found that the burns, although not very painful whilst in the water, became very painful when exposed to the air.'

Cramp

Survivor from SS Sheaf Mount. *North Atlantic. August*
Cadet J. L. Oliver: 'I swam round two and a half hours before being picked up by the Rescue Ship. I was suffering from cramp in my legs, through the cold, and could not walk.'

Channel Swimmer
Commander C. G. Forsberg: 'I am not much affected by cramp in the water. On every occasion I have been struck it has been through a combination of tired muscles, extreme cold and, above all else, some action which differs from the past pattern, e.g. changing from long periods of even-paced crawl to a tread-water posture for feeding. I cure it by letting the affected limb "idle"; this has never failed to work. Very occasionally I have a brief dig at the affected part with my fingers. But the contortions necessary to do this may produce another spasm in some other part of the body.'

Ear, Nose and Throat

Survivor from SS City of Corinth. North Atlantic. November
Captain G. T. Law: '—— was blown overboard by the first torpedo
and decided to swim for the shore. He had his lifejacket on, but had
swam about eight and a half miles. Apart from a sore throat and
ears, he was in excellent condition.'

Survivor. Gulf of Mexico. November
Second day. Air Force Captain Paul Shook saw some seaweed
floating by. 'After chewing it for a while I noticed that my mouth
was sensitive to touch and that my tongue was sore and swollen. I
gave up the seaweed and decided it was a total loss.'

Exhaustion

Survivor from MV Thiara. North Atlantic. July
Robert Thompson, Master of MV *Thiara*, reported that the ship
was abandoned with way on. It went round in a circle and came
towards him so he had to swim out of the way. He swam for about
four hours, was in a lifeboat for about one hour and was then rescued.
The Rescue Ship reported: 'On the 27th this gentleman was brought
on board this ship suffering from extreme exhaustion due to exposure
and immersion for some considerable time in the sea. He had a large
circular bruise on the left thigh and some skin abrasions due to salt
water and friction on the left arm. I prescribed rest and warmth and
also administered one injection of camphor oil. On examination
today (28th) I find no symptoms except that of extreme fatigue.'

Eyes

Survivor from MV San Victorio. Doldrums (Atlantic). May
Mr A. Ryan, the sole survivor from a tanker loaded with benzine
and paraffin: 'The water was quite warm but there was a terrible
glare from the sun which was very painful to the eyes. . . . By sheer
providence the [rescue] vessel spotted me and picked me up after I
had been in the water sixteen and a half hours. I was quite conscious
when picked up, but I could not see and I felt very weak. After I
was safely rescued, however, I completely lost consciousness.'

Hyperventilation

Dr Stanley Miles: 'A sturdy and experienced swimmer volunteered
to examine a mooring anchor on the sea bed at a depth of 50 feet.
He took twelve deep breaths to reduce his alveolar carbon dioxide
and dived in. He remembers swimming down and looking at the
anchor but passed out as he turned to come up. A companion
standing by with a breathing set, seeing he had not surfaced in

four minutes, swam down and found him lying prone and unconscious. He was brought to the surface very cyanosed and was revived
with artificial respiration.'

Nausea and Vomiting

Survivor from MV Mary Slessor. *North Atlantic. February*
Captain C. H. Sweeny: 'After three and a half to four hours in the
water —— picked us up. I was very hazy about what happened, but
remember distinctly being hauled up by a line on to the deck. I was
almost unconscious, having swallowed a greal deal of oil fuel, which
made me very sick.'

Swimmer. English Channel. September
Harry E. Hinken: 'The grease put on my body to keep out the cold
washed off my shoulders and I swallowed some. This made me vomit
continuously for six or seven hours. I was unable to take down any
food and I gradually got weaker.'

Survivors and Casualties from SS Lakonia. *North Atlantic. December*
Dr W. R. Keatinge: 'Two survivors mentioned being sick at the time
they were taken from the water and one of them said most other
people rescued from the water were also sick, though the sea was
calm by then. A rescuer reports that most of the dead on board the
Montcalm had their mouth, nose and ears coated with vomit.'

Ditched Airman. Gulf of Mexico. November
Second day. Paul Shook: 'Up to this time I never felt hunger but I
was becoming extremely thirsty. . . . In the afternoon of the second
day my thirst had become so great I began to drink sea water. After
I had drunk a considerable amount I became nauseated.'

Paralysis

Survivors. Pacific Ocean. August
'The vessel finally sank at 2125 on 11 August 1961, after which the
Master and three crew members swam towards the shore, clinging
to pieces of timber. The Master and one crew member are stated to
have been carried ashore by breakers at about 0400 on 12 August
1961 and it would appear that the other two crew members may
have landed somewhat earlier than this. The Master stated that
both he and the crew member who landed with him were unable to
walk on first hitting the shore as the legs of both men were paralysed.'

Speech

Survivor from SS Lulworth Hill. *Doldrums (Atlantic)*
Kenneth Cooke, in the course of one day, abandoned ship in shark-
infested water, was picked up by an enemy submarine and washed

off the deck of the submarine, saw the enemy ram a lifeboat, saw his fellow survivors attacked by sharks, struck out for a patch of oil fuel and became very fatigued. A survivor on a raft saw him and shouted out 'Stop'. Kenneth Cooke heard the shout but was speechless: 'I tried again, summoning up every mite of strength remaining in me, but although my mouth opened and I expelled breath, only a small hoarse rattle came from it. Then Providence did what I was unable to do. As I gulped air into my lungs a wave smashed into my face and I found myself choking and vomiting. It was enough. I was heard.'

PSYCHOLOGICAL ASPECTS OF IMMERSION

Boredom, depression and despair, fantasy, self-preservation to the point of selfishness, and other emotional disturbances are reported by survivors and long-distance swimmers.

Boredom

Swimmer. English Channel. July
Elaine Gray, who swam from England to France in record time in July 1966, gave up the struggle because of boredom in two previous attempts to swim the English Channel—on getting into the pilot boat she said, 'I just thought, what a long way to swim.'

Despair

Ditched Airman. Gulf of Mexico. November
Second day. Air Force Captain Paul Shook reported that an aircraft flew within five hundred feet of him. 'I moved, yelled and kicked the water but again he failed to see me. It was a terrible disappointment to see him fly away knowing that my chances of rescue were diminishing with each hour. Again I am at a loss for words to describe the feeling of despair I felt each time this happened during the second day but I still had hope or else refused to believe the seriousness of my situation.'

Dissociation

Ditched Airman. Gulf of Mexico
Night of second day. Paul Shook reported: 'Sometimes . . . I seem to divide myself. It seemed as though my mind had departed from my body but yet was aware of what was taking place. I kept imagining that a small boat had found me and that I was telling the man to go to notify the coastguard of my position so that they could come and get me. Then I was telling him that this was not too good a plan, and

that I had better go with him because I couldn't last much longer. This all seemed real and vivid to me at the time.'

Fantasy

Ditched Airman. Gulf of Mexico
Second day. Paul Shook: 'Again I felt the cold and misery and once more drifted off into fantasy.'

Survivors from USS Indianapolis. North Pacific. July
By the second night in the water, following the torpedoing and sinking of the *Indianapolis* it is reported that 'many of them passed from the world of sanity into the world of fantasy'. On the third day many of the survivors had hallucinations that the ship was not sunk, that there was an island very close and that the mother of one of the survivors ran a hotel on the island. During the night they had hallucinations that the enemy were after them and attempting to kill them.

Some of the survivors dispensed with their lifejackets, swam towards the imaginary island and perished in the attempt. During the hallucination at night some of the survivors fought and killed each other.

Swimmer. South America
The Argentinian long-distance swimmer Antonio Abertendo reported that during an eighty-hour swim in South America in 1957 he was greatly comforted by visions of dogs which appeared to be swimming with him.

Swimmer. English Channel
Commander Forsberg: 'For a few brief moments off the French coast I had the distinct impression that I was swimming downstream in a muddy river—probably the setting sun was making the water look brown. This was after eleven hours in the water. A calm patch of water with no immediate worries probably left me nothing to concentrate my mind on.'

Forgetfulness

Long-distance Swimmer
Commander Forsberg: 'During the Lulworth to Weymouth Swim, I found myself unable for several minutes to recollect what town I was swimming towards. Everything else was normal, I was swimming towards a plain leading-mark, felt fit and knew exactly how far I was from the finish. I just could not think what town, or part of Britain, the finish was in! I had only been swimming four hours on this occasion.'

Humiliation

Swimmer. English Channel. August
Sam Rockett took part in the France to England race of 1950, when within a short distance of England the tide turned against him and he had to swim parallel to the shore for a time. He touched ground after swimming for fourteen hours seventeen minutes and recorded: 'Vaguely I recall laying flat on my face on the treacherous rock, whimpering with exhaustion and emotion . . . unable to move.' He finally managed to get on to the beach. 'I lay on the shingle and opened my eyes in a daze to stare into my wife's face. And suddenly I recognized her and had a great feeling of shame that she should see me in such a supine, grease-besmeared, whimpering state.'

Morale

Survivors. North Atlantic
Lieutenant Commander W. G. Ogden, commanding officer of HMS *Lady Madeleine*, engaged in picking up survivors in the second World War, reported: 'Sally sent me a record called "Off she goes to the North", which was a Scottish reel, and in her honour I used to play this over the ship's loud-hailer system when we were picking up survivors from sinking ships. Many of the exhausted sailors we rescued from the drink [sea] told me afterwards that the music gave them hope, and courage to hold on a little longer, until we could get them on board the *Lady Madeleine*.'

Panic

Underwater Swimmers. Pacific. January
Bernard Gorsky: 'It was a very large shark . . . it made straight for Roger. . . . We fell back to the reef on the point of panic.'

Prayer

Man-overboard. North Atlantic. September
Franz Streycharczyk, sixteen hours in water. A ship passed close to him after four hours; 'he prayed and was very frightened'.

Ditched Airman. Gulf of Mexico. November
Paul Shook: 'I noticed dark clouds ahead. I observed rain falling some distance from me and prayed that it would come my way.'

Selfishness

Survivor from SS Nova Scotia. Indian Ocean. November
Senior Second Officer, Mr N. Robertson (in the water thirty-five hours): 'Later I contacted a raft with seven prisoners of war on it, but they would not let me board it, so I hung on to the side. Once

these prisoners were on a raft they would not let the British sailors get on, but pushed them back into the water. During the night several fell off the raft and an Italian assisted me to get them back on it each time, but finally I was exhausted, and did not have the strength to help them any more. When morning came only three remained on the raft.'

Survivor from SS Laconia. *Doldrums (Atlantic). September*
Nursing Sister Doris M. Hawkins was in a lifeboat alongside a torpedoed ship. The lifeboat capsized. 'I found myself among numbers of Italians screaming and struggling in the water. One in his terror grasped me, both arms around my neck, and dragged me down, down into the water. Thoughts came to me in that moment with amazing clarity, and in rapid succession. . . . I saw too my parents eagerly awaiting my return after five years' service overseas. I struggled and I came to the surface. . . . My hand touched a piece of wood and I clung on. Another Italian began to drag at me. Finally I came up to a raft.'

Vision
Survivor in Water. Doldrums (Atlantic)
'I had lost all sense of perspective and what I thought had been a large light, quite distinct, was in reality a very small light close up. Where there was a lifejacket light there was a survivor, so I struck out.'

LANDING

Survivors may require to reserve their strength for the final effort of getting ashore.

Clothing protects the skin from abrasions, but it adds to the effect of the undertow. It may be better, under difficult landing conditions, to dispense with clothing and accept abrasions, rather than risk being swept back to sea.

It is better to cling to small pieces of flotsam than to large pieces which may crush the survivor.

Swimmer in high seas. Rocky shore. English Channel. May
Ann Davison attempted to land on Portland Bill in a Carley float. 'I dug away with the handhold (used as a paddle) for all I was worth. Then was caught up in a blind white rush, hurled towards the rocks. The float turned over and I was flung into the sea. Surfaced for a moment, still gripping a lifeline. High overhead hung

a wave, breaking. Instinctively I let go and was lost in a green confusion, rocks beneath, sea above. The water receded. I was lying on my back on a rock with the float on top of me. The float was empty. I tried to push it off. Tried again and succeeded. Another wave towered. Tumult. Then air and peace and the float atop again. Again I pushed it off. Crawled to another rock, clung to it as the next wave broke. Between waves I had glimpsed a cavern whose floor was above the level of the breaking seas, and between waves I worked towards it, pursued by the float, and thinking with idiotic simplicity, so this is how you land on rocks, cling like a limpet and keep your head down.'

Non-swimmer in high seas. Rocky Shore. Irish Sea. December
The *Royal Charter* grounded in hurricane and high seas, ten yards from the rocky shore of Anglesey in 1859. Men and women in the water who clung to heavy pieces of wreckage, such as masts and spars 'were crushed to death, the bodies dreadfully mutilated against the rocks by the great weight of these materials. Mangled corpses, arms, legs and even heads were discernible on the crest of many a retreating wave.' Those who grasped lighter pieces of wreckage were more fortunate. Upon landing on the rocks those who were wearing heavy clothing staggered under the weight of the sodden mass and suffered most from the undertow. Those who survived were nearly naked.

A swimmer from the same wreck let himself go limp and was unhurt on impact with the rocks. On grasping the rocks the undertow caused him to slip back and he was cut. He was not wearing clothing and managed to scramble free.

Swimmer in Breakers. Coral Shore. Indian Ocean. September
C. O. Jennings at the end of a 127 days' voyage: '. . . another wall of water curling right over us. . . . There was no dodging this one. . . . I went into the water. My lungs were ready to burst as I rose to the surface, only to see another monster towering high above me. I had just chance to take a deep breath, and dived again. . . . Again I came to the surface, to see a piece of *Gilca*'s false freeboard floating past me. Clutching it, I looked round for Hall, but saw no sign of him. Our craft had been smashed completely, and I was alone among the breakers, a quarter of a mile from the beach. . . . Swimming harder than I had ever done in my life, I tried to get as far shorewards as I could before being compelled to dive in order to miss the next breaker. Releasing my hold on the plank prior to diving, it became obvious that I was making little headway, because no sooner was I under the water than the undertow caused me to spin like a

catherine wheel head over heels, and when I came to the surface my plank had disappeared. I was afraid of becoming completely exhausted. Diving again, I felt a stinging pain in my leg. Putting out my hands I gripped a rock, a pinnacle of coral, to which I clung: and I found I could put my head above the surface of the sea. For five minutes or more I clung to it, not daring to let go. I waited until my breathing became fairly normal. Then at what seemed a favourable opportunity I stepped forward, found no bottom, and started swimming shorewards as fast as I could. Again I barked my shins on rock, but the pool had been crossed, and again my grip tightened on the coral to prevent my being swept out to sea. . . . I was bleeding freely where my body had come in contact with the coral and, half-drowned, I clung to the submerged rock, trying to regain my breath and energy. Summoning all my courage, I made another effort shorewards, and although repeatedly touching bottom, I seemed unable to make any progress, due I presumed to the undertow. . . . Looking shorewards I heard Hall shouting . . . "Crawl, Skipper, crawl!" Only then did I realize what was wrong with me. My legs not having been used for so long, coupled with weakness due to starvation, they were not strong enough to carry the weight of my body. So down I went on my knees, head under water, and crawled along the bottom, coming up only for occasional breaths, and, when I was some twenty yards from shore, Hall staggered into the water and helped me up the sandy beach. He too, I noticed, was bleeding where he had caught the coral.'

Swimming in Surf. Rocky Shore. North Pacific
Eugene Burdick: 'I went body-surfing with two Hawaiian friends and it was not until we were past the surf line and treading water and waiting for a "big one" that I realized what they intended. Body-surfing is a much more intricate art than surf-boarding, because you must catch the wave at exactly the right point, arch your shoulders exactly right, and if you know the art, shoot into the beach with your body out well in front of the wave. Once mastered, it is not particularly dangerous. But what my companions proposed to do was to ride the storm waves directly towards an outcropping of rock and coral against which the waves shattered themselves into the maddest spume I had ever seen. The trick, they patiently explained, was to duck out of the wave just before it hit the rocks, dive deep to escape the turbulence and swim underwater back towards the surf line. It called for exquisite timing.

'They demonstrated for me a few times. Just as the wave was about to shatter on the rocks I saw their feet flash into the air, their bottoms rolled forward and they disappeared. A half minute later

74

their heads popped to the surface just beyond the churning white water.'

ADVICE TO MEN IN THE WATER

Man-overboard

If you are doing work where there is a danger of your falling overboard, wear warm unrestricted clothing, protective clothing (when in cold climates) and a lifejacket. As with all persons at risk at sea, the man-overboard should be able to swim; the non-swimmer is a liability to his companions.

Shout as you go overboard, get clear of the ship and continue shouting as long as there is a chance of being heard. Splash the water all the while there is a chance of being seen. Then float, on back, so as to conserve body heat; you are more likely to be seen from the air in this position. If a surface craft appears tread water and splash; the emergence of the head will increase the chance of being seen.

Do not panic, nor swim unnecessarily. Man can remain afloat for a long time even in rough seas. Franz Streycharczyk was in mid-Atlantic, sea state 5–6, for sixteen hours and did not know that it was rough.

Survivors at Sea

Keep together. Encourage one another.

If it is cold retain all clothing, the thicker the better, but loosen all restrictions, especially neckwear, before the hands become too numbed to do so. A tightly knotted tie will shrink when it is wet and may cause choking. Remain still and conserve body-heat. Do *not* swim unless a refuge is near.

Avoid oil-covered patches, unless sharks are around. If in an oil patch, keep on back or otherwise keep eyes, nose and mouth clear of the oil. Oil will not kill, but it blurs the vision and causes smarting for a day or two, and oil swallowed is nauseating and may cause vomiting. If the oil is alight swim underwater and proceed as described on page 49.

If there is any possibility of an explosion swim away from the ship as quickly as possible and endeavour to get out of the water, by climbing on to a raft or flotsam. If it is not possible to get out of the water, turn on the back and lift the

75

chest and abdomen out of the water as far as possible and also keep the ears and nostrils out of the water; the lifejacket will enable these precautions to be taken.

Underwater Swimmers

Do not undertake underwater activities on an empty stomach nor soon after a heavy meal, nor after a hang-over.

Do not hyperventilate. The taking of rapid, deep breaths for two minutes or so will increase the breath-holding time but it washes out the alveolar carbon dioxide (carbon dioxide normally present in the deep, minute air spaces of the lungs) which provides the danger signal forcing one to surface for another breath. Restrict yourself to normal breath-holding time and do not undertake sudden spasms of activity. Hyperventilation leads to unconsciousness and drowning.

Swim in pairs and have a safety boat available. Get out of the water immediately you feel below normal.

ADVICE TO MEN IN SHARK-INFESTED WATER

Survivors at Sea

Retain all clothing, particularly on legs and feet. Keep quiet and as stationary as possible, move only to keep the shark in sight. If in a group, form a tight circle and face outwards. Get on to some flotsam if available, do not trail anything from it. Get into an oil patch if available. If it is necessary to swim, use regular strokes, strong or lazy, fast or slow, but always rhythmic.

Do not urinate if a shark is near. Bind bleeding wounds. Do not wear or trail a bright object. Do not carry or trail wounded fish. Stream a shark repellent if available.

A piercing shriek underwater may scare a shark away, but this is not always effective. If a shark approaches stiff-arm it on the snout, between the eyes, with the bare fist if nothing more suitable is available.

Swimmers and Bathers

Pleasure beaches where sharks are a hazard are protected by netting, equipped with shark-alarm sound signals, usually a siren, and appropriate first-aid equipment, and are patrolled by lifeguards.

THESE SHARKS ARE DANGEROUS

Great White Shark
or White Pointer (20-35 ft)

Tiger Shark (12-18 ft)

Mako or Blue Shark (12 ft)

Whaler or Grey Shark (12 ft)

Hammerhead Shark (10-14 ft)

Great Blue Shark
or Blue Pointer (10-13 ft)

Sand or Grey Nurse (10-12 ft)

The sizes given here are those
of the mature shark

Bathe and swim in the protected area. Do not bathe or swim alone. If the shark alarm is heard, leave the water immediately.

Victims of Shark Attack

Shark attack produces severe shock and usually massive tearing of the flesh and loss of blood.

The Surf Lifesaving Association of Australia practises the following treatment:

In the water

Get the patient to the beach as quickly as possible.

If a boat is available, use it. Begin control of haemorrhage by tourniquet, pressure or otherwise, as soon as the patient is brought into the boat.

On the beach

Immediate, urgent treatment—

Carry the patient above the waterline.

Place with the head below the level of the feet. Keep the patient quiet. Restrict movement of the patient to the very minimum.

Stop the bleeding. Use immediate pressure with fingers and hands on spurting blood vessels. Fill firmly with clean handkerchiefs or any other clean material available. Apply a tourniquet immediately if necessary.

Cover the wound with a clean towel or other material when bleeding is controlled.

Ask a bystander to call a doctor and ambulance; if possible the Red Cross Blood Bank or its local branch. In cases of serious shock and injury, a blood transfusion on the spot is much more important and likely to save the patient's life than immediate transfer to hospital.

Wait.

While waiting—

Keep the crowd away.

Resist suggestions by onlookers to do something more.

Do not warm the patient. This means no hot-water bottles, no blankets, no hot drinks, no alcohol. A light cover only is recommended. The patient's mouth may be moistened by sips of water. *No further food or water to be given.*

If a special shark kit is available, bring it to the patient's side.

On the doctor's arrival—
He will inject pain-killing drugs.

He may give fluids into the veins.

He may decide to give an immediate transfusion or wait for further recovery before arranging transport to hospital.

If no doctor is available—
Control of haemorrhage must be maintained.

Wait for thirty minutes to enable some recovery from shock to make transport safer.

Transport to hospital. The patient must not be moved except on a rigid frame. Movement must be *slow, gentle* and *smooth*. The vehicle must be driven to conform with these requirements. A rough journey could kill the patient by aggravating the shock.

ADVICE TO SURVIVORS MAKING THE SHORE

Do not panic; most currents usually go back to shore at some stage.

Tidal Streams

Whereas ocean currents rarely exceed a speed of 2 knots, tidal streams in some places reach speeds of more than 4 knots. Strong currents formed by the tides occur off headlands, and the bigger the headland the faster the current. There is an added danger in that the current off a headland is likely to be to seaward. Estuarial currents have speeds from 3 to 8 knots.

The average swimmer in still water has a speed of about 1 knot and this is reduced if clothing and a lifejacket are worn. In general, therefore, do not attempt to swim against a current but conserve energy and warmth, and await rescue from local shore-rescue forces who are familiar with the currents.

Rip Currents

Rip currents flow at right angles to the shore, are intermittent, mostly offshore but sometimes onshore. They are generally very narrow, sometimes less than 100 feet across at their inshore end, and fan out at their seaward end, the water feeding round the sides back to the shore. Lengths of between 200 feet and 2,500 feet have been measured.

Do not attempt to swim directly against a rip current. Keep the body horizontal and close to the surface; this will reduce the effect of the current. If there is reason to believe that the current is narrow, swim across it; otherwise drift with the current and await rescue, or, when the current has petered out at its seaward end, swim into the feed-back to the beach.

Longshore Currents

Longshore currents are induced by waves breaking obliquely on a beach and flow in the direction of the wave motion.

Swim in the general direction of the current.

Undertow

Undertow is the flow of water to seaward along the bed of the beach, returning to the sea the water which has been brought shoreward along the surface; it occurs, for example, when steep waves and an onshore wind are pushing surface water towards the shore.

Keep the body horizontal on the surface to take advantage of the shoreward movement. Do not stand in the undertow. Water 3 feet deep can be troublesome; more than that depth, and with large waves breaking, it can lead to disaster.

Surf

Select the swell whose crest is longer than average, as these travel furthest up the beach before breaking up. In a sea where there are both high and low waves, if the low wave is also of the greatest length along the crest, so much the better.

Having selected the wave, the practised body-surfer will tread water and wait for where the surface breaks, push on to it with several quick, strong, strokes, place the arms close to the body, hunch the shoulders, slightly hollow the chest, propel by the palms or crawl-kick if necessary, keep the head down and raise only for a breath.

If the wave is thought to be a dumper (which crashes down suddenly, unlike an ordinary breaker; the crest curls over almost into a cylinder before it collapses), pull off it by sweeping the arms forward to force the body backwards and throw the head back as far as possible; continue to do this until the calmer water behind the dumper is reached. Escape from the dumper well before the dumping develops; if left too late, go to the bottom and wait for the wave to pass.

Survivors who are not practised body-surfers should swim steadily towards the shore keeping a careful watch on waves in front and behind. When a wave breaks behind, watch it until it is about five yards away, take a deep breath and dive or submerge as deeply as possible and re-surface when it is considered that the wave has passed; repeat this procedure with every wave.

A survivor who does not feel able to proceed as described above should take a deep breath just before a wave strikes him; he will be dragged under and tumbled around. Do *not* attempt to regain the surface but wait for the natural buoyancy to do this. By keeping afloat between waves and letting each successive wave push the body further in, the shore is soon reached.

If the surf is light, tired and weak swimmers should keep the body vertical and let the waves push them towards the shore.

If there is any flotsam around, a weak swimmer should select a small piece of adequate buoyancy for clinging to, rather than a large piece which might get out of hand and crush him.

Storm-waters
Avoid calm areas in an otherwise stormy sea; they are sometimes due to strong currents which flow seaward.

Seaweed
Do not attempt to swim through thick seaweed, but make overhand movements, grasp the weeds and pull over the top.

RESCUE BY BEACH LIFE-GUARD

The following signals, which are in general use by the Surf Lifesaving Associations of Australia, Great Britain and South Africa, should be understood by swimmers and surfers in distress. There are some other signals used by the Associations which are of no direct interest to the survivor and are not included here.

Beltman or Patient to Linemen and Beach

Signal	*Signification*
One arm raised perpendicularly above head until certain that signal has been received.	'All clear; Secured patient; Haul in'
Both arms raised perpendicularly above head.	'Lost patient. Pay out if necessary'
One arm raised and lowered three times in quick succession.	'Hauling too fast'
Both arms waved to and fro crossing above head until signal has been understood.	'Distress'

Beach to Beltman, Surf Boats, Boards or Skis

Two signal flags, orange with a 4-inch blue diagonal stripe, are used, except for the shark alarm, which is red and white quartered.

Signal	*Signification*
One flag held above head.	'Return to shore'
Two flags held above head.	'Proceed further out to sea'
One flag held at arm's length parallel to the ground in the required direction.	'Proceed to the right (or left)'
Two flags held at arm's length parallel to the ground.	'Remain stationary'
One flag waved above the head.	'Message not clear; repeat'
One flag held stationary above the head and cut away quickly.	'Message understood; all clear'
Two flags moved to and fro crossing above the head.	'Attention'
One flag waved in circular manner around the head and a second flag pointed in the direction of the patients.	'Pick up swimmers'
Shark-alarm flag (red and white quartered) waved above head.	'Shark alarm'
Three strokes of alarm bell or three blasts of siren.	'Mass rescue'

Surf Boat to Beach

Surf boats carry a signal flag (orange with a 4-inch blue diagonal stripe) and a shark-alarm flag (red and white quartered).

Signal	*Signification*
Wave shark-alarm flag above head; if flag is not available, raise oars.	'Shark alarm'
One signal flag raised above head and swept down; if flag is not available, one arm waved horizontal in front of body.	'Shore signal received and understood'
One signal flag waved above the head; if flag is not available wave one arm from side to side across the head.	'Shore signal not understood'

Surf Boards and Surf Skis to Beach

Signal	*Signification*
One arm raised above head.	'Beltman required'
Right arm waved to and fro above head.	'Another board required'
Both arms held vertically above the head, or the paddle in the case of surf skis.	'Shark alarm'
Both arms held in horizontal position, or the paddle held above the head in a horizontal position at the full extent of the arms.	'All clear'

3

Afloat

The chances of survival are much greater if the body is supported clear of the water, but a prolonged period afloat leads to many disabilities and may even result in death. Survival depends on the degree of protection against the elements, the availability of drinking water and to a much lesser extent of food, and the maintenance of the will to live.

The greatest hazards to men adrift at sea are exposure to cold and dehydration.

EXPOSURE TO COLD

Lifeboat from SS Induna. *Arctic. March*
A three days' ordeal. The Second Officer, Mr E. Rowlands: 'It was bitterly cold during the [first] night and the six or seven bottles of whisky which were in the boat were passed round. I myself only had a mouthful, but unfortunately some of the men drank a good deal of the spirits; several of the older men fell asleep and died during the night. In fact, most of the men who drank the whisky died in their sleep that night. . . . We continued sailing for three days, seven men died during the first night, including the donkeyman who was severely burned, one or two died each day and on the last day four men died. It was bitterly cold, everyone suffered from frostbite in their hands and feet but not their faces.'

Stowaway. North Atlantic. November
Mr M. W. F. Dunning, VRD, FRCS, reported on a youth 'aged fifteen years, stowed away on a ship from Montreal, hiding in a lifeboat, under a tarpaulin cover for four days. During this period the weather was extremely cold and the air temperature was often below $-4°C$. There was no water in the lifeboat. When found he had severe frostbite of both feet. He was treated with bed rest and penicillin (one mega unit daily) for the remaining five days of the voyage and then transferred to the Royal Southern Hospital, Liverpool. On admission . . . the terminal phalanges of all his toes were gangrenous. Large blisters were present on both feet. . . .'

Ship's Boat from HMS Endurance. *Weddell Sea. April–May*
A six days' ordeal. Commander F. A. Worsley, RN, writing of

Shackleton's boat voyage from an ice floe to Elephant Island, stated that on the fifth day Blackbarrow's feet were badly frostbitten. 'Blackbarrow, the youngest of the party, was twenty years old. This may have accounted for the fact that he was the only one to suffer permanently from frostbite. . . . Most of us suffered no more than frostbitten fingers, which we were all liable to. . . . We made a practice of eating our food and swallowing our milk at a far greater heat than normal men could have borne. So we gave our chilled bodies warmth enough to keep us alive against cold, fatigue and lack of sleep.'

On landing at Elephant Island, on the sixth day, 'The most serious invalid was Blackbarrow. His right foot appeared to be recovering and there was hope that it might even be saved. But in the toes of his left foot gangrene had already set in. McIlroy [Surgeon] who was attending him was chiefly concerned with preventing the affected parts developing what is called "wet gangrene".'

Lifeboat from MV Shillong. *North Atlantic. April*
A nine days' ordeal. Apprentice David E. Clowe: 'Our feet were badly frostbitten. . . . I was the only survivor to escape amputation of some kind, all the other survivors had to have finger, toes or feet amputated. One apprentice had to lose both legs. I can only attribute my good fortune to the fact that I kept as active as possible in the boat and even did exercises whenever I could to keep my circulation going.'

Lifeboat from SS Aldington Court. *South Atlantic. October*
Thirteen days' ordeal. Third Officer Mr J. R. Mitchell: 'After seven days in the boat it was noted that the men's feet started swelling, those without shoes or boots being the first to complain. After about ten days, everyone was complaining of their feet being sore and painful despite the fact that all were using the massage oil for their feet as well as their bodies. We found the oil helpful in keeping out the cold, but everybody was suffering from trench feet by the time we boarded the rescue ship (on the thirteenth day). The Bosun found it quite impossible to use his feet at all, so we had to put a rope around him, and hoisted him in board. He was afterwards taken to hospital, where one leg was amputated.'

Ship's Boat from HMS Endurance. *Scotia Sea. April–May*
A sixteen days' voyage from Elephant Island to South Georgia on the 22 foot 6 inch *James Caird*. Commander Worsley: 'After the third day our feet and legs had swelled and began to be superficially frostbitten. . . . During the last gale (on the ninth day) they assumed a deadwhite colour and lost surface feeling. To prevent my feet

85

getting worse, I adopted a system of wriggling them constantly, contracting and relaxing my toes until quite tired, waiting a minute, then wriggling them again, and so on.' By the thirteenth day, 'Each successive frostbite on a finger was marked by a ring where the skin had peeled up to, so that we could count our frostbites by the rings.'

Sir Ernest Shackleton: 'On the tenth day Worsley could not straighten his body after his spell at the tiller. He was thoroughly cramped, and we had to drag him beneath the decking and massage him before he could unbend himself and get into a sleeping-bag. . . . Skin frostbites were troubling us and we had developed large blisters on our fingers and hands. I shall always carry the scar of one of these frostbites on my left hand, which became badly inflamed after the skin had burst and the cold had bitten deeply.'

Lifeboat from SS Britannia. *Doldrums (Atlantic). April*
A twenty-three days' ordeal. Lieutenant Frank West reported on the thirteenth day: 'Sunday night was very cold and everyone was miserable.' Fifteenth day: 'It was late in the day when the rain stopped and we were very wet and cold. . . . McIntosh rinsed his clothes with salt water and felt appreciably warmer. In the evening it rained again and we were all soaking wet and very cold. I got cramp badly and spent a horrible night. How I loathe being cold. For me it is worse than the heat.'

Ship's Boat from HMS Bounty. *South Pacific (Tropics). April–May*
A forty-two days' ordeal, including stops at islands. Captain William Bligh reported, ninth day: 'Our limbs were dreadfully cramped, for we could not stretch them out, and the nights were so cold, and were so constantly wet, that after a few hours' sleep, we could scarcely move.' Twenty-third day: 'The little sleep we got was in the midst of water, and we constantly awoke with severe cramps and pains in our bones.' Twenty-seventh day: 'The weather and sea continued very bad, we now dreaded the nights, for we were all benumbed with the cold, being constantly wet. To act against the evils attending such a situation, I could only order everyone when our clothes became filled with water, to strip naked and wring them, and when only wet with the rain, to dip them first in the sea, so that this was the only resource we had for dry clothes.'

Sailing Ship. Cape Horn. March
Apprentice seaman Eric Newby: 'The cold struck at us from the deck through the soles of our boots. Those with rubber sea-boats were the worst off. The Finns and Alanders . . . all wore leather boots which they kept greased.'

86

Yacht. Circumnavigation
Marcel Bardiaux, of his time in Aguirre Bay: 'On a small boat such as this, the cold is more formidable than the sea itself.' Near Cape Horn, 'The chain ran out of my hands. . . . It tore out the palms of my fabric gloves as well as the skin and a little flesh from three fingers. At this temperature healing was slow . . . my face and ears were covered by chilblains and one ear seemed to be completely frozen.'

Sailing Yacht Suhaili. *Cape Horn. January*
On the 218th day after leaving Falmouth in his single-handed round-the-world voyage, Robin Knox-Johnston recorded: 'I've just finished the dried peaches and I've consumed a quarter of a bottle of whisky since yesterday morning. In fact, I prefer coffee or cocoa to whisky which explains my low consumption; I find that they warm me up more.'

Sailing Ship Santa Maria. *North Atlantic. February*
The journal of Christopher Columbus records on the thirty-second day of the return voyage: 'This night [Saturday] the Admiral took some rest for since Wednesday he had not slept nor been able to sleep, and he was crippled in his legs, owing to having been constantly exposed to the cold and water, and owing to the small amount he had eaten.'

Rowing-Boat English Rose III. *North Atlantic. July–August*
Chay Blyth reported, forty-third day: 'I was very cold and very wet and every inch of my body was one long irritating rash.' Fifty-seventh day: John Ridgway had 'a rash from knees to hips and his neck was encircled with salt-water boils. The only thing in the first aid pack which gave him any relief at all was foot powder.'

EXPOSURE TO WIND

Relief Ship Morning. *Antarctic*
Admiral Lord Mountevans: 'All hands remained ready for any emergency, clothed, seabooted and protected by oil-skins on top of their cold-weather clothing. The look-outs were doubled and perched in the eyes of the ship and had to be relieved every half-hour to prevent them from becoming frostbitten. Yes, I remember that gale which developed into a three-day hurricane.'

Convoy. Arctic
'The wind sprang up and increased in strength. On the morning of

the twenty-eighth an icy gale was blowing. . . . The men on watch were swiftly transformed into blocks of ice and had to be relieved every hour.'

Sailing Yacht Pagan. *South Pacific. September*
John Caldwell, sailing the 29-foot cutter *Pagan* single-handed, was caught in a hurricane north of the Cook Islands. He wrote: 'Before jumping on deck I bound a heavy line round my middle, and made it fast to the handrail on the deckhouse. I waited a moment when the decks were water free and leapt out of the hatchway, closed it, jumped into the windward waist, and lay flat, facing up deck. The prying fingers of the wind caught the loose fold of my shirt, filling it at the front, tearing away the buttons, and ripping it down the back and sides. It hung by tatters. My full strength was required to lie flat on deck. I didn't dare to stand into that wind, or even sit. When I looked into it for a second, I could feel my eyes depress; I could feel my hair whip against my cheeks.' He worked his way along a knotted life-line to replace a broken shroud by the forestay. 'I lay on my back on the blown decks with only my hands and forearms in the wind. . . . The job completed, I made the gross error of sitting up to check it. An explosive wind bent me to a helpless angle. A flurry of bubbling water lifted me bodily and bounced me against the deck-house and into the shrouds, then whelmed me over the rail on to a churning sea.' His life-line held and he managed to reboard.

Sailing Boat from HMS Endurance. *Scotia Sea. April–May*
Eighth day, Commander Worsley wrote: 'Constant peering to windward to ease her into the heaviest seas and the continuous dash of salt water into my face had almost bunged up my eyes.'

Warship HMS Lady Madeleine. *Off Iceland*
Lieutenant Commander W. G. Ogden, commanding officer of HMS *Lady Madeleine*, reported that the hurricane 'reached its height at about 1800 when its official speed was given as 120 m.p.h. The barometer showed 26·4 inches—this was the lowest I have ever seen it. Water was driving past the bridge (which was 27 feet above normal sea level) in a solid sheet. I couldn't see the sky and I couldn't see the surface of the sea. The effect of the hurricane when at its height was like being in a tunnel. It was impossible to stand up and the only way one could see anything at all was by putting one's face into the large end of the hand megaphone and quickly squinting into it.'

EXPOSURE TO HEAT

Prisoner-of-War Ship. Banda Sea. September
Flight Lieutenant W. M. Blackwood: 'All the men lay spread on
the uneven bundles of firewood blistering horribly in the tropical
sun. Tongues began to blacken . . . and all vestiges of sanity deserted
many. . . . One youngster, delirious with sunstroke, shouted the
thoughts of his disordered mind for thirty hours before he became
too weak to utter another word. Just before he died he grabbed a
full tin, that was being used as a bed pan, and drank the contents
greedily, before he could be prevented.'

Tanker MV Miraflores. *Westerschelde. February*
The *Miraflores* caught fire following a collision; oil spread on the
water and some of it became alight. Captain van den Bosch, master of
a rescue vessel: 'The heat became too much at the end. At one time I
thought I had gone blind. You could not look at the flames any more.'

Lifeboat from SS San Demetrio. *North Atlantic. March*
Burning oil tanker and fire on the water. The Master, Captain C.
Vidot: 'After pulling clear of the ship's side I saw the Chief Wireless
Operator still hanging on the rope ladder at the water's edge, and
we had to pull back through the flames to get him into the boat.
After a desperate struggle due to the suffocating smoke and flames
which enveloped this lee-boat, we finally succeeded in getting clear
of the ship and blazing sea which surrounded her. The heat in the
boat was so fierce that four men were unable to withstand it and
jumped overboard, and I'm afraid that they were lost. Fortunately
the boats were made of steel and did not suffer any serious damage
from the fierce flames.'

Liferaft from SS Britannia. *Doldrums (Atlantic). March*
A five days' ordeal. Lieutenant A. H. Rowlandson RN reported on
the second day: 'Welby, who had been without covering most of the
day, began to behave queerly and there is no doubt that his mind
was wandering. He needed much support and was quite unable to
help himself. [Surgeon Lieutenant] Marks said he was definitely
suffering from sunstroke and was not likely to survive the night. . . .
Cox and I shared the weight of Welby, who became unconscious
after dark. It was difficult to keep his head above water and I'm afraid
he must have swallowed a lot. . . . During the night Welby died.'

Lifeboat from SS Britannia. *Doldrums (Atlantic). March*
A twenty-three days' ordeal. Lieutenant Frank West RN reported,
third day: 'Beck is suffering badly from exposure and has severe

sunburn on his legs and thighs. This is in the form of huge blisters, some containing watery fluid and others thick pus. I have tried to evacuate them and have put dressings on them; he must be in great pain and is quite unable to keep still for even a few minutes.' Fifth day: 'Beck fainted during the night [of the fourth day] owing to the heat and the congestion. His sunburn and blisters are very bad. . . . Blank appeared to have sunstroke and failed to wake up properly on being roused after his hour's rest. He was most quarrelsome and wanted to fight. . . . After a further two hours he woke up quite well, not knowing anything about the earlier attempt to waken him. Apparently some rowing he did yesterday had tired him greatly.' Sixth day: 'Our lips were swollen and cracked and some, who had failed to keep arms and legs covered, were badly sunburnt.'

Lifeboat from SS Laconia. *Doldrums (Atlantic). September–October*
A twenty-seven days' ordeal. Nursing Sister Doris M. Hawkins: 'Until they became too weak, most of the men used to go over the side for a dip once or twice a day, and they used to pour tins of water over my bare head and shoulders and limbs, and then we used to sit during the heat of the day with our clothing soaked in water, and with cloths which we kept perpetually wet tied above our heads. I believe that in these ways water was absorbed through the skin. By night the clothing had dried on us and the burning heat gave way to cold.'

Lifeboat from SS City of Cairo. *South Atlantic. November–December*
A thirty-six days' ordeal. Fifty-four persons in boat, only two men and one woman alive at the time of rescue; the woman died five days later. At the start of the voyage there were three meals a day, each meal consisting of 4 oz. of water, biscuits, pemmican, chocolate and Horlicks tablets. Some natives started drinking salt water from about the tenth day. Mr J. C. Edmead, Third Steward and Ship's Writer: 'From noon until 1800 each day the sun beat down on us unmercifully and it was impossible to keep cool. An old flag was torn up, each man was given a small piece to put over his head. On the eleventh day the first native died, and during the next few days they died, two and three at a time. It was about this time that some of the Europeans began to lose heart, several of them dying at various intervals. Death in each case appeared to follow an attack of delirium lasting about three hours. From this time onwards the crew gradually lost their appetites and the water situation became very grave. . . . One of the Quartermasters developed a high fever which lasted for three days before he died. . . . The men now died on various days until on the twenty-eighth day there were only six of us

left.' Three men died during the night of the twenty-ninth day. On being rescued by the German blockade runner *Rhakotis* on the thirty-sixth day: 'We were taken to the sick bay and put straight to bed. The woman passenger was in a serious condition and continued to get weaker, the German doctor told me that all the tissues in her throat had collapsed and she was unable to eat anything. She died on 17th December (five days after rescue). . . .'

Liferaft from SS Lulworth Hill. *Doldrums (Atlantic). March–April*
A fifty days' ordeal. Fourteen men on a raft, only two survived. The survivors' clothing, which had been torn by explosion and turbulence when their ship sank, gave little protection against the sun. Kenneth Cooke, the ship's carpenter, reported, first day: 'Some of us are already feeling the effects of sun and salt on our exposed skins and these cases of sunburn caused agony at the slightest touch.' Second day: 'It was not long before the men were shifting uneasily and grumbling about the sunburn they were beginning to suffer, which coupled with thirst and rough salt-dried clothing was getting unbearable.' Fifth day: 'So badly burned were our bodies that the slightest touch seared them like a red-hot iron.' Eighth day: 'Huge water blisters had resulted from our compulsory sunbathing.' Tenth day: 'Salt-water boils were increasing and combined with the effects of sunburn made movement horribly painful. Each time a man moved his neighbour would scream aloud in the agony caused by the slight knock or blow. The screams were hard to bear.' Fifteenth day: 'Although by that time our sunburn had eased, leaving our bodies so deeply tanned that we looked like a crew of Lascars, the sun still caused us acute suffering from its heat and overpowering dryness.'

Sailing Yacht Gipsy Moth IV. *Doldrums (Atlantic). September*
Sir Francis Chichester: 'I don't get hungry in these 85°F heats until the middle of the night, or early morning. . . . At night I was troubled by cramp in my legs which would hit me after I had been asleep about two hours, and would let go only if I stood up. This meant that I never got more than about two hours' sleep at a time. It was hot and I sweated profusely; I wondered whether my body might be losing too much salt. I decided to drink half a glassful of sea-water a day to put back salt.'

DEHYDRATION

Liferaft from SS Britannia. *Doldrums (Atlantic). March*
Ten men on a raft and planks, waist-deep in water, for five days.

No food or water. Lieutenant A. H. Rowlandson reported, third day: 'Marks showed signs of exhaustion and it soon became clear that his mind was wandering. . . . He was able to picture a scene of his own fishing village and carried on conversations with imaginary boatmen round him. He was very anxious to swim ashore which he said he had often done from there before and I had to use force to restrain him on several occasions. . . . During the night Marks at last swam away from us and swam into the darkness.' Fourth day: 'The heat was intense. Cox and Dwyer seemed very exhausted, both appearing to be rather light-headed, and on one or two occasions tried to strike each other. During the night Dwyer's mind went completely and he too eventually fought his way off the raft and swam away to "buy an evening paper". We saw and heard nothing more of him.' Fifth day: 'Lobo became completely out of control. . . . About midday he became weaker and could not help himself, and I found it impossible to get him fully on the raft. Soon after this one of the sharks seized his leg and savaged it. . . . He became unconscious and died soon afterwards.'

Ship's Boat from HMS Endurance. *Scotia Sea. April–May*
Six men in the boat *James Caird* for sixteen days' passage from Elephant Island to South Georgia. The daily water ration in the later stages was 1 gill (= 142 ml). All survived. Commander Worsley wrote of the fourth day: 'There had been no time to lay in a stock of ice for drinking water. All hands were suffering from the sensation of thirst.' Sixth day: 'Our poor fellows lit their pipes—their only solace—for our raging thirst prevented us from eating.' Sixteenth day: 'The water finished, our mouths and tongues were so dry and swollen.'

Sir Ernest Shackleton: 'Thirst took possession of us. . . . Lack of water is always the most severe privation that men can be condemned to endure and we found, as during our earlier boat voyage (from the ice field to Elephant Island) that the salt water in our clothing and the salt spray that lashed our faces made our thirst grow quickly to a burning pain. . . . Our mouths were dry and our tongues were swollen.' On the sixteenth day Sir Ernest found himself on a lee shore. 'Our thirst was forgotten in the realization of our imminent danger.'

Lifeboat from SS Britannia. *Atlantic (Doldrums). March–April*
Eighty-two men (19 Europeans, 24 Sikhs and 39 Lascars and Goanese) in 28-foot lifeboat (official capacity 56 persons) for twenty-three days. Sailed 1,535 miles. Daily ration of condensed milk and water determined by dividing total quantities in the boat

by the number of men and by 28 (the estimated time for making a landfall). At the start of the voyage the ration was a spoonful of milk at sunrise, and at sundown a third of a dipper of water (10 ounces), a biscuit and milk spread on the biscuit. Deaths commenced on the seventh day; during the voyage a total of 44 died (6 Europeans, 14 Sikhs and 24 Lascars and Goanese). Frank West reported, fourth day: 'We are feeling rather weak and tired. . . . This time it took the combined efforts of five men to hoist the mainsail, whereas two men had done it easily on the second day. . . . Some of the British used to suck a button and thought it helped. I tried it several times but it did nothing at all to alleviate my thirst, but David Purdie recalls that he kept a button in his mouth for days on end and lost count of how many he sucked completely away.' Fifth day: 'Throughout the day we pour tins of water over ourselves to help keep cool. A wet cloth round the throat seems to ease our thirst a little.' Sixth day: 'Our lips were swollen and cracked. . . . We are also by now terribly thin. Just skin and bone. I think we lost all the weight we could in this first week. . . . The majority, certainly the British, ate very little after the third or fourth day, though Wheater was able to eat a biscuit every day while any remained. I was quite unable to swallow biscuit after the third day and, except for trying some of the soaked biscuit (soaked in condensed milk and water), did not eat until we landed. I do not recall any great feeling of hunger.' Seventh day: 'The Indian chief cook either threw himself, or fell, overboard. He had been drinking a good deal of sea-water and had gradually become quite ill. . . . Our conversation continually centres round what we shall drink. . . . A number were suffering from badly swollen and cracked lips and swollen tongues. This was caused by the formation of a white fur on the gums and teeth which gradually spread on to the lips, dried and caused cracking and bleeding, sometimes quite severe.' Eighth day: 'We all seemed a little short-tempered until after our morning-bath ritual.' A small increase was made in the milk ration. Ninth day: 'Daylight showed a number of the Indian crew in a very weak state, through drinking sea-water, and though we gave these a small extra issue of milk and fresh water, one died. . . . All of us are getting very touchy and it is sometimes hard to keep the peace. I have at this moment suggested that we cut out all swearing. . . . We had now existed for nine days on a total of well under a pint of water each, less than a quarter of a tin of condensed milk and, at the most, a couple of biscuits. Such meagre nourishment, under a tropical sun and with many duties to perform, was beginning to tell on us all, strangely enough, more on those who were less occupied. So an increase of $1\frac{1}{2}$ ounces to 2 ounces of water each day was decided upon.' Tenth day: 'So few can now eat the biscuits, even with milk on, that we have discontinued putting milk on biscuits and made the milk ration in the usual way and gave biscuits only to the one or two who asked for them.' Eleventh day: 'I had not the strength to finish my notes yesterday. Beck and Carney fainted in the afternoon and I had a job to bring them round—the strain is telling on us all—Liddell is near passing out.' Twelfth day: 'We are all getting terribly weak and how thin we are. . . . We all spent a fair amount of time day-dreaming, in a state of lethargic drowsiness, neither awake nor asleep.' Thirteenth day: 'Harman and Beck died. . . . Heavy rain fell. . . . We all got very wet and cold but feel most refreshed.' Fifteenth day: 'Six more Indians were found dead. It rained hard for several hours. All had as much as they could drink and 6 gallons were collected.' A ship passed very close. 'Many of the men in the boat shouted, sometimes single voices, but many times in a combined effort, but they were pathetically weak and useless cries.' Seventeenth day: 'Another Sikh passenger died during the night. . . . Like others I am feeling very weak. The only time we have any strength is at dawn . . . I found that I frequently fell asleep.' Eighteenth day: 'I had my first bathe for some days this morning for I have not had the strength to hang over the side of the boat. I also feel better as last night I had the first bowel movement for seventeen days, caused by having drunk a lot of rain water, I think. Few, if any, have been so fortunate as I in this respect, though we are all able to urinate twice a day since the additional water issues. . . . Smith is weakening and I seem to be able to do little for him. There is something wrong with his joints, which are seizing up. It was quite a usual thing for anyone who became delirious to want to throw things overboard, even going so far as to ask for things and then immediately throwing them away.' Nineteenth day: 'A cupful of milk again for breakfast was delicious, and we also soaked the remains of the biscuits in some fresh water which made them very soft but very few people ate any, for they stick in the throat.' Twentieth day: 'It now not only required a physical effort to write, but a mental one as well. It was difficult to think back and more so to put words and sentences together and the little I did write took a long time. So often I would fall asleep or just lie or sit in a comatose condition. . . .' Twenty-first day: 'We felt no hunger though many of us had not eaten for about eighteen days. We suffered badly from thirst but not as much as earlier, and we were getting used to that too.' Twenty-third day: 'The last night in the boat was one of the worst for all of us. . . . Two Indians died and those who went for'ard to bury them had the utmost difficulty in lifting the bodies from the bottom of the boat and became completely exhausted, for it took them a long time. . . . I weighed only 84 pounds on arrival instead of my normal 145, but within a few weeks had picked up to 112. It took several years to regain normal weight.'

Lifeboat from SS Laconia. *Doldrums (Atlantic). September–October*
Sixty-eight persons in thirty-foot lifeboat for twenty-seven days. Only sixteen survived. Nursing Sister Doris M. Hawkins: 'Our daily ration of food was as follows:

Morning: Four or five Horlicks tablets, three pieces of chocolate (size $1\frac{1}{2}$ in. × $\frac{3}{4}$ in. × $\frac{1}{8}$ in.). No water.

Evening: Two ship's biscuits (size of petit beurre, but very dry and hard); one teaspoonful of pemmican. Two ounces of water.

'Our worst torture was thirst. After a time we could easily bear the lack of food, but the lack of water tried us sorely. . . . When we received our precious drop, we took a sip, ran it round our teeth and gums, gargled with it and finally swallowed it. We repeated this until not a drop nor a drip was left clinging to the little biscuit tin from which we drank. After five minutes we could not tell that we had had any, so quickly did our parched bodies absorb the fluid. As we grew weaker and our mouths more and more dry, we only spoke when necessary. . . . Our pores closed up completely after a few days, and we did not perspire at all, in spite of the intense heat. Our nails became brittle and broke easily; many of us found our cuticles peeling away, and our nails became very pale. After a few days we all became a little light-headed, and were unable to sleep, but dozed lightly, and dreamed always of water, cool drinks, fruit— and of rescue. . . . Over and over again, teasing and tormenting, like a cinematograph show, the scenes passed and repassed. . . . We became thinner daily, and we were hollow-eyed. The men's beards grew. . . . Our tongues became hard and dry and our lips swollen and cracked. Many of us kept our teeth clean by rubbing them with a piece of cloth soaked in sea-water. When we talked our mouths were curiously mis-shapen and our voices became harsh and weak. . . . It was impossible after a few days to eat our biscuits or malted-milk tablets. The biscuits blew out of our mouths as we chewed them, and they just would not go down. . . . We tried to make our mouths less dry by chewing bone buttons from clothing and rubber bands from the pemmican and biscuit tins.

'Towards the end of our third week at sea, when I could no longer eat at all, because I was devoid of saliva, and depended for life on my water ration, we ran out of water. We prayed for rain. Next

morning we had a torrential downpour, lasting nearly six hours. . . .
Our dried-up bodies took on new strength as we absorbed this life-
giving water and drank as we had dreamed of doing for so long. That
day I managed to eat two biscuits again, and two or three Horlick's
tablets. Several of us had earache; even that could not depress us
now. The Polish cadet-officer and one of our own men, however,
developed large painful swellings of the parotid gland, making them
look as though they had mumps. The Pole soon recovered, but the
Englishman's condition did not improve.'

Liferaft from Transport Ship Skaubryn. *Indian Ocean. February–March*
Two men on raft. $1\frac{1}{2}$ litres of red wine in a rubber water bottle. One
man died on the seventeenth day, the other was rescued on the
thirty-second day.

Ensio Tiira reported, third day: 'We had drunk the last of the
wine. Our tongues were parched, our saliva dried up, now came the
rain and we had cold, refreshing, sweet beautiful water.' Fourth day:
'All we wanted was water.' Fifth day: 'It was over forty hours since
we drunk anything and my thirst was awful. My tongue was thick
and dry and I could smell my foul breath.' Some rainwater was
caught. 'I could feel my strength returning. There was saliva in my
mouth again and I could talk without strain. The tight constricted
feeling in my throat disappeared. I felt I was no longer going to
choke . . . we were full of water. My stomach, which had shrivelled
with the days, was now puffed out with water. . . . Thirst had left us
but we were very hungry.' Seventh day: Ericsson 'was haggard and
his skin yellow and unhealthy. Under his swollen eyes there were
deep dark shadows. . . . He'd lost a great deal of weight. Ericsson
tried to sing in the cool of the evening. His voice lost itself in his
throat. It was very difficult for me to talk. My voice was a whisper
. . . we couldn't talk even in our hoarse whispers for more than a few
sentences without breaking off into fits of coughing and there was
nothing we felt like doing. . . . Life was slowing down.' Eighth day,
some rain was caught: 'The temptation of having water and not
drinking it presented a new problem.' Ninth day: 'Our promises
shattered as the first drops rolled down our dried-up throats. We
couldn't take the bottle away from our lips. . . . By nightfall the bottle
was empty and we were left with our thirsts which had never
properly been slaked.' Tenth day: 'Our thirst was very bad.' Twelfth
day: 'My tongue wasn't swollen, but when I touched it with my
fingers it was hard, like coarse cloth. I was listless and weak.' A
turtle was caught. 'Between us we must have taken a pint of blood
. . . the blood was warm and sweet and sickly, refreshing at first.'
Some rainwater was caught. 'I felt much stronger . . . but Ericsson

hadn't improved at all. He said he was tired and fell asleep as soon as it was dark. The exertions of the day seemed to have outweighed any value he might have had from the food and water.' Thirteenth day: the water was exhausted. Ericsson would not eat any of the turtle scraps and slept nearly all day. Fourteenth day: Ericsson 'lost interest in everything and was failing fast. He revived somewhat when some rain fell, and we held up our faces to drink. Ericsson was in a strange mood.' Fifteenth day: Ericsson became unconscious. Sixteenth day: 'I felt that I was sinking too. Ericsson was much weaker. The colour had gone from his eyes. Usually they were very blue, but now they'd changed to a sort of milky white. . . . They were glassy and I doubted whether he could see.' Seventeenth day: rain fell. Ericsson 'gasped for breath through lips that were so swollen and cracked I couldn't bear to look at them. He no longer knew where he was. He kept trying to move his body but no position was better than the last. I helped him on to his stomach and there at last he found peace. He was groaning softly. I knew that he was going to die. Nothing but water would save him now.' It rained, the water bottle was three-quarters filled, but Ericsson had died. Eighteenth day: 'My thirst grew . . . I think it was worry and the upset of my friend's death that brought on this increased demand for water. . . . I was not hungry at all, though the fresh water had started my gastric juices working and that night I dreamed about food.' Nineteenth day: 'Eighteen hours after the rain about half a bottle of water remained and I decided, by keeping all my movements to a minimum, to make it last a long time. . . . My worst trouble I was so very tired and when I decided to do something the co-ordination took a long time. My legs and arms responded very slowly to instructions from my brain. I dreamt of food again during the night, but my urge to eat was purely sub-conscious and in the morning I was only thirsty, not hungry.' Twentieth day: 'I felt better and stronger and less tired than I had for days. My policy of resting was paying off. I finished the last of the water in the evening before going to sleep. I'd done my best to make it last until the next rain, but it was beyond the capacity of my willpower now to have water in the bottle and not drink it.' It rained heavily during the night. Twenty-second day: 'I drained my waterbottle in the morning.' It rained heavily for two or three hours during the night. Twenty-third day: 'Rain fell again—I got a fresh supply of perhaps half a bottle and I drank the equivalent of several cups while I was gathering it. . . . I'd lost so much weight that my belt wouldn't hold up my trousers. I had to hold on to my trousers every time I moved. I estimated I'd lost twelve inches from my waist line. . . . With the water supply now fairly constant, my physical condition improved somewhat—once I tried to whistle, but the sound wouldn't come to my lips. They were too cracked and broken to assume the whistling shape. It had become difficult to drink water. My throat appeared to be shrinking and tightening and I couldn't swallow well. Even a small sip took some seconds to make the passage down my throat, and it brought no relief to the pain there, only stirring up the hurts. My mouth was vile and I tried to wash its smell away with salt water.' Twenty-fourth day: 'I swore at daylight to keep my quarter bottle of water until it rained again. I took a sip, no more.' It rained heavily during the night and it filled about half the bottle. It rained again on the twenty-sixth day. Twenty-eighth day: 'The skin on my feet hung in unwholesome patches and was sore to touch. The leather merely aggravated the ulcers which were spreading to all parts of my body. My mouth was awful with foul sores along my gums and between my teeth. It hurts like the devil, but I rinsed out my mouth with salt water and afterwards felt better for it—I had several big and especially painful ulcers in my armpit and the poison from there gradually spread down my arm and I could no longer use it.' Twenty-ninth day: 'My mouth was much worse. I still had some water and about noon rain fell again. . . . I got about half a bottle and drank all I could. After the rain I tried to sing and was shocked to discover that I had no voice left. . . . My throat had become so sore I could not swallow any more. Water had to find its way down by itself and in the smallest quantities. The sun was worse after the rain. . . . I was being grilled. . . . No sweat came out of my pores, no moisture.' Thirtieth day: 'Only the heat again, worse than ever. Hour after hour, gasping and twisting in pain. The hurts from my ulcers was one great hurt. . . . I was in a semi-coma and saw myself walking out of the raft and into the sea and up a sandy, tropical beach. I came to and found my feet over the edge of the raft in the water. Twice this happened. And I didn't care. All the water went a long time before sunset, most of it spilled over my shirt.' Thirty-first day: 'Sometimes I thought I had died.' It rained in the early morning. 'Sometimes I slept whilst I was gathering the water. . . . I got half a bottle. My fingers were so weak I couldn't put the stopper back in the bottle. They shook and I couldn't find the opening. . . . Though I was often unconscious I moved constantly in the raft, turning from side to side, rolling and struggling. Lapsing into unconsciousness I felt drawn all the time from the raft. . . . There was little relief in the water now. I'd lost all sense of a second person being on the raft.' Thirty-second day: 'My nerves produced a final effort, my muscles worked and my mind co-ordinated . . . completely conscious now. . . . My feet were so thin. I seemed to have no backbone and several times I fell forward. My eyes were weak and I couldn't focus properly—I held the water in my mouth and tried to swallow it, but my throat was bound up. The muscles had ceased to work. I got a little water down . . . trying to hold on I fainted and fell into darkness. . . .' He was rescued and taken aboard a ship. 'They cut away my clothes and my flesh came too, in long strange pieces.' Ensio Tiira's normal weight was 132 lbs but after five days on the rescue ship, where he had been well looked after, his weight was only 56 lbs.

Liferaft from SS Lulworth Hill. *Doldrums (Atlantic). March–April*
A fifty days' ordeal. Fourteen men on a raft, twelve died, two survived. The water ration was 6 ounces a day to start with, increased to 9 ounces on the twenty-ninth day and reduced to 4 ounces on the forty-second day. Kenneth Cooke reported, fourth day: 'With the movements of waking, slight as they were, the hands were aware of the desire to pass water. Many of us had experienced great difficulty over this natural function and when we were successful our urine was only too often tinged with redness, showing the presence of blood.' Fifth day: 'My tongue seemed to fill the whole of my mouth with the feeling I was gagged with cotton wool.' Eighth day: 'No one had bothered about conversation in the past forty-eight hours. Tongues were swollen and blackened and even cursing one another had become an effort. Food had lost its appeal, it was water we needed. Food needed forcing down and to eat it dry was impossible. Our lips were cracked and bleeding. Rain fell about midnight, I shouted excitedly, causing my cracked lips to bleed so freely that I felt blood trickle down my chin.' Tenth day: 'Realizing how weak the chaps were becoming, I cut down the watches from two hours to one. The move was popular and I think a wise one. . . . Two hours of concentration was more than minds could stand. I noticed that on coming off watch most men were completely exhausted.' Fourteenth day: 'The First Officer showed signs of insanity, and attempted suicide. . . .' Fifteenth day: 'The First Officer recovered his sanity but he lost his senses again soon after.' Eighteenth day: the First Officer 'spent a very bad night, shouting and raving incoherently nearly all the time. Twice he had attempted to get over the side, but had been so weak that the weight of a restraining hand proved sufficient to hold him down. He recovered sanity at 4 p.m. and asked for water. He died at 4.30 p.m.' Twenty-first day: 'The deadly thirst was our greatest enemy.' Twenty-second day: 'A night of horror, one of the boys was drinking seawater all night long—gulping it down in bulk, using an empty biscuit tin for a

cup. Now he's sat in the well, his eyes glassy and uncomprehending. All night he had kept us awake with his shrieks, groans and shouts— Several men were suffering from delirium.' Twenty-fifth day: 'The task of sharing the water had become so great that two of us had to help Platten to pass it round. . . . Even with my eyes open I was no longer free from visions. The most persistent and frequent was the one of my mother with the pink water jug.' Thirty-eighth day: the last of the biscuits was eaten. 'The loss did not disturb us overmuch. They were terribly hard things and our mouths, throats and tongues were by that time so swollen that the effort of chewing was hardly worth while. . . . I sipped my morning water and with difficulty swallowed my meagre rations. Life was rapidly becoming too much for me. . . . We were almost too weak to move. Longish spells of unconsciousness came to both of us.' Forty-second day: 'I leant over the side and ladled a tin of water over my head. The refreshment gained was lost in the effort required for the act. . . . My hand reached for my spear, but I have not the energy to use it and I let it lie undisturbed.' Forty-fifth day: 'Great effort was expended in obtaining five barnacles from the side of the raft. The effort of attaching the aerial wire [dropped from an aeroplane] to the mast was too great.' Forty-sixth day: 'Colin signed to me to cast the line over again. His had been the effort of handling, mine was the effort of shooting it again.' Forty-eighth day: Kenneth Cooke collapsed after paddling a short distance in a rubber dinghy dropped by an aeroplane.

Inflatable Boat L'Hérétique. *North Atlantic. October–December*
Dr Bombard: 'My skin became dehydrated and I had a rash covering my whole body.'

HUNGER

Landing Craft from SS Fort Lamy. *North Atlantic. March*
A thirteen days' ordeal without food or water. Fourth Engineer, Mr F. H. Millbank: 'For the first four days we felt desperately hungry, but after that the hunger wore off and we were more or less content to live off snow.'

Inflatable Boat L'Hérétique. *Mediterranean. May–June*
Dr Alain Bombard and Jack Palmer made a fourteen days' voyage, in which they attempted to live off the sea. Dr Bombard: 'We had spent ten days out of the fourteen without food or fresh water and on the other four had a raw sea perch and fish juice. . . . The symptoms of hunger were these; cramp-like pains extending to the shoulders

during the first and part of the second day. On the third day these pains ceased and were followed by somnolence and a permanent sensation of fatigue. To reduce the need for food it is essential to induce an effect of physical hibernation by leading a vegetative existence. Our blood pressure hardly varied, but in this respect I do not think the experiment lasted long enough for concrete results.'

Raft from the Frigate Medusa. *North Atlantic. July 1816*
A seventeen days' ordeal. The French frigate *Medusa* grounded on the Arguin Bank, near Cape Blanco. A raft, some 20 m by 7 m, was constructed and boarded by 10 seamen and 147 landsmen, soldiers and their officers. They had 5 barrels of wine, 2 casks of water and 25 lbs of biscuits which were damaged by sea water. With such a heavy load on the raft the survivors were waist high in the water. Many men were washed off the raft by rough seas. Mutiny broke out and there were many deaths from violence. Of the fourth day, J. Savigny, an engineer, recorded: 'Those whom death had spared in the disastrous night fell upon the dead bodies with which the raft was covered, and cut off pieces, which some instantly devoured. Many did not touch it; almost all the officers were of this number. Seeing that this horrible nourishment had given strength to those who had made use of it, it was proposed to dry it, in order to render it a little less disgusting. Those of us who had firmness enough to abstain from it took a larger quantity of wine. We tried to eat sword-belts and cartouche-boxes, and succeeded in swallowing some little morsels. Some ate linen, others pieces of leather from the hats, on which there was a little grease, or rather dirt. A sailor attempted to eat excrement, but he could not succeed.' About another dozen died during the morning; their bodies were cast into the sea, one corpse only being retained as food for the survivors. A shoal of flying fish became entangled in the raft. 'We dressed some fish which we devoured with extreme avidity; but our hunger was so great and our portion of fish so small that we added it to some human flesh, which dressing rendered it less disgusting.' Another mutiny occurred and on the fifth day only thirty men were left. About half the survivors were seriously wounded, and as they could not be expected to last for more than a few days it was considered that their rations would be wasted on them; the wounded were therefore thrown into the sea. Only fifteen men were on the raft when rescue was effected on the seventeenth day.

Dinghy from Sailing Yacht Mignonette. *South Atlantic. July 1884*
A twenty-four days' ordeal. Four men in dinghy, sixteenth day: 'Dudley suggested to Brooks and Stephens that lots should be drawn

for one of the four to be sacrificed so as to provide food for the others. Brooks would hear none of it, protested at the suggestion and wept. Stephens was also opposed to the suggestion at first, later asked to be given another day to think it over.' Nineteenth day: Dudley took a penknife and plunged it into the side of Parker's neck. The blood was caught in a bailer and drunk. The body was cut open, the heart and liver were removed; the liver was eaten whilst still warm. All three men fed upon the body for the next few days.

Lifeboat from SS Laconia. *Doldrums (Atlantic). September–October*
A twenty-seven days' ordeal. Nursing Sister Doris Hawkins: 'With our exceedingly small water ration it was impossible after a few days to eat our biscuits or malted-milk tablets. . . . The Horlicks tablets stuck to the roof of the mouth, and stayed there. I tried to eat my pemmican ration each day, as I had read that it has high food value, but it often took an hour to swallow one teaspoonful. The chocolate dissolved easily and I was able to eat the three little squares ($1\frac{1}{2}$ in × $\frac{3}{4}$ in × $\frac{1}{8}$ in) daily, until the supply ran out. . . . Some of our number ate small barnacles scraped from the sides and bottom of the boat, and we chewed our skin as it peeled from sunburnt surfaces.'

Liferaft from Transport Ship Skaubryn. *Indian Ocean. February–March*
A thirty-two days' ordeal. Fourth day. Ensio Tiira: 'Our hunger had worn off during the morning. We were over the first acute need for food.' Fifth day: 'We were terribly hungry. I tried all I knew to think about anything but food, but always food won.' Seventh day: 'We needed food but we didn't want it. The first two days had been the worst, the next two only slightly less bearable, the fifth and sixth much better, and now we had got over our thoughts of food. We wanted water, we craved for water, but food no longer mattered.' Eleventh day: 'I was not hungry and it was long since Ericsson complained. We knew we had to eat to live, but always it was water that we wanted.'

Sailing Yacht Pagan. *South Pacific. October*
John Caldwell, sailing single-handed from Panama towards Australia, short of food and his boat dismasted, wrote: 'Hunger pains irked me all morning. . . . My careful plans for apportioning out my food had gone glimmering. What did it matter. I was full and happy. I had no worries. If there was no food, there was no food. Better to eat and be at peace than talk and fret over a morsel. My spirits rose. Tomorrow I'd catch a fish.' He made repairs to his boat but was dismasted a second time. 'I took a sip of water. As it coursed down my throat, I felt a return of strength. Putting the water flask back, I saw the shave lotion. I opened it, sniffed it—it was unbearable.

Throwing my head back I downed a hearty portion of what remained of it. As I capped it, I felt an electric surge through my body. The next thing I was walking over the deck, and before I realized what I had done, I had jerked the mast off the deck, had pointed it like a broom handle, and it was stepped. Everything I did in the next hour was effortless.' He caught a small white seabird. 'Crazed by the thought of food . . . I tore the head from the body in one motion. Thrusting the pulsing stump into my mouth, I drank every particle of its life-giving blood. When it no longer yielded a drop, I bit the delicate neck off and chewed it up, bone and all. Before I could stop myself, the greater part of the bird was gone. Even then I couldn't stop. I bit wolfishly into the mass of feathers, tearing at what met the tooth; whether it was bone or feather didn't matter. Not one bone of the fowl's body escaped the mill of my teeth. Each one I smashed to fine splinters and ground to pulp and swallowed.'

Sailing Yacht Moana. *North Atlantic. November*
Bernard Gorsky: 'Rough sea continues . . . we were neither hungry nor ever really thirsty, we merely dreamt of enormous green salads and masses of fruit. We ate and drank almost nothing.'

Sailing Ship. South Atlantic/Antarctic Ocean
On Admiral Pizarro's voyage of 1540, hunger drove the crew to eat rats, which were bought for four Spanish dollars each.

Sailing Ship Vittoria. *Circumnavigation*
Antonio Pigafetta, who sailed with Magellan 1519–22: 'We ate biscuit, but in truth it was biscuit no longer, but a powder full of worms, and in addition it was stinking with the urine of rats. So great was our want of food, we were forced to eat the hide from which the main yard was covered. These hides, exposed to the sun, rain and wind, had become so hard we were first obliged to soften them by putting them overboard for four or five days, after which we put them on the embers and had them thus. We also used sawdust for food and rats became such a delicacy that we paid a ducat a piece for them.'

Whaleboats from Whaleship Essex. *South Pacific. December–February*
The whaleship *Essex* was rammed twice by a whale near the equator on 20 November 1820 and the ship foundered. The crew took to three whaleboats and landed at Henderson Island on 20 December, where they replenished their water. They sailed from the island on 27 December. One boat parted company on 12 January 1821 and another, presumed lost, on 28 January.
'The Captain relates . . . on the 14th January, the whole stock of

provisions belonging to the second mate's boat was entirely exhausted. On the 25th, the black man, Lawson Thomas, died and was eaten by his surviving companions. On the 21st, the Captain and his crew were in the like dreadful situation with respect to their provisions. On the 23rd, another coloured man, Charles Shorter, died, and his body was shared for food between the crews of both boats. On the 27th, Isaiah Shepherd, a black man, died in the third boat (second mate's), and on the 28th another black man named Samuel Reed died out of the Captain's boat. The bodies of these men constituted their only food while it lasted. . . . On the 1st of February, having consumed their last morsel, the Captain and the three other men that remained with him were reduced to the necessity of casting lots. It fell upon Owen Coffin to die. With great fortitude and resignation, he submitted to his fate. They drew lots to see who should shoot him. He placed himself firmly to receive his death and was immediately shot by Charles Ramsell, whose hard fortune it was to become his executioner. . . . On the 11th, Braxilla Ray died. The Captain and Charles Ramsdell, the only two that there were then left, subsisted on the two bodies until the morning of the 23rd of February, when they fell in with the ship *Dauphin* . . . and were snatched from impending destruction.'

Owen Chase, writing of the boat that parted company on 12 January, recorded that one man gave up the struggle to live on 7 February, and on the following day 'he lay in the greatest pain and apparent misery, groaning piteously until four o'clock in the afternoon, when he died in the most horrid and frightful convulsions I ever witnessed. We kept his corpse all night. In the morning my two companions began, as a matter of course, to make preparations to dispose of it in the sea when, having reflected on the subject all night, I addressed them on the painful subject of keeping the body for food! Our provisions could not possibly last us beyond three days. Within this time it was not in any degree probable that we should find relief from our present sufferings, and, accordingly, hunger would at last drive us to the necessity of casting lots. It was without any objection agreed to, and we set to work as fast as we were able to prepare the body so as to prevent its spoiling. We separated the limbs from the body and cut all the flesh from the bones, after which we opened the body, took out the heart, closed it again—sewing it up as decently as we could—and then committed it to the sea.

'We now first commenced to satisfy the immediate cravings of nature from the heart, which we eagerly devoured. We then ate sparingly of a few pieces of the flesh, after which we hung up the remainder, cut in thin strips, about the boat to dry in the sun. We made a fire and roasted some of it to serve us during the next day.

'In this manner did we dispose of our fellow traveller. . . .

'The next morning, the 10th of February, we found that the flesh had become tainted and had turned a greenish colour. We concluded to make a fire and cook it at once to prevent it becoming so putrid as not to be eatable at all. We, accordingly, did so and, by that means, preserved it for six or seven days longer. Our bread during the time remained untouched. . . .

'We contrived to keep body and soul together by sparingly partaking of our flesh, which was cut up in small pieces and eaten with salt water. By the 14th, our bodies became so far recruited as to enable us to make a few attempts at guiding our boat again with the oar. By each taking his turn, we managed to steer it and make a tolerably good course.

'On the 15th our flesh was all consumed. We were driven to the last morsel of bread, consisting of two cakes. Our limbs had, for the last two days, swelled very much and now began to pain us most excessively.'

The three survivors were rescued by a ship on 18 February.

EXPOSURE TO MOTION

Sailing Yacht Cardinal Vertue. *North Atlantic. June–October*
On the second day of the single-handed transatlantic race, 1960, in his 25-foot sloop, Dr David Lewis reported: 'As yet I had not found my sealegs, I was falling about heavily each time the ship lurched and I tried to move, and now I was cut and bruised all over.' Ninth day: 'I was at last mastering the knack of wedging my hips in the main hatchway so that my trunk remained upright and the sextant could be held steady, while the ship rolled and pitched under me and my body swayed to the sea's rhythm.' Forty-eighth day: 'The yacht rolled violently up to 20° to starboard and 30° to port. The cabin lamp had gone out. Feeling sick and exhausted, I filled it with paraffin and lit it. Lowering sail and making all secure, heaving to and filling and lighting the lamp, had occupied one and a half hours. For a time the fury of the gale increased but I felt too ill and tired to care.'

Twentieth day of return voyage, after experiencing another gale: 'I was irritable and drained of energy as always after a gale. Every joint ached where it had been jerked and snapped to and fro.'

Lifeboat from SS Trevessa. *Indian Ocean. June*
Third day. Captain Cecil Foster: 'By this time all hands were feeling

sore and stiff. It was impossible to get any exercise, or even to sit still, owing to the jumpy motion of the boat.' Sixth day: 'We were raw and sore, as owing to the motion of the boat we were not able to sit still.'

Lifeboat. Indian Ocean. June
Captain Foster, reporting on First Officer Smith's boat, twenty-first day. The second engineer stood up to step over a thwart. 'Just as he was in the act of stepping over, the boat gave a sudden and unexpected lurch, which made him lose his balance and fall over-board. . . . The boat could not be brought near enough for him to be hauled in.'

Sailing Yacht Lively Lady. *North Atlantic. August*
Forty-fifth day. Sir Alec Rose, of his 36-foot ketch: 'The motion is sharp and jerky and catches one unawares and throws one right off balance. Every smallest job is therefore a thought-out plan of action —taking four times as long as usual. This goes on all the time—every minute—and is rather wearing and tiring, coupled with the constant whine of the wind in the rigging.'

Sailing Yacht Tzu Hang. *Southern Ocean. December*
Miles Smeeton, describing the 46-foot ketch *Tzu Hang*: 'Because of the constant and often violent motion, we found these handrails most useful, and as necessary as the straps in the London Under-ground. . . . There was the cook's seat . . . it faced forwards and had a curved seat with two arms, so that the cook was held firmly in place, whatever the antics of the ship.'

Sailing Yacht Gipsy Moth IV. *Roaring Forties. October*
Fifty-sixth day. Sir Francis Chichester, in his 53-foot ketch, in bad weather, with little appetite and having to make repairs, recorded: 'I was up two or three times in the night to tend the tiller. . . . Around six o'clock in the morning *Gipsy Moth* did gybe and began rolling wildly. . . . It took me an hour to dress, make tea, collect my tools and generally screw myself to make a start. The rolling was frightful, and I felt as feeble as a half-dead mouse.'

Balsa Raft Seven Little Sisters. *South Pacific. June–October*
William Willis: 'The *Seven Little Sisters* [length 33 feet, beam 20 feet] took the seas as if born to them but laboured incessantly and with unpredictable movements. Sometimes it took quite a while to get a cup of coffee to my lips. . . . Taking a sextant sight was a job on account of the incessant movement of the raft and its low position on the sea. It was almost impossible to get a level horizon. . . . It was

impossible to take star sights due to the movement of the raft, but I was satisfied with the sun.' Forty-fifth day: 'There was so much work that I was often near exhaustion. The balancing, the ceaseless shaking I was subjected to, also threatened to wear me down.' Forty-seventh day: 'My legs, from continuous balancing and bracing to keep from being thrown were . . . hard.' Seventy-sixth day: 'She was rolling a lot tonight. If I had tried to go on sewing I would have punched myself all over with the needle. A few times during the afternoon, when I was tired, I had almost jabbed my face.' Eighty-seventh day: 'The raft was rolling badly now. . . . The result was that I sewed my pants to the sail, besides jabbing the needle into my fingers several times; a couple of times I barely missed my face. I was forced to stop often. . . . I purposely used short threads so I wouldn't have to raise my right arm so high.'

Sailing Yacht Pagan. *South Pacific. September*
John Caldwell in the 29-foot cutter *Pagan* was caught in a hurricane north of the Cook Islands. He rigged his storm sail on the mast, sheeted it flat and crammed the staysail below. '*Pagan* commenced dancing nervously. Instead of rising gently to the oncoming crests she broke abruptly into them. Instead of a quick roll before the more forceful seas, she made a sharp lurch which found her often heeled over far enough to throw me. In my bunk I was forced to grip its sides. . . . *Pagan* was no longer riding comfortably. Her bow was lying five points off the wind . . . the port rail was under and the windward bow was throwing spray high into the rigging and beating into the seas. Rain was the heaviest yet. It was impossible to look straight into that wind and rain. . . . For the first time I lashed myself in my bunk and waited. . . . In the deep trough formed by the hills of sea, the wind was unable to strike; and *Pagan* righted abruptly. As she neared the curled peak on the climb up the oncoming roller, she once more encountered the blast. She careered before it. I couldn't stand. . . . It was then *Pagan* pounded most. Her bow was pitched as though dynamited and she yawed wildly until heavy seas, boarding her, weighted her down so that she wallowed clumsily, her lee rail out of sight. She would then shake herself free of her load and go reeling down the backside of another great, rolling swell of water.' He went on deck to repair some damage, was washed overboard and managed to board again. 'I was too sick and weak to care what happened next. For long hours I rolled to and fro on the floor knocking against the bunks as *Pagan* tilted high. . . .' There was a sudden change of behaviour; *Pagan* was in the eye of the hurricane. 'Her pitching and rolling became suddenly beyond what I had ever felt before. She inclined to flatness on both beams; and pitched so

high that it seemed incredible she didn't jerk her keel off. . . . Not a
breath of air stirred. There were no rollers or combers as such, only
peaks of water shooting up or falling away flatly. . . . Great pyramids
of water bolted masthead high from the sea surface. . . . *Pagan* lay to,
her scuppers beneath a constant deck of water. Her sea-anchor was
helpless; she danced to all points of the compass, her mast scoring
the water on either side. Suddenly she was high and suddenly she
was low. Nausea assailed me. The sickening surge of the boat and the
unstable watery sight set me to vomiting. I couldn't hold myself up
longer. I stumbled to my bunk and lashed myself down. I realized
that I should get up and pump the bilges; also plug the broken port
hole—but I was too dead sick to move. I couldn't even brace myself
against the lurch; I just lay there, rolling against my lashings.'
Pagan got into the outer circle of the hurricane again. 'The seasickness was pacified by the more consistent motion of the boat. Now
that the wind had set upon her again, there was a system in her wild
behaviour that was kindred to my experience.

'There is only one safe way to ride out a hurricane in a small boat;
flat on your back lashed in the bunk with ports and hatches dogged,
and everything strapped down.'

Sailing Yacht Pen Duick II. *North Atlantic. May–June*
Eric Tabarly, who won the single-handed transatlantic race in
1964 in his 44-foot ketch, had an adjustable motor-cycle saddle
fixed to the chart table and another one at the look-out position;
they enabled him to work 'on an even keel'. He wrote on the fourth
day: 'Go below and get into the starboard bunk. . . . I wedge myself
up against the sail-bags but the boat is pitching about so heavily
that it is impossible to sleep.' Following the crossing, he wrote: 'A
snag about small sailing boats is that when the weather is clear but
the sea is rough it is often difficult to use the sextant. The pitching
and rolling prevent you standing steady enough to get the sun's
reflection at an angle to the horizontal. Besides, the horizon itself is
often obscured by the swell, and spray splashes on the apparatus,
which does not help matters.'

HAZARDS FROM SEA CREATURES

Fish

Canoe. North Atlantic
Dr Hannes Lindemann reported that a hornfish bit him in the ball
of the hand and a few days later a small abscess appeared and the
lymph glands enlarged.

Inflatable Boat L'Hérétique. *North Atlantic. November–December*
Dr Bombard: 'This pleasant interlude was succeeded at about
2.0 p.m. by twelve hours of terror, which lasted till 2.0 the next
morning. There was a violent blow on the rudder. . . . What I saw
was a large swordfish of undeniably menacing aspect. He was
following the dinghy at a distance of about 20 feet, seemingly in a
rage, his dorsal fin raised like hackles. In one of his feints around the
boat he had collided with my rudder oar. Several times his back
bumped the underside of the dinghy, but he still seemed a little
afraid of me. He never approached from ahead and every time he
came at me he changed course at the last moment before striking
the floats.
'It was during this period of uneventful calm that I had the most
dangerous encounter of all. Sitting in the stern of *L'Hérétique*,
watching the feeble wake, I saw appear, still some way off, a flat,
black undulating mass in the water. As it came nearer, I saw it had
white patches which caught the sun. When it was about fifty feet
away I realized that it was a giant ray. It followed me for about two
hours, keeping its distance all the time. Then it suddenly disappeared
as if sucked down to the depths.'

Fishing Sampan Helen. *North Pacific. September*
'The 43-foot fishing sampan *Helen* from Honolulu was attacked and
nearly sunk by a large swordfish some 240 miles south-east of Oaku.
The three people on board sustained no injuries although the vessel
had been severely damaged.'

Cargo Ship Richmond Castle. *South Atlantic. December*
'Bound from Mauritius to Hull the crew of the *Richmond Castle* got
an outsized catch—a giant manta ray measuring 14 ft from wing to
wing, 10 ft from head to tail and weighing 1,500 lb. Rammed by the
ship off Lobito Bay, Portugese West Africa, the ray, which was
impaled on the bows, had a mouth 3 ft 6 ins long and 10 ins wide.
. . . The fish had struck the ship and wrapped itself round the
bow. . . .'

Liferaft from SS Britannia. *Doldrums (Atlantic). March*
Lieutenant A. H. Rowlandson RN: 'A giant ray came and circled
round us and sailed under the raft with each fin-tip out of the water
and well clear of us on each side.'

Liferaft from SS Treworlas. *Caribbean. December*
Second Radio Officer Mr R. J. T. Webb: 'We were troubled by
sharks which rubbed against the raft several times, nearly upsetting
us. We were also troubled by barracoutas which tried to leap on

board the raft and we beat them off with four iron weather-screen stanchions.'

Ship's Boat from HMS Bounty. *South Pacific. April*
First day. John Fryer: 'We got the boat's foremast up and set the sail and rowed and sailed for the island of Tofoa—a very large shark struck at one of the oars.'

Lifeboat from MV Cressington Court. *North Atlantic. August*
Chief Officer S. R. Gardner: 'I noticed one or two small stumpy sharks near the boat and now and again one or two would bang the boat with its tail. I was afraid that the seams would open up so decided to do something about it. The next time a shark approached I gave him a terrific jab with the boat hook; it soon disappeared and we were not troubled again that morning. During the afternoon however . . . I saw another shark near the boat. This shark came right alongside with his fin out of water and before it realized what was happening I had grabbed hold of its fin and it was in the boat— I don't know which was the more surprised, the crew or the shark. I set about it with an axe, chopped it in pieces and offered it round. Several of the crew refused to eat it, but the rest of us ate the raw shark—it was not too bad. I saved the liver for myself and it was good.'

Liferaft from SS Lulworth Hill. *Doldrums (Atlantic). March–April*
Eighth day. Kenneth Cooke: 'Without thinking I dipped the knife into the sea to wash. I soon realized my mistake. A thin line of blood from the fish gut streamed away from the knife just as an eight-foot shark put his snout around the stern of the raft. He went mad— stark, staring, raving mad. He came at us viciously and with a power-ful flick of the tail sent the raft crabbing sideways. We beat him off with oars. For a while he stood off, then diving beneath us, came up under our bow, catching it with his ugly scarhead and knocking several planks adrift. He sheered off, then attacked again, sending us spinning completely round with one glancing blow. Again he swam alongside, so close that his cold glassy eyes were within arm's length of me. I grabbed my harpoon at the target offered; the point must have reached a tender spot, for the brute sheered off with good speed.'

Fiftieth day. Kenneth Cooke burst a boil while working a Very Pistol. He squeezed the boil, wiped it with a piece of kapok from one of the buoyancy tanks and threw the kapok overboard. 'For a second the bloody, pus-soaked piece of cottonwool-like material floated behind us. A small shark swam to it, then old scarface. They snapped together and the young shark streaked away with blood streaming from its bleeding mouth. This blood drove the other sharks insane. Sharks from all directions pounced on the wounded shark. Scarface came for us at the rate of knots, dived underneath us and lashed out with his tail. The raft spun round twice on its own axis for two complete circles. There was another crash. Then the shark swam alongside the raft, striking with its tail every thirty seconds or so. Four or five times he struck us, then he dropped back to his usual position astern.'

Liferaft from Transport Ship Skaubryn. *Indian Ocean. March*
Twenty-fifth day. Ensio Tiira: 'Some [sharks] went for the sides, others came up from the bottom against the canvas. This was even more terrifying than the side attacks. They shot up against me into the four-foot square of canvas and water that was my home, jostling Ericsson's body and sometimes taking some of it before they fell back into the sea.'

Ship's Boat from the Merchant Cruiser Voltaire. *North Atlantic. April*
R. V. Coward: 'Sitting next to me in the cutter was a man named Palmer. . . . He had swallowed a lot of oil and was being violently sick. As he held his head over the side a shark shot by and just missed biting it off.'

Jelly-fish

Liferaft from SS Laconia. *Doldrums (Atlantic). September*
Nursing Sister Doris M. Hawkins: 'I felt a sudden sharp pain in my right hand which was hanging in the water. A purple jelly-fish, said to be deadly poisonous, had stung me; its sting—a long violet-coloured tentacle—was wound round my hand, completely detached from the jelly-fish itself. I shook my hand and the sting fell off, but unfortunately it hit one of the men and wound round his hand, stinging him in turn. Our hands and arms swelled rapidly. With a stick another man beat the jelly-fish against the side of the raft and killed it. Sometime later a third man grasped the end of the stick which had killed the jelly-fish on which some of the poison must have remained. Immediately he felt a stinging pain in the palm of his hand, and his hand and arm swelled too. The pain was intense and we each held our affected limbs in the sea for hours, and nothing worse than the pain and swelling occurred. They took several days to subside.'

Mammals

Whaler Sumi Maru. *Antarctic. March*
'Japanese whaler *Sumi Maru* No. 5: Two blades of five-bladed

propeller were broken off by a whale during operations on the Antarctic whaling grounds on 9 March.'

Dory. North Atlantic. August
'Preston Newell . . . was about a mile from the mother ship in a dory and hauling in a swordfish when a whale surfaced underneath him. It hit the boat with its nose, throwing it three feet into the air. The dory landed squarely on the whale's back and for several seconds it moved through the water. The whale swished and slid under the water, leaving the dory clear. Newell said that the most dangerous part of his adventure was when the whale swished its tail as it went under the water. It came close to striking the dory.'

Steamer Mariposa. *South Pacific. March*
'Steamer *Mariposa* will go into a Cockatoo Island dockyard tomorrow for repairs to rudder damage caused by a giant whale. . . . the repairs to the vessel would take several days. The pintle bolt, which weighs about 2,500 lb, was damaged.'

Lifeboat from MV Corbis. *Indian Ocean. April*
Chief Engineer Mr T. E. Simpson: 'One afternoon we made little or no headway as the wind dropped, so after darkness when the wind rose, I persuaded the Second Officer to continue sailing to make up for lost time. I was keeping a lookout forward when I suddenly spotted a dark shape right ahead: I yelled to the Second Officer who was at the tiller, he swung the boat away and we just managed to slide past the tail of a huge whale about seventy feet long which had surfaced and was about to blow. Had I not seen him in time we should have sailed right into him and one flip of his tail would have shattered the boat, with the loss of all in her. We never tried to sail after dark again.'

Whaleboats from the Whaler Cachalot. *Indian Ocean*
F. T. Bullen: 'Without any of the desperate flounderings generally indulged in on first feeling the iron, he [a cachalot] turned upon us . . . leaping half out of the water he made direct for our comrades [in the Second Mate's boat]. Then ensued a really big fight, the first, in fact, of my experience, for none of the other whales had shown any serious determination to do us injury, but had devoted all their energies to attempts to escape. . . . Without attempting to "sound", the furious monster kept mostly below the surface; but whenever he rose, it was either to deliver a fearful blow with his tail, or, with jaws widespread, to try and bite one of our boats in half. Well for us it was that he was severely handicapped by a malformation of the lower jaw. . . . Once he delivered a sidelong blow with his tail, which, as

we spun round, shore off the two oars on that side as if they had been carrots, at last the Second Mate got fast to him. . . . The whale now started off to windward at top speed with the two boats sheering broadly out upon either side of his foaming wake. . . . He had not gone a couple of miles before he turned a complete somersault in the water, coming up behind us to rush off again in the opposite direction at undiminished speed. . . . With a roar like a cataract, up sprang the huge creature, head out, jaw wide open, coming direct for us. . . . The Mate raised his bomb-gun, firing the bomb directly down the great livid cavern of a throat facing him. Down went that mountainous head not six inches from us . . . up flew the broad tail in the air and a blow struck the Second Mate's boat fairly amidships. It was right before my eyes, not sixty feet away, and the sight will haunt me to my death. The tub oarsman was the poor German baker . . . that awful blow put an end summarily to all his earthly anxieties. As it shore obliquely through the boat, it drove his poor body right through her timbers—an undistinguishable bundle of what was an instant before a human being.'

Sailing Ship Hoorn. *South Atlantic. October*
It is reported that the 110-ton ship *Hoorn*, sailing before the trade wind in deep water, felt a shock and dipped and rolled. The blue sea turned red 'as if a fountain of blood were gushing up from the keel'. When the vessel was beached the tusk of a narwhal was found protruding from the bilge; it had pierced three heavy planks, grazed a timber and entered the ship for more than a foot.

Whaleship Essex. *South Pacific. November*
Owen Chase, Second Officer of the 238-ton whaleship *Essex*, reported that the ship was twice attacked by a sperm whale and sank on 20 November 1820. Chase and nineteen others in three boats made for the coast of Chile; only eight survived.

Kayaks. Arctic. June
Dr Fridtjof Nansen: 'All day long we saw herds, that often followed us a long way, pressing in round the kayaks. . . . Just then we saw a solitary rover pop up a little in front of us. . . . Suddenly the walrus shot up beside me, threw himself on to the edge of the kayak, took hold further over the deck with one fore-flipper, and as it tried to upset me aimed a blow at the kayak with its tusks. I held on as tightly as possible, so as not to be upset into the water and struck at the animal's head with the paddle as hard as I could. It took hold of the kayak once more, and tilted me up, so that the deck was almost under water, then let go and raised itself right up. I seized my gun, but at

the same moment it turned round and disappeared as quickly as it had come.' The kayak began to fill with water. Dr Nansen managed to get it to a sunken ledge of ice, where it sank. 'It is a good big rent that he has made, at least six inches long; but it is fortunate that it was no worse. How easily he might have wounded me in the thigh with that tusk of his!'

Molluscs

Sailing Dinghy. Coral Sea
David Lewis reported on an Enterprise dinghy at Port Moresby, where an octopus 'slithered enough of its arms aboard to embrace the gunwale, immobilize the tiller and seriously embarrass the helmsman and crew for several minutes before they managed to prise it free.'

Prau. Ceram Sea
Evelyn Cheesman: 'I noticed a large patch of white foam on the waveless blue of Fak-Fak Bay. . . . The space between the patch and the shore was altering so there was movement.' She was informed that it was a binatung [giant squid]. 'By my watch the path must have remained for at least a quarter of an hour after I had noticed it. I surmised that the squid might be swimming in a circle. . . . This giant squid had a personal name, there was a smaller specimen which inhabited another bay. Apparently they were only known to surface at very long intervals. If a prau happened to be crossing to gardens on the other side it would be seized and dragged down. The occupants would spring overboard and swim ashore. After a while the prau would reappear either entire or in fragments but anything edible—fruit, vegetables or fish—would have vanished. One human victim had been known, a woman who had turned back to rescue her basket of vegetables. A giant limb clamped her to the prau and she went down with it and was never seen again.'

Shellfish

Liferaft from Transport Ship Skaubryn. Indian Ocean. March
Fred Ericsson died on the seventeenth day and was buried on the twenty-fifth day. Ensio Tiira reported, twentieth day: "Little fish were all the time inside the raft and I could not bear to see what they and the crabs were doing. My mind and stomach revolted.'

FIRST AID AND PRESERVATION OF HEALTH

Survivors at sea may be wounded, exhausted, chilled, in a state of shock or covered with oil. The survival craft must protect them from the environment and provide them with the means of survival. Every craft carries a first-aid pack which is used as on shore to protect wounds, prevent haemorrhage, support fractures, etc. The pack should contain a list of simple instructions suitable for use by a survivor who has no previous knowledge of first aid.

Health sometimes improves under conditions of stress. Able Seaman James McGreen of SS *Trevessa* suffered from a discharging hip bone when he abandoned ship. The wound healed after two or three days in the lifeboat and remained clean with no pain for the rest of the twenty-three days in the Indian Ocean; but it broke out again a few days after rescue.

There are some special health hazards at sea and their prevention and first-aid treatment are considered here.

The resources which can be made available in small boats and survival craft are very limited. It is therefore essential to apply preventive and first-aid measures immediately and thus obviate a serious situation arising.

Medical treatment which ordinarily cannot be given until after rescue is described in Chapter 8.

Blisters
Unusual friction, frostbite and sunburn may produce blisters. Protect the skin so as to prevent their formation. Do not prick blisters, but if they break clean the area and cover with a dressing.

Burns
Burns may occur on the hands due to friction when handling ropes, and on other parts of the body exposed to sunburn and oil-fire on water. All burns are liable to sepsis. Do not touch them, nor try to remove clothing which is stuck to a burn. Keep the burn dry and apply a sterile dressing or clean cloth immediately. Firm bandaging will help to prevent blisters, but if blisters form they must not be pricked. Prepare to loosen bandages if the tissues swell.

When large areas of the skin are burnt there will be severe pain and shock. Relieve the pain with morphine. To treat surgical shock keep the patient at rest and give him plenty of water in frequent small quantities. A large quantity of water given at one time may make him vomit.

If the burns become septic apply antiseptic **cream** and clean dressings. For severe burns, give antibiotic tablets immediately.

Buttocks

The buttocks become very sore from sitting in boats, particularly under wet conditions. Blisters, boils and sores sometimes develop. Endeavour to keep the buttocks dry, sit on something soft, avoid friction and change the position frequently.

Calluses

Calluses are formed where there is a combination of friction and pressure, as on the hands and buttocks of oarsmen and canoeists. They are best left alone, but any cracks in the skin on raw areas where calluses have been accidentally removed should be kept very clean.

Chilblains

Chilblains are formed on skin exposed to cold wet conditions. Avoid unnecessary exposure to cold and dampness. Endeavour to keep blood circulating by wiggling fingers, toes and face muscles. Keep affected parts clean and dry. If sores are present apply antiseptic cream and dressings, or strips of clean cloth.

Cold

Wear warm clothing in cold climates. Take warm clothing when abandoning ship. Erect a shelter to avoid windchill. Solitary survivors should keep their limbs tucked close to the body; a group of survivors should huddle close together for warmth. A chilled person should be hugged or wrapped up well and given a hot drink if possible. Alcohol must *not* be taken; it could cause death.

Take off wet clothing, wring it out and put it on again. If it is wet by cold rainwater, rinse it in the sea before giving it a final wringing out. Exercise with care, do not overdo it to the point of exhaustion; have rests between periods of activity.

Do not massage damaged tissue. Take care of minor cuts and abrasions; they heal more slowly in the cold and are more likely to become infected.

Take care when handling petrol or other liquids with a low freezing point; a drop on the skin will cause immediate freezing.

Constipation

The survivor should not worry if he becomes constipated; on the contrary he should be glad, for bowel movement involves a loss of valuable water from the body. There is no useless residue in the emergency food rations provided in survival craft; in consequence there is less to be passed from the bowels. Some of Captain Bligh's companions had no bowel movement for thirty-five days.

Cramp

Muscular cramp occurs when survivors are confined to small craft for many days, especially in cold weather. Endeavour to flex the muscles and bend the joints whenever possible. Knead the affected area.

Seafarers, particularly single-handed sailors who sweat profusely when working their boats in hot climates, may experience cramp due to loss of salt from the body. Relief is given by drinking seawater, but do not do this if there is any shortage of fresh water. Under conditions of water-lack salt hastens dehydration, which is more deadly than cramp.

Death

Survivors should recognize the signs of death, remove from the body anything likely to be of help in the survival of others, and dispose of the body promptly, particularly in shark-infested waters. The signs of death are:

The pulse in the artery deep in the neck is absent. Feel your own (just behind and below the angle of the jawbone) to make sure you know where it is.

The skin blanches on pressure, but does not become pink again when the pressure is removed.

The pupils of the eyes (central dark circular areas surrounded by the coloured part of the eyes) are large, and do not alter in size when light is directed into the eye. If morphine has been given the pupils may be small after death, but generally *after death the pupil remains large when a light is shone into it.*

If there is any doubt about the above three signs, the following can be found later:

The muscles stay flat after being pressed.
The body becomes cold.
The skin is stained red-blue in parts.
The body will become stiff as *rigor mortis* occurs.

Debility

Survivors will become debilitated if exposure is prolonged. They should therefore take all necessary measures to secure their position whilst still active in the early days of their exposure and whilst their rations last. A reserve supply of glucose is advisable, for use when called upon to undertake some essential activity.

Dehydration

Early in the exposure period, whilst still fresh and active, make all necessary arrangements for collecting and storing rainwater, dew and water of condensation. Stream solar stills if provided.

Reduce water losses from the body as much as possible. Avoid unnecessary activity and thus reduce sweating. Take seasickness tablets to avoid vomiting. Do not eat anything likely to result in diarrhoea. Keep as dormant as possible.

Particular care is necessary in the tropics. Rig an awning to keep the sun off the body and arrange it to allow plenty of airflow to cool the body by day. In the daytime douse the awning with sea water. If an awning is not possible, wear light clothes; during daytime soak the clothes in the sea and put them on whilst still wet—the evaporation of the moisture will have a cooling effect. Repeat the soaking during daytime, but one hour before sunset rinse the clothes to remove as much of the salt as possible, and wring throughly. Clothing and the survival craft should be as dry as possible before the temperature begins to fall at night.

Keep a good look-out for rain, day and night. Navigate if at all possible towards the rain clouds. Clean catchment surfaces of accumulated salt before the rain falls. Sample the rainwater caught and do not start storing it until all traces of salt have been eliminated. Long hair and moustaches have been found useful in collecting rainwater. If rainfall is plentiful, take the opportunity of cleaning the body, but rainwater usually feels cold, especially at night, so avoid undue exposure.

Do not drink seawater or urine and restrain anyone who attempts to do so. Do not mix fresh water with seawater. The salts in seawater and urine need so much water for excretion that they increase dehydration.

Do not drink any water the first day adrift, it would only be lost in the urine. Start the water rations on the second day. A daily ration of about one pint is adequate if the survival drill is followed (by taking anti-seasickness tablets for first two days at least, not eating protein foods, protecting the body from hot sun, cooling the body in hot climates with wet clothes). Sip the ration, let it roll around the mouth and trickle slowly down the throat. Any drinking water obtained from rain, solar stills or desalting kits should be consumed before continuing with the survival ration, as it will not keep so well.

If rescue has not occurred by the day on which only one ration is left, save some of it for the next day.

Diarrhoea

Survivors should avoid any foodstuff likely to cause diarrhoea, as it is a serious drain on body water and thus hastens dehydration. Food should be avoided, or taken in very small quantities, until the attack has passed, but drink as much as the rations allow, to replace the loss of fluid.

Drowning

Drowning has occurred in lifeboats and inflatable liferafts where water has been allowed to accumulate. Keep the survival craft bailed dry and ensure that survivors' heads are raised above floor level. Apply artificial respiration, mouth to mouth or mouth to nose, as follows:

Lay the victim on his back. Clear his throat of water, mucus, false teeth or other matter. Tilt his head right back.

Either pinch his nose and blow through his mouth, *or* cover his mouth and blow through his nose.

Blow air into him until his chest rises. Remove your mouth to allow him to breathe out and to allow you to take a fresh breath.

Repeat quickly three times, then continue at a steady rate of about ten times per minute. When he breathes for himself or if gurgling noises are heard, he may vomit. Immediately turn him on to his side and treat for unconsciousness (see page 129). Keep a watch on his breathing; it may stop again.

These instructions are summarized and illustrated in the diagrams opposite.

Exhaustion

Cease activity before becoming completely exhausted, keep a supply of glucose for use before further exertion and only undertake arduous essential duties at the most favourable time of day.

Eyes

Conjunctivitis and ophthalmia (inflammation of the lining of the eyelids or the membrane over the eye with soreness, discharge and often a 'gritty' sensation in the eye), leading to headache and temporary loss of vision, sometimes occur. Protect the eyes from direct or reflected ultra-violet radiation, and from wind, cold, rain and spray. Wear glasses, preferably coloured ones, or improvise with a bandage around the head, with slits for the eyes. Limit look-out duties as much as possible; one hour or less may be appropriate where glare is pronounced.

Do not rub the eyes. If inflamed, lightly smear the lids with soft paraffin. If contaminated with oil, remove oil from eyelids and areas near the eyes, particularly above the eyes, and protect from bright sunlight; the eyes normally recover in one or two days.

Fainting

After remaining in cramped conditions for a long time, and with shortages of sleep, water and food, sudden changes of posture may cause giddiness and fainting. Avoid rapid movements. If the survivor feels faint he should rest with his head low for a few moments.

Feet

The feet are very vulnerable to exposure. A condition known as immersion foot commonly occurs in crowded open lifeboats. The cold, wet, cramped conditions interfere with the circulation of the blood in the feet, and sometimes in the hands, causing swelling, numbing, pallor or purplish discoloration and ulceration.

Prevention is by keeping the boat bailed and having the feet clear of water, as high and warm as possible. Loosen footwear,

ARTIFICIAL RESPIRATION

Lie the patient on his back, clear his nose and throat and tilt his head back as far as possible.

Pinch his nostrils, keeping his head back. Take a deep breath.

Cover his mouth with yours and blow until his chest rises.

Uncover his mouth to allow him to breath out. Watch his chest fall. Repeat until he breathes for himself. Keep his head back as far as possible all the time

THE COMA POSITION

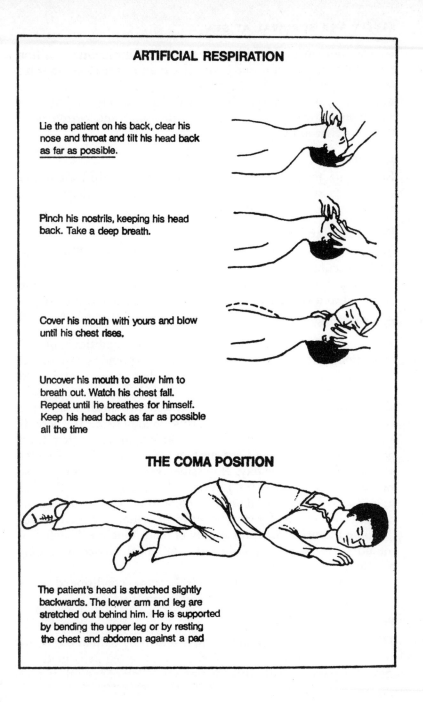

The patient's head is stretched slightly backwards. The lower arm and leg are stretched out behind him. He is supported by bending the upper leg or by resting the chest and abdomen against a pad

wiggle toes, flex ankles, put legs into a horizontal position for a few minutes in every hour. If a man has trouble with his feet a companion should put them in his lap, between his thighs or under his armpits; warm them slowly and do not rub them. Cover ulcers with clean dressings and cotton wool from the first-aid pack.

Fingers

Endeavour to keep the fingers clean. This is difficult under survival conditions, but uncleanliness leads to festering and, sometimes, to loss of nails.

Fish Bites and Stings

Do not handle jelly-fish and take care when handling other fish, particularly if they have spikes or spines.

Treat a bite or sting as any other wound—apply antiseptic ointment and cover with a dressing or a strip of clean cloth.

Food

The appetite for food is soon lost under conditions of dehydration, but survivors should make every endeavour to eat their food ration, starting on the first day adrift, and should adhere strictly to the ration routine. Regular meals are a great aid to morale. The emergency food rations are specially selected because of their water gain during metabolism. If there is any choice to the survivor, select carbohydrates rather than protein foods, and never eat protein unless two pints of water are drunk in the same day. If possible, keep a supply of glucose sweets for use when extra physical effort is required. Rations to a group of survivors should be equal, and seen to be equal.

Long-distance seafarers who have to remain active most of the time require a plentiful supply of food. One meal each day should be cooked—unpolished or half-polished rice is recommended.

Once the digestive system has become conditioned to a uniform diet, avoid any sudden change in the food.

Fractures

The presence of a break in a bone is shown by pain and tenderness which are very much increased if an attempt is made to move the part. Usually there is some swelling of the soft tissues around the broken bone and, if a limb bone is broken, the injured person cannot move the limb.

Immobilize the fracture; a broken arm can be supported in a sling or tied across the chest, a broken leg can be tied to the sound leg with padding between. For a fracture of the spine gently place the casualty in a comfortable position; this is usually on the back. Place soft padding under the natural curves of the back. When the spine is broken in the neck region, place padding on both sides of the head to prevent any rolling movement. Every two hours gently turn him partly to one side and then the other, and support him in the new position to prevent the development of pressure sores.

Frostbite

Frostbite occurs on exposed parts of the body, particularly the extremities, during very cold weather and is due to impaired local circulation caused by chilling. The sensation of cold at the injured part suddenly and completely ceases and the skin becomes hard, grey or yellowish white.

To prevent frostbite wear plenty of clothing and protect all exposed skin, keep dry, avoid sweating and do not touch bare metal. Wiggle fingers and toes, use facial muscles, wrinkle nose and manipulate ears and nose to keep the blood circulating. Loosen light footwear. If the craft is dry remove boots or shoes and wrap the feet in dry clothing.

First-aid treatment is to put the palm of a warm hand over the spot and apply steady pressure, but do not rub; or cup the hand over the spot and breathe on to it. Put frostbitten fingers under the armpits or between the thighs, and frostbitten feet on the belly or between the thighs of a companion. Do not massage frostbitten areas.

Gangrene

Gangrene arises from poor circulation due to burns, frostbite, immersion foot (see page 120) and wounds. In dry gangrene the affected part becomes dry, dark and shrivelled. Wet gangrene is complicated by infection of the part which swells, becomes painful and produces an offensive smelling liquid. There is inflammation of the tissues adjacent to the gangrene, and absorption of the poisons causes a fever.

Prevention is by keeping all injured parts, including frost-bitten areas, clean and dry.

If gangrene develops keep the part clean and dry, cover it with a dressing or clean cloth and, if possible, keep it rested and in a raised position. If there is much inflammation and fever, give an antibiotic.

Head

There is a considerable heat loss from the head, so protect it from exposure to cold; a spare woollen stocking pulled down over the head will do. Keeping the head warm will help to keep the rest of the body warm. Protect the head from the sun; improvise with a handkerchief with part hanging down the back.

Heat Stroke

Heat stroke arises from undue exposure to heat. The signs are hot and dry skin, slow pulse rate, diarrhoea, dizziness, fever, headache, nausea and vomiting, mental confusion and unconsciousness.

Loosen clothing; bathe head, face, wrists and body in cool sea water. Place patient in a reclining position shaded from the sun, with good air flow; fan and keep him cool.

Hygiene

Keep the skin clean; infection may arise from ingrained dirt and salt, and from salt-encrusted clothing rubbing against the skin. Depending on the temperature, exposure to rain, bathing and short air or sun baths are beneficial. Survivors going over the side should be secured with lifelines and should not attempt vigorous swimming. When crossing the Atlantic in a canoe Hannse Lindemann had a 'hygienic hour' each day when the weather permitted; John Ridgway and Chay Blyth in their rowing boat kept fresh water for a weekly shave and washdown; Cecil Foster and his companions in the *Trevessa's* lifeboat found combing the hair beneficial.

Keep the mouth clean; suck a button, or frequently wipe the inside of the mouth, tongue, gums and teeth with a damp rag; rinse the rag in sea water, to keep it clean, and wring it out before putting it in the mouth. Sub-Lieutenant (now Admiral) Ian McIntosh sucked through two buttons during a twenty-three days' lifeboat voyage in the Atlantic.

When fresh-water supplies are adequate and there is no risk of dehydration, allocate some for hygiene.

Do not foul the survival craft; keep it clean.

Joints
The joints tend to swell, seize up and become weak and painful. Avoid remaining in one position for very long. Move all joints and stretch them several times a day, particularly in cold climates.

Medical Attention
Establish a routine of medical attention; it keeps troubles in check and helps morale.

Mental Disturbances
Engage the mentally disturbed in cheerful conversation and give them something useful to do. In extreme cases give injection of morphine.

Oedema (Swelling)
Swelling of the feet and hands commonly occurs. The swelling of any part of the body indicates that something is wrong. Check that survival technique is being followed, endeavour to correct any deviation as far as circumstances permit.

The feet and ankles often swell if the survivor remains in a sitting position for a long time, due to gravitational effects. Stretching the limbs and exercising the muscles will help to keep the circulation going and reduce the chance of a gravitational oedema. Gentle massage will also give some relief and help the circulation in the veins, but do not massage any part affected by immersion foot or frostbite. Regular changes of posture, especially if the feet are raised, will help to prevent oedema.

Oil Contamination
Survivors from shipwreck are sometimes covered in oil. Oil in the eyes blurs the vision and causes them to smart; if swallowed it causes nausea and vomiting. These disabilities pass off in a day or two.

Clean the hands using paper or rag, then clean round the eyes, nostrils and mouth. A de-oiling cream for this purpose is supplied in the Royal Navy's first-aid pack; it is also used as a sun deflectant. The cream is not toxic, for in the event of great hunger survivors may be tempted to eat it; it has a rum flavouring to make it more palatable.

A tube of paraffin jelly is provided in the first-aid pack in lifeboats of British merchant ships. A little of the jelly is smeared on the eyelids when cleaning the eyes.

Pain

Cramped conditions will be uncomfortable. A regime of exercise and movement should be started at an early stage before pain and cramp occur.

Pain due to injuries may be severe and need special treatment. With burns and large wounds morphine may be needed. It is usually provided in ampoules of 15 milligrams fitted with a needle; it should be injected deeply into a muscle. If it is injected superficially just under the skin, it will take a long time to be absorbed. Morphine must not be given to an unconscious person, he cannot feel the pain and the morphine may further affect an already injured brain. Morphine also tends to suppress respiration; it should not be given if the person has difficulty in breathing.

The injection of morphine may be repeated after thirty minutes if the pain is not relieved, but after these two injections no more may be given for a further six hours.

Less severe pain may be relieved by swallowing two compound codeine tablets. These should be chewed into a powder and swallowed with some water.

Parotitis

Swelling, inflammation and pain in the salivary glands sometimes occurs. It is prevented by strict attention to oral hygiene.

Salt

Survivors should avoid salt in any form. Salt taken into the body will hasten dehydration and death.

Seafarers who use sea water or salt for cooking purposes should use minimum quantities only and then only when plenty of drinking water (about 4 pints) is taken on the same day. They should likewise be on their guard when taking salt to ward off attacks of muscular cramp.

The skin should be protected from salt. Take the opportunity of a rain storm to clean salt from the body and the clothing.

Salt-water Boils

Salt-water boils, sores or ulcers are due to the skin becoming sodden with seawater and may appear within the first few days of exposure. They are painful and leave holes as big as pigeon eggs.

Keep the body as dry as possible and avoid chafing. Unfortunately this advice conflicts with that about keeping the body wet by day in hot climates in order to lessen dehydration. Dehydration is more serious than boils, so the boils must be tolerated when drinking water is short. Kenneth Cooke, carpenter of SS *Lulworth Hill*, who was rescued after being fifty days on a raft in the Doldrums wrote seventeen years after the event that he still had over sixty deep scars on his body.

Cover the boils with bandages; do not open or press them.

Seasickness

Survival craft are very lively if there is any movement on the water and the difference in motion from that of the ship predisposes to seasickness. This is particularly the case with inflatable liferafts; most men who take to them soon become seasick and some are prostrated. Seasickness generally ceases after two days.

Various types of anti-seasickness tablets are available. They usually take about an hour to become effective and should therefore be swallowed before abandoning ship. Ascertain the type which is most suitable and have a tablet handy in the event of shipwreck. It should not be a type which produces undue drowsiness, as there may be work to be done urgently; this applies particularly to leaders in survival craft—proof against seasickness should be an important factor in their selection and they should avoid becoming drowsy in the early stages in the craft.

The Royal Navy uses tablets of hyoscine hydrobromide and an immediate supply is provided in a special pocket in the inflatable liferaft; the leader distributes them and everyone has to swallow one, whether he is normally prone to seasickness or not. An exception is where morphine has been administered; a tablet is not then taken for at least twelve hours. The main supply of tablets is contained in the first-aid pack and a tablet is taken every eight hours for the first forty-eight hours, or longer if necessary. Six anti-seasickness tablets for each person are provided in the liferafts of ships which conform to the International Convention for the Safety of Life at Sea, 1960.

There is no shame about seasickness; even the greatest seafarers suffer at times. Accept it as a temporary disability which will soon disappear. Fight against the lethargy which it produces; if anything is required to be done in the raft make every endeavour to do it.

If spectacles are normally worn, keep them on at sea; eye-strain may induce seasickness. A tight bandage round the body gives some relief in rough weather.

If fluids cannot be kept down, stop taking them until the seasickness has ceased; the loss of water and electrolytes will have serious physical effects.

Shock

Injuries are usually accompanied by shock, the signs of which may be irrational behaviour, weakness, pale and moist skin, nausea and vomiting, and a pulse which is weak and fast or even indetectable.

Keep the patient lying down and warm but do not overheat him; raise the legs provided there is no head injury, no difficulty in breathing and no pain when the legs are moved. If there is difficulty in breathing keep the head and chest raised.

Skin

Boils, rashes, 'spots', etc., are common. Pustules and septic spots will tend to occur when clothing cannot be changed and the skin cannot be washed and dried.

Protect the skin from exposure to cold, sun and salt and keep it as clean and dry as possible. Wear clothing which does not fray and irritate the skin. The principles of dealing with skin disorders are cleanliness, protection and avoidance of scratching or interfering in any way. Keep the affected parts as clean as possible, use antiseptic ointment if the skin is infected and cover with clean cloth.

Sunburn

Sunburn is caused by exposure to ultra-violet radiation, direct from the sky or reflected from the water, and occurs mostly in the middle part of the day in summer months and also near the Equator. The skin becomes inflamed and blisters form, the lips crack and the eyes become sore.

Avoid exposing the skin to radiation. Survivors in tented rafts should keep well inside the raft, and where so fitted, as in the RN raft, an awning should be rigged over the entrance to increase the shade without stopping the airflow in hot climates. Look-outs should smear some de-oiling cream over their faces.

If exposed in an open boat or raft, keep the clothes on, cover head and neck, tie handkerchief over head and under the eyes, cover bare areas with bandages, pin bottom of trouser legs to socks, wear glasses to protect the eyes, or wear a bandage round the head with narrow eye-slits. Smear de-oiling paste on exposed skin.

First-aid treatment is to apply the ointment from the first-aid kit as soon as blisters appear.

Unconsciousness

An unconscious survivor should be lifted aboard the survival craft carefully and placed on one side, leaning the body slightly towards the face-down position with the side of the face on the floor (see page 121). He can usually be kept in this position by bending the top leg or by supporting the trunk with folded clothing. Open the mouth and clean it out if necessary and loosen tight clothing—these measures will help to prevent obstruction to breathing.

Never give a drink to an unconscious person, as it will choke him. Never give him morphia, it will poison an already damaged brain and may kill him. Wrap him up well if the weather is cold.

Urination

Regularity is very important; it should be at the rate of about $\frac{2}{3}$ pint a day. The urine will become darker and thicker as dehydration proceeds, but do not worry as long as it is passed.

Weight

A massive loss of weight occurs during prolonged survival, or near-survival, conditions, but there is no need to worry if the survival drill is followed. Men who have lost more than half their normal weight have survived and made a full recovery.

The record appears to be held by Ensio Tiira, who drifted for thirty-two days on an open raft in the Indian Ocean. His normal weight was 132 lbs; he weighed 56 lbs after being on a rescue ship for five days during which he had food and drink.

Wounds

If the wound is dirty, clean it with seawater and if the wound is also large, give an antibiotic.

Cover all wounds as soon as possible with sterile wound dressings from the first-aid pack. If these dressings are insufficient, use clean cloth. If the wound is on a limb, lay the victim down and raise the limb. This, together with the pressure of the bandage, will usually stop the bleeding. Add further pressure over the wound if necessary. If a large artery has been severed, apply pressure immediately over it as it enters the wound. The use of a tourniquet is not recommended. For large flesh wounds, pack the cavity with sterile dressings, then bandage firmly.

Wounded parts will swell; if the limbs are wounded keep them raised to reduce the swelling. It may be necessary to loosen the bandages after a few hours, but do not disturb the wound dressings.

If the wound is severe treat for shock.

If the wound becomes septic, with pain, redness, swelling and discharge, remove the dressing, wash the wound with seawater, and redress. Give antibiotics at the first indication of sepsis.

ADVICE TO MEN AFLOAT IN SHARK-INFESTED WATER

If there is not sufficient room for everyone on the liferaft, only those who are not wounded should go outboard.

Maintain a watch for sharks if anyone attempts to bathe or swim; have a lifeline on the survivor as he may have overestimated his strength. Do not swim at night or when the water is dirty. If a shark appears, leave the water immediately. Stream a shark repellent.

Do *not* trail arms or legs in the water. Do *not* jettison blood, vomit, garbage or any foul matter, but use containers in the liferaft. Do *not* fish if sharks are near; abandon a fish if a shark appears.

SIGNS OF LAND

Survivors should maintain a look-out for signs of land. Where the signs are good and a pyrotechnic distress signal might be useful, one should be fired.

The following signs of land have been reported by seafarers.

Sign	*Signification*
Sky	
A fixed cumulus cloud in a sky which is otherwise clear, or where the other clouds are moving.	This cloud is hovering over, or slightly downwind of, an island.
A line of cumulus cloud.	Over a coastline.
Greenish-blue tint in sky or on underside of cloud (in low latitudes).	Reflection from shallow water of a lagoon or over a reef.
Light tint (in high latitudes).	Reflection from icefield or snow-covered land. A dark tint indicates open water.
Glare (at night).	Urban area.
Air	
Bird flight at dawn.	From land to feeding area.
Bird flight at dusk.	To land from feeding area.
Insects (flies, butterflies, bees, gossamer threads).	Wind-borne from land.
Odours.	Odours of earth and vegetation (especially after rain), smoke, etc., are wind-borne. Some parts of the world have characteristic odours, e.g. peat from Ireland, eucalyptus from Australia.

Sounds.	Sounds travel a long way over water. Surf and breakers are usually heard before they can be seen.
Morning and evening breezes in opposite directions.	The breeze is from the land in the morning and towards the land in the evening.

Sea

Light colour (as opposed to dark green or blue of deep sea).	Shallow water.
Muddy colour, sweet taste.	River water. Some rivers flow out to sea for many miles.
Fish.	Usually become more numerous near land. In moderate and high latitudes seals and sea-lions are usually close to shore.
Flotsam.	Driftwood, vegetation, kelp, etc., carried offshore by ocean currents. An exception is seaweed in the Sargasso Sea, 20°–40°N and 40°–70°W.
Swell.	A regular open sea pattern is deflected by presence of an island.

Survivors should be on their guard against mirages. A mirage will change in appearance or may even disappear when viewed from different heights.

LANDING IN SURF

Many men have survived exposure over long periods, only to perish when attempting to land through breakers and surf.

Ship's Gig from Paddle-Steamer Saginaw. *North Pacific. December*
The US paddle-steamer *Saginaw* broke up on the reef at Ocean Island. Lieutenant J. G. Talbot and four volunteers took the ship's gig and attempted to sail to Honolulu for assistance. They reached Kauai in the Hawaiian group at night-fall, after covering 1,700

miles in thirty-two days. During the night the boat fell off and ran before the wind directly toward the breaker line; an attempt to bring the boat back into the wind failed, the boat broached and capsized, with the loss of two men. Lieutenant Talbot attempted to climb on to the bottom of the boat, but the next roller washed him away.

The coxswain, Halford, managed to get into the bottom of the boat. The sea forced the boat over the reef and righted it. Halford found the fifth man in the boat, having been pinned down in the entrapped air when the boat capsized. He got the man ashore but the man died soon after.

Whaleboats from Whaler Cachalot. *Tristan da Cunha*
F. T. Bullen: 'All round the island the kelp grows thickly, so thickly indeed as to make a boat's progress through it difficult. This, however, is very useful in one way here, as we found. . . . On approaching the black pebbly beach which formed the only landing place, it appeared as if getting ashore would be a task of no ordinary danger and difficulty. The swell seemed to culminate as we neared the beach, lifting the boats at one moment high in the air, and at the next lowering them into a green valley, from whence nothing could be seen but the surrounding watery summits. Suddenly we entered the bed of kelp, which extended for perhaps a quarter of a mile seaward, and, lo! a transformation indeed. Those large, waving fronds of flexible weed, though swayed hither and thither by every ripple, were able to arrest the devastating rush of the gigantic swell, so that the task of landing, which had looked so terrible, was one of the easiest.'

Whaleboats from Whaler Cachalot. *South Pacific*
F. T. Bullen: 'As we drew near the beach we found . . . the ocean swell broke upon the beach in rollers of immense size. In order to avoid any mishap, we turned the boats' heads to seaward, and gently backed towards the beach, until a larger breaker than usual came thundering in. As it rushed towards us, we pulled lustily to meet it, the lovely craft rising to its foaming crest like sea-birds. Then, as soon as we were on its outer slope, we reversed the stroke again, coming in on its mighty shoulders at racing speed. The instant our keels touched the beach we all leapt out, and exerting every ounce of strength we possessed, ran the boats up high and dry before the next roller had time to do more than hiss harmlessly around our feet.'

Boats approaching surf

Stay near the land, outside the breaker line; make a distress signal and await assistance if there is any prospect of help becoming available. In any case, wait for several hours or more if necessary in order to make a thorough study of the surf. Remember, an observer to seaward sees the smooth backs of the waves, not the curling, breaking front, and this sight might give him a false sense of security.

Observation	*Inference, comment and action*
Landfall from windward side of island.	Surf on windward side is usually higher than on leeside. Depending on size of island, there may be an area on the leeside where there is little or no surf. In determining whether to work round to the leeside of the island or a headland without risk of being swept out to sea, consider the capability of the craft and the prevailing conditions of wind and sea.
Surf approaches parallel to the shore.	Rip currents will be produced; look out for them (distinguished by sediment in the water, green water, foam belts, agitated water and confused surf, breaks in the surf, gaps in the advancing breakers, the breaker line being further seaward than in adjacent areas, the seaward drift of flotsam). The rip current may extend to 1,000 yards offshore, being 50 to 100 feet wide at the shore and much wider at the seaward end. Rip currents result in more severe breakers and in them breaking further out. Avoid them.
Surf approaches at an angle to the shore.	A longshore current, away from the direction of the approaching waves, will be produced. Avoid it, but if unavoidable, take it into consideration when planning the landing. Failing a more suitable landing

area, choose a beach which is turned away from the direction of the waves by an angle of more than 45°.

Coast is regular.	A rip current is likely to exist.
Coast is irregular.	Do not make a direct approach to headlands, but select a spot on the leeside or choose an indentation, narrow bay or valley—the surf will break further in and be less severe.
Coast rises sheer out of the water.	Avoid it. Look for a gradually sloping beach, preferably a sandy one.
Coast is inhabited.	Look out for a fishing settlement. In all probability it will be at a suitable place for landings. Signal the shore. Natives will come out and assist, or will signal the best place to land.
A wind blows.	This will produce a sea-surface current of about 1/30 the wind speed. In the equatorial belt (10°N to 10°S latitude) this drift will be in the direction of the wind; in more northerly latitudes it will be 30° to the right of the wind direction, and in southerly latitudes 30° to the left.
The wind is offshore.	Wind will cause waves to steepen offshore, but waves on breaker zone will be less severe if the land is high enough to shield them.
The wind is onshore.	May produce whitecaps outside the breaker line, making it difficult to determine where the surf begins.
There is a 'sea breeze'.	This will affect the waves, as for an onshore wind. The breeze will die down at night and early morning, but do not attempt a landing at

K

night unless assisted by local inhabitants.

The tide runs. Tidal streams will probably run along the coast, except at the entrance to bays, where they run directly in and out. For islands in the northern hemisphere the stream is stronger on the right side of the island in the direction of the current movement; in the southern hemisphere it is to the left. If the tidal stream is judged to render landing difficult, wait for slack water.

Streams at ebb tide off a gap in a reef will make the surf more severe. Wait for slack water.

The waves vary in height. Watch for the wave which is higher than the others (one in every seven or so) or the group of three or four large waves followed by smaller ones. Get a rough idea of the sequence. Take observations (particularly for gaps in reefs) when on the high waves. Ride in on the low ones.

The waves vary in breadth. The broader the wave (that is the greater the distance along its crest) the further will it travel towards the beach without breaking up. Use it for running in. If it is also a low wave the chance of a successful run in is so much greater.

The lines of breakers vary in number along the beach. There is a difference in the slope of the bottom. A greater number of breakers means that the slope is gradual, the backwash is less severe and the bottom firmer.

There are different colours in the sea. May indicate a rip current; check with other distinguishing features given above.

136

	Reefs appear to an observer down-sun as dark purple, deep water as blue, shallow water greenish-blue.
The land is a coral atoll.	Resist the temptation to land on it, especially from the weather side. Search for an opening into the lagoon.
An opening in the reef or bar cannot be found.	Wait for high tide. The waves may pass over without breaking and the surf on the shore will be much reduced.

The Run-in

Select the best spot for landing and the best time for running in. Manœuvre the craft into the correct approach for the run-in, allowing for the effect of currents, and bring the boat end-on to waves. Keep end-on by the use of a sea anchor if necessary.

Select the best wave for the run-in, dispense with the sea anchor and use oars or paddles to 'catch the wave'. Keep the boat end-on to the waves to avoid broaching and maintain speed by rowing or paddling in order to prevent somersaulting.

Row or paddle as far up beach as possible; wait for the craft to ground before jumping out. If the craft capsizes during the run-in, grab hold of it and stay with it.

4

Living off the sea

There are various forms of life at sea from which man can obtain sustenance, but their presence in sufficient quantity and the ability to bring them aboard cannot always be relied upon.

Food and rainwater are more plentiful in some seas and seasons than in others.

The great danger to man is the lack of drinking-water. Although some practised seafarers have found seawater of use in cooking and in mixing with fresh water, the drinking of seawater by shipwrecked people has proved almost always fatal.

Barnacles

Liferaft from SS Lulworth Hill. *Doldrums (Atlantic). April*
Forty-second day. A painter [rope] left over the side had collected barnacles. It was a painful effort to pull the painter aboard. Kenneth Cooke reported: 'We opened the shell of those goose barnacles. We munched them slowly so as not to lose the flavour and the wonderful softness of the flesh that acted like balm to our parched mouths. Colin was the first to tackle the long juicy stems. "Water, Ken, they're full of water!" As always the case with us, fresh flesh gave us immediate strength. Colin cast the line over again in the hope of another crop in the future—a hope that was realized some days later. I had the luck to find several more barnacles growing on the side of the raft.'

Sailing Boat Gilca. *Indian Ocean. August*
C. O. Jennings reported on the 115th day: 'I noticed several barnacles on the waterline. . . . We reached down into the water and cleared as many barnacles as we could; about half a mug full. They looked rather like whelks, and as we pulled them off the boat-side a blob of grey camouflage paint came with them. Devouring them we crunched shells and paint, the while likening them to oysters owing to their pleasant taste. They proved to be most sustaining.'

Whaleboat from Whaleship Essex. *South Pacific. December*
Twenty-fifth day. Owen Chase, First Mate: '. . . observed the bottom of the boat to be covered with a species of small clam, which upon being tasted, proved a most delicious and agreeable food. This

was no sooner announced to us than we commenced to tear them
off and to eat them for a few minutes like a set of gluttons.'

Birds

Inflatable Boat L'Hérétique. *North Atlantic. October*
Dr Bombard, on the ninth day of his voyage from Las Palmas to
Barbados, trailed a fishing line; the hook was baited with a piece of
flying fish. A shearwater pounced on the bait and was caught. Dr
Bombard: 'My strong advice to those who catch a sea bird is not to
pluck it but to skin it, as the skin is very rich in fat. I cut my shearwater in two, ate one half immediately, and left the other to dry in
the sun for the next day. . . . The flesh was excellent, but it had an
undesirable taste of fish.'

Ship's Boat from HMS Bounty. *South Pacific. May–June*
Twenty-eighth day. Captain Bligh: 'At noon some noddies came so
close to us that one of them was caught by hand. The bird was about
the size of a small pigeon. I divided it, with its entrails, into eighteen
portions. . . . In the evening, several boobies flying very near to us,
we had the good fortune to catch one of them. This bird is as large
as a duck. . . .'

Sailing Boat Gilca. *Indian Ocean. July*
Sixty-second day: a seagull perched on the bowsprit. It was shot by
revolver, decapitated, the blood was caught in a mug and the body
was squeezed dry of blood. C. O. Jennings: 'Not being able to
contain ourselves any longer, we added fresh water with just a dash
of sea water for flavouring, and enjoyed a mugful of the most
delectable drink in the whole world. . . . The physiological fact of
giving ourselves a blood transfusion was sufficient to prevent us from
tearing the bird to pieces there and then. . . . No plucking was to
be done, that process was much too slow, and while skinning the gull
Hall said it reminded him of many ducks he had handled in similar
fashion. . . . Neither of us ate one single piece of flesh until the
division had been completed. . . . This was the first food we had eaten
for twenty long days. Six hours later . . . we were still chewing bones,
chewing them to destruction, in the process of which I broke two
teeth off my dentures, but such a thing could not dismay one who
felt as I did. The flesh of the bird had been deliciously tender, and,
most surprisingly, did not taste of fish. . . . We settled down with
renewed vigour to the task of reaching land.'
Sixty-third day: another gull was shot. 'In pumping the bird dry
(of blood) several squid came from its gullet and these we ate with
relish.' A third gull was caught and, on the seventy-second day, a

fourth gull. The ammunition was then exhausted and gulls were caught by hand; in order to do this it was necessary for the hunter to be unseen by the gull. Intestines and their contents, eyes and brain were eaten. On the seventy-sixth day a second perch was erected and eight birds were caught by hand. The skin and feathers were hidden by day, so as not to scare birds away, and disposed of by night.

Sailing Ship. Antarctic
Admiral Lord Mountevans wrote on his experiences of the Antarctic: 'None of us ever could stomach the slightest taste of . . . penguin fat or blubber.' He stated that the Adelie penguin, properly prepared, tastes like hare and quoted another authority claiming that it tasted like 'a piece of beef and odiferous cod fish and a canvas-backed duck roasted in a pot with blood and cod liver oil for sauce'. He regarded the skua gull as of great value for their tasty and nourishing flesh; roasted it was almost as tasty as roast duck.

Ship's Boat from HMS Endurance. South Georgia. May
Sir Ernest Shackleton and two companions landed on South Georgia. Commander Worsley: 'We found a plateau with baby albatross on the nest. . . . These chicks gave 12 or 14 lbs of delicious food, and were a godsend to a weakened man. . . . We even ate the bones, as they were soft and juicy. A little of the liquid that was left in the cooker cooled down into a fine rich jelly. It was far better than chicken broth.' A grown albatross was caught. 'Though well flavoured, he was very tough. . . .'

Research Ship Quest. South Georgia. May
Commander Frank Wild: 'We were able to catch also Cape pigeons and albatross, which when properly cooked make good eating. The former have an oily taste which can be largely removed by soaking them for twenty-four hours in diluted vinegar.'

Crabs

Liferaft from Transport Ship Skaubryn. Indian Ocean. February
Fifth day. Ensio Tiira: 'About noon one of our crab passengers climbed through the canvas at the bottom of the raft. . . . Ericsson could no longer endure his hunger and he seized the crab, and broke off one of its legs. There was little edible meat on it, but with his fingers Ericsson managed to roll off a few shreds of white flesh which he ate and said were good. I snapped off a claw and tasted it. Then we broke up the body and ate that. Not that we got very much. . . . We looked for crabs underneath the raft and as soon as a claw appeared we grabbed at it, we ate another crab between us. From the two, I suppose we got two or three ounces of flesh.'

Collapsible Sailing Canoe. North Atlantic
Dr Hannse Lindemann, towards the end of his voyage, gathered some seaweed, shook it over the spray deck of the canoe and ate the crabs, shrimps and small fish that fell out.

Dew

Inflatable Boat L'Hérétique. *Mediterranean. May*
Dr Bombard: 'The nights that followed were to bring us a pleasant surprise. We found that very nearly a pint of fresh water condensed in the bottom of the boat. The atmosphere was very humid, and the quantity of the deposit by no means negligible. The dinghy had yet to ship a drop of sea-water and we managed to collect our windfall with a sponge. It was not enough for our total needs but it was a great help. Above all it was fresh water and tasted like nectar.'

Fish

Liferaft from MV Larchbank. *Indian Ocean. September*
A twenty-three days' ordeal. Fourth Engineer Mr Douglas Goodall: 'I stretched the spare canvas between the two paddles and rigged an awning under the shade of which the fish were attracted. We had no bait or hooks so I tried the large safety pin from my lifejacket as a hook, but it proved useless so my only course was to catch the fish with my hands. By pulling the fish into the side of the raft I caught two during the first day and six during the second, which was my biggest catch. They were fairly large fish. I tried to eat the first one with a piece of chocolate, after cutting it up with the lid of the biscuit tin. Eaten this way the fish tasted quite good, but after the chocolate ran out I was unable to carry on with this type of food. I therefore tried to get rid of the salt by cutting the fish into strips, and hanging them out to dry, and found that this was fairly successful.'

Lifeboat from MV Cressington Court. *North Atlantic. August*
A twenty-three days' ordeal. The Chief Officer Mr J. S. Gardner: 'Some of the crew managed to catch several small fish with bent pins from the medical box. We chopped up some wood from the boat and built a small fire in one of the biscuit tins and cooked these fish, which were excellent.'

Sailing Yacht Pagan. *South Pacific. May–October*
John Caldwell in his 29-foot cutter, sailing from Panama to the Fiji Islands: 'I sought to harpoon the dolphins; but I landed only three of them the whole trip. . . . Those of the dolphin I speared I cut into strips and dried on strings tied between deckhouse and traveller. The meat kept indefinitely if re-dried often enough. I alternated this

with my decreasing supply of turtle, which too I had to keep drying over and over again.'

Liferaft from SS Lulworth Hill. *Doldrums (Atlantic). March–April*
A fifty days' ordeal. Kenneth Cooke reported that on the eighth day, in bailing seawater over one another, a long stream of jelly-like substance was found. It was pulled apart, giving a mouthful all round. 'We found them salty but delicious. They were soft and cooling to the tongue, and although they made our lips smart, we were only too willing to suffer the pain. Altogether we found over a dozen strings, and felt much stronger and refreshed in consequence.' Nineteenth day: he caught a shark fifteen inches long. Twenty-fifth day: 'That evening a blue fish fell prey to my harpoon. The strength given me by my share of the fish brought a return of my determination to live. I told all hands that from then on watches must be kept, however ill and feeble we felt.' Twenty-ninth day: 'I caught a fish last evening. The vitality derived from a little fresh fish was unbelievable. It made one feel new strength flowing through veins and arteries.' The fish he caught was a ray.

Liferaft from MV Sutlej. *Indian Ocean. February*
A forty-nine days' ordeal. Chief Engineer Mr R. H. Rees: 'The birds and fish caught . . . were responsible for keeping us alive. . . . We managed to catch quite a lot of rainwater.'

Inflatable Boat L'Hérétique. *North Atlantic. October–December*
Dr Bombard: 'For sixty-five days (from the Canaries to the West Indies) I lived exclusively on what I could catch from the sea. . . . My intake of proteins and fats was sufficient. The lack of carbohydrates doubtless contributed to my loss of weight (55 lbs), but I had proved that the safety margin, calculated in advance in a laboratory, was a correct estimate.'

Balsa Raft Seven Little Sisters. *South Pacific. June–October*
William Willis left Callao on 22 June 1954 and landed at Samoa on 15 October. He wrote, twenty-third day: 'For a few days I found a lot of flying fish on the raft and feasted on them. The flesh is tender and not as firm as that of larger fish. They are six to eight inches long, and ten or twelve made a good meal.' Forty-ninth day: 'I sat beside the wheel and had my breakfast, the raw liver of a 25 lb. dolphin and about half lb. of meat. I had soaked the liver and the meat in lemon juice. It tasted fresh and clean, like raw scallops.' Seventy-first day: 'My stove had now failed completely. No more fried fish. I only ate it raw, when it was absolutely fresh, within an hour or so after it was caught. . . . I liked to chew on dried fish, too. I

had dried some dolphin meat in the sun; it was something to chew on when the weather was bad and there was no time to fix up my flour paste. An old Florida fisherman had shown me how to do it with mackerel. But it had to be taken in at night while drying, especially when the moon was out, this old fisherman had said.'

Bamboo Raft Tahiti-Nui. *South Pacific. January*
Eric de Bisschop: 'After lunch, everyone on board was suffering from a stomach upset, Alain especially. He turned deathly pale and was violently sick over the side. Soon we were all complaining of the same symptoms: aching head, palpitating heart. . . . This was not the first time we had eaten dried fish, and we had never had any trouble with it before. . . . Francis now confesses that he had forgotten that one must never leave dried fish out overnight when the moon is shining! Polynesian fishermen knew this fact very well.'

Ship's Boat from HMS Bounty. *South Pacific. May*
Captain Bligh reported, eleventh day: 'This afternoon I suffered great sickness from the nature of part of the stomach of the fish, which had fallen to my share at dinner.'

Whale Factory Ship Acushnet. *Southern Ocean*
Dr R. B. Robertson: 'It is only necessary to bait a cod hook with a smell of bacon and throw it overboard anywhere in the inlets, or over the banks surrounding South Georgia or the other southern islands, to haul up a large meal for six men.'

Balsa Raft Kon-Tiki. *South Pacific. April–August*
Thor Heyerdahl wrote of the *Kon-Tiki* sailing in the South Equatorial current: 'There was not a day on our whole voyage on which fish were not swimming round the raft and could not easily be caught. Scarcely a day passed without at any rate flying fish coming on board of their own accord. It even happened that large bonitos, delicious eating, swam on board with the masses of water that came from astern, and lay kicking on the raft when the water had vanished down between the logs as in a sieve. To starve to death was impossible. . . . We could eat shark; it tasted like haddock if we just got the ammonia out of the pieces of fish by putting them in seawater for twenty-four hours. But bonito and tunny were infinitely better.'

Canoe. North Atlantic
Dr Lindemann reported that the slower a boat the more fish will accompany it. Fish are easiest caught by an underwater gun, secondly with a trident and last of all with fishing tackle.

Inflatable Liferaft. Mediterannean
Surgeon Commander F. W. Baskerville RN reported on the first day: 'No fish had been seen and no one claimed a bite.' Third day: 'Fishing produced no bites and it was difficult to maintain interest in the lines. . . . There is no simple explanation why no fish were caught. The two types of tackle used were that recommended for survival and used by local fishermen.'

Inflatable Boat L'Hérétique. *North Atlantic. October*
Dr Bombard reported, seventh day: 'I managed to catch my first dolphin (or, to be correct, dorado). I was saved; not only did I have food and drink, but bait and hook as well. Behind the gill cover, there is a perfectly natural bone hook, such as has been found in the tombs of prehistoric men.' To catch dolphins newly arrived (the old ones knew the trick) Dr Bombard used the bone hook fixed to a length of string, 'baited with the flying fish picked up every morning on my tent. I pulled the bait rapidly across the surface of the water as if it were a flying fish skidding over the surface before diving again. The dolphins fairly fought for it. All the new arrivals fell for this trick.' Thirtieth day: 'Still plenty of flying fish; not daring to put out lines in case I catch a swordfish and make him lose his temper.'

Rowing-boat Puffin. *North Atlantic. July*
Fifty-second day. David Johnstone: 'So much for the Coast Guard's fishing kit, which John has used repeatedly without a fish of any sort being caught except in the net, or hit with the harpoon. . . . The entire kit is a failure, or else the fish are the wrong sort for all the various attractions in it.' Fifty-fourth day: 'Just before rowing this evening John had his first big fishing triumph. . . . A small lump of Oxo and beef and pork bar dropped over the side and he [a big grey fish] came straight out hungrily to get a crumb. The next piece had a hook in it, and the big fellow was hooked.'

Bamboo Raft Tahiti-Nui. *South Pacific. April*
A sunfish was harpooned. Eric de Bisschop: 'An odd fish. . . . And what a stink! The creature consists almost entirely of thick gristle, with nothing edible but a tiny strip of flesh on its upper part. I didn't fancy it myself, but the others tried some; they tell me the taste is somewhere between a turtle and a crayfish.'

Sailing Yacht Kurun. *Circumnavigation*
Lieutenant Jacques-Yves le Toumelin, when sailing in the Gulf of Papua during monsoon weather in August: 'The boat was now rolling and shipping a considerable amount of water. . . . One wave

left some fifteen fair-sized fish on the deck.' Indian Ocean, 7 September: 'I finished my last piece of dried dorado. . . . Before nightfall, a roller deposited some twenty small fish on deck.' 9 September: 'I picked five flying fish off the deck.' 10 September: 'At dawn I picked up seventeen flying fish on the deck.' 29 September: 'At dusk, before darkness had properly set in, the boat passed through a shoal of flying fish, of which several fell on deck. They rarely fell on deck in daylight for they see the boat and avoid it.'

North Atlantic. Doldrums, 10 May: 'My trailing line did not catch me a single fish for hundreds of miles.' North Atlantic, 27 May: 'The dorados followed me faithfully and I caught quite a few. I had to stop the fishing, in the end, for otherwise I should have filled the boat. . . . I dried the fish on deck in the hot sun which preserved them for several months. . . . In my view a long cruise is based on economy and foresight, and I see no reason why every opportunity to add to one's store of dried and salted fish—excellent food—should not be seized.'

Sailing Yacht Moana. *North Atlantic. October*
Bernard Gorsky: 'We now salted down about two hundredweight of fish, cutting off heads and tails, splitting them down the spinal ridge and taking out the fillets, to be carefully washed and layered in salt for three days, after which they were strung up in the rigging to dry, afterwards to keep indefinitely and provide excellent eating. The best fish for this purpose is indubitably the grouper, which gives fillets weighing several pounds.'

Lifeboat from SS Laconia. *Doldrums (Atlantic). September–October*
A twenty-seven days' ordeal. Nursing Sister Doris M. Hawkins: 'One night a small flying fish came into our boat. It was divided among eight of us and we ate it with relish.' Attempts to catch fish with improvised hook and line were unsuccessful.

Fish Juice
Reports differ as to the value of the fluid extracted from fresh fish.

Balsa Raft Kon-Tiki. *South Pacific*
Thor Heyerdahl: 'The old natives knew well the device which many shipwrecked men hit upon during the war—chewing thirst-quenching moisture out of raw fish. One can also press the juices out by twisting pieces of fish in a cloth, or, if the fish is large, it is a fairly simple matter to cut holes in its side, which soon become filled with ooze from the fish's lymphatic glands. It does not taste good if one has anything better to drink, but the percentage of salt is so low that one's thirst is quenched.'

Sailing Canoe. North Atlantic
Dr Hannse Lindemann reported that, unlike the *Kon-Tiki* crew who
had put fish in bags on which they had chewed, drinking the juice,
he personally, had had absolutely no success and only obtained a
fish pulp.

Boat. Atlantic
René Lescombe: 'In the course of an experiment lasting ninety-
eight days and for the execution of which I was equipped with
fishing tackle ranging from a shrimp lure to live bait I managed to
catch only about 22 lbs of fish. I must further stress that 70% of this
was no help against thirst, being dogfish from which only blood
could be extracted.'

Molluscs

Underwater Swimmers. Gilbert Islands
Sir Arthur Grimble: 'The Gilbertese happen to value certain parts
of it [the octopus] as food, and their method of fighting is coolly based
upon the one fact that its arms never change their grip. They hunt
for it in pairs. One man acts as the bait, his partner as the killer. . . .
The human bait dives and tempts the lurking brute by swimming a
few strokes in front of its cranny, to give himself into the embrace of
those waiting arms. . . . The killer dives, lays hold of his pinioned
friend at arm's length and jerks him away from the cleft; the octopus
is drawn adrift from the anchorage of its proximal suckers, and
clamps itself more fiercely on its prey. In the same second, the
human bait gives a kick which brings him, with the quarry annexed,
to the surface. He turns on his back, still holding his breath for
better buoyancy, and this exposes the body of the beast for the kill.
The killer closes in, grasps the evil head from behind, and wrenches
it away from its meal. Turning the face up towards himself, he
plunges his teeth between the bulging eyes, and bites down and in
with all his strength. That is the end of it. It dies on the instant; the
suckers release their hold; the arms fall away.'

Balsa Raft Kon-Tiki. *South Pacific. June*
Thor Heyerdahl: 'Young squids continued to come aboard. . . . I
have often eaten squid; it tastes like a mixture of lobster and india
rubber. But on board the *Kon-Tiki* squids came last on the menu. If
we got them on deck gratis we just exchanged them for something
else. We made the exchange by throwing out a hook with the squid
on it, and pulling it in again with a big fish kicking on the end of it.
Even tunny and bonito liked young squids, and they were food which
came at the head of our menu.'

146

Plankton

Inflatable Boat L'Hérétique. *Mediterranean. June*
Thirteenth day. Dr Bombard: 'The days grew longer, more monotonous and even more exhausting. A small ration of seawater was our only drink and the plankton, which disgusted us more every day, was our only food.'

Canoe. North Atlantic
Dr Lindemann: 'I have eaten plankton once but it burned my mouth—perhaps through the Portuguese Galley nettles—so I gave up eating this sort of food. Plankton for shipwrecked persons appears to be justified only when there is adequate fresh water available.'

Balsa Raft Kon-Tiki. *South Pacific. May*
Thor Heyerdahl reported that a silk net with almost three thousand meshes per square inch was used to collect plankton. 'It was sewn in the shape of a funnel with a circular mouth behind an iron ring, 18 inches across, and was towed behind the raft. . . . The catch varied with time and place. Catches diminished as the sea grew warmer further west, and we got the best results at night. . . . Where the cold Humboldt Current turned west south of the equator, we could pour several pounds of plankton porridge out of the bag every few hours. And bad as it smelt, it tasted correspondingly good. . . . If this consisted of many dwarf shrimps, it tasted like shrimp paste, lobster or crab. And if it was mostly deep-sea fish ova, it tasted like caviare and now and then like oysters. The uneatable vegetable plankton were either so small that they ran away with the water through the meshes of the net, or they were so large that we could pick them up with our fingers. "Snags" in the dish were single jelly-like coelenterates like glass balloons and jellyfish about half an inch long. These were bitter and had to be thrown away. Otherwise everything could be eaten, either as it was or cooked in fresh water as gruel or soup. Tastes differ. Two men on board thought plankton tasted delicious, two thought they were quite good, and for two the sight of them was more than enough. From a nutrition standpoint they stand on a level with the larger shellfish, and, spiced and properly prepared, they can certainly be a first-class dish for all who like marine food.'

Seals

Ship's Boats from HMS Endurance. *Weddell Sea. April–May*
Commander F. A. Worsley reported, near Elephant Island, 9 April: 'A crab-eater seal . . . was soon killed and cut up. . . . Green, aided by Howe, cooked the best joints.' 14 April: 'We then resorted to

chewing pieces of raw bloody seal meat. This stayed our thirst as well as our ravenous hunger for a while, but later we were more parched than before. Probably this was due to the salt in the seal's blood.' 15 April: 'We chewed biscuits, nut food, pemmican and raw seal meat. A queer mixture, but we could have eaten leather. . . . Green soon converted a sea-elephant, that we killed, into glorious hoosh. . . . All night the blubber fire burned. Each watchman cooked and ate seal liver, brains and steak. After the enforced absence from food and drink we took gluttonous delight in sizzling seal meat and hot tea or milk.' On passage to South Georgia, 30 April: 'We drank our seal oil, black and odoriferous, as it was not worth keeping (for damping the waves) for one day of the gale, and its calories were so valuable. A matter of latitude—what would have made us ill in the tropics was nectar here.' In South Georgia: 'We came across a seven-foot sea-elephant. Not having a stick, I stunned him by hurling a small boulder on his nose, then, turning butcher, took heart, liver, some flesh and blubber for food and fuel.'

Research Ship Quest. *Antarctic*
Dr A. H. Macklin: 'The meat of whales, seals, sea-elephants, sea-leopards and penguins is all very similar, being composed of a dark red coloured flesh of coarse texture. They have a somewhat strong oil taste, which one learns not to dislike in cold regions. The organs such as the brains, hearts, livers and kidneys are edible and are said to be rich in anti-neuritic vitamin. One has to beware of parasites. Fish form the diet of most of these animals, and are a prolific source of tape-worm, round worm and small thread worms. Often, also, the liver contains small trematodes. Weddell seals and sea-leopards especially seem to be infected with these parasites; on being cut open they often have an unpleasant toxic smell, the intestines swarm with worms, the heart may have small cysts on its surface, small animal-culae may be detected in the bile which flows from the cut liver, and the spleen and lymph glands are often enlarged, showing that the animal is suffering from a general poisoning. Unless the party is starving, such an animal should naturally be rejected in toto, al-though the meat may appear to be sound.'

Seawater Drinking: Planned Voyages

Inflatable Boat L'Hérétique. *Mediterranean and North Atlantic*
Dr Bombard: 'I had no rainwater for the first twenty-three days [in the Atlantic]. During the whole of that period I proved conclusively that I could quench my thirst from fish and that the sea itself pro-vides the liquid necessary to health. After leaving Monaco, I drank

seawater for fourteen days in all and fish juice for forty-three days. I had conquered the menace of thirst at sea.

'I had been told that seawater was laxative, but during the long period of our Mediterranean fast neither Palmer nor I had a single motion for eleven days. There was no sign of the predicted auto-intoxication, and my mucous membrances never became dry.'

Dug-out Canoe Liberia II. *North Atlantic*
Dr Lindemann reported that when he drank 200–500 c.c. of sea-water with 500–700 c.c. of fresh water his feet began to swell after twenty-four hours. After thirty-six hours the oedema extended to the knees. Static congestion also played a part. When he did not drink seawater he had no oedema.

Balsa Raft Kon-Tiki. *South Pacific. June*
Thor Heyerdahl: 'The special rations we had on board included salt tablets to be taken regularly on particularly hot days, because perspiration drains the body of salt. We experienced days like this when the wind died away and the sun blazed down on the raft without mitigation. Our water ration could be ladled into us till it squelched in our stomachs, but our throats malignantly demanded much more. On such days we added 20 to 40 per cent of bitter salt seawater to our freshwater ration, and found to our surprise that this brackish water quenched our thirst. We had the taste of seawater in our mouths for a long time afterwards, but never felt unwell, and moreover had our water considerably increased.

'One morning as we sat at breakfast an unexpected sea splashed into our gruel and taught us quite gratuitously that the taste of oats removed the greater part of the sickening taste of seawater.'

Sailing Yacht Pagan: *South Pacific. July*
John Caldwell: 'Invariably breakfast consisted of a cooked cereal. I mixed about six parts of fresh water with one of salt, boiled it on the Primus, and stirred in the cereal—corn meal, oat meal and such—with a heaped spoon each of powdered milk and sugar.'

Sailing Yacht Gipsy Moth IV. *Circumnavigation*
Sir Francis Chichester: 'I could cook potatoes in sea water but not rice.'

Sir Francis was troubled with muscular cramp of the legs and found that half a glass of seawater a day did him good. This was more effective than salt tablets which he tried three times and each time made him sick.

Sailing Yacht Cardinal Vertue. *North Atlantic. July*
Dr David Lewis: 'The dehydrated food presented the biggest

149

problem. Most solid foods contain 60–80 per cent water, which has to be added to reconstitute dehydrated food. Some salt water can be used for the meat and vegetables, but the highest rates I could tolerate was one part of salt water to three of fresh. I tried more but it made me sick.

'However, I found that if the tins or packets were opened, and their contents were exposed to the moist sea air in the cockpit for about twenty-four hours, they would absorb a good deal of moisture. For instance, the brittle dehydrated "plastic chips" which used to need ten ounces of fresh water, only required two ounces of fresh and two ounces of salt, after twelve hours "airing".'

On a later voyage, in the Coral Sea in July, David Lewis reported: 'Macaroni and potatoes were boiled in seawater, pumpkins in equal parts, and soups in one part of salt water to two of fresh.'

Seawater Drinking: Survival Situations

Ditched Airman. Gulf of Mexico
Second day. Air Force Captain Paul Shook: 'In the afternoon of the second day I began to realize a change was coming over me. I no longer seemed to care about my physical wellbeing and my thirst had become so great. I began to drink seawater. I knew this was wrong and was aware of the consequences, but I no longer cared. After I had drunk a considerable amount I became nauseated. I did not feel any relief from thirst or any degree of satisfaction. I knew if I continued to drink salt water I would die but I could not have cared less. I continued to drink it and became nauseated each time my stomach content reached a specific level. The desire to drink more salt water left me as the nausea increased. I finally arrived at the point where I was dry-heaving. This condition gradually subsided and was replaced by a growing pain in the kidneys and stomach.'

Lifeboat from MV Mosfruit. *North Atlantic. June*
A nine days' ordeal. Captain J. L. Ugland: 'In addition to the crew we had on board three dogs (two terriers and an Alsatian) and a cat. It was agreed to give the animals the same water ration as the crew, and a supply of biscuits was given to them throughout the trip. All the dogs survived the ordeal, but the cat died on the third day in the boat because it was continually sucking the salt water off its fur.'

Lifeboat from SS Arletta. *North Atlantic. August*
Two men in boat. Chief Officer Mr W. M. Duncan: 'The water became too salty to drink so I threw the tank overboard (on the tenth day). The sailor then started to drink seawater and soon became delirious. On one occasion he told me he was going for a

walk and he went over the side; after a struggle I managed to drag him back into the boat and he became normal for a short time but again lapsed into indistinct sentences about going to dinner with his Aunt. I struggled with him throughout the greater part of the night of the eleventh day. By the morning I too was becoming weak and delirious and could not restrain the sailor any longer. He went overboard sometime on the twelfth day.'

Lifeboat from SS Empire Chaucer. *South Atlantic. October*
A fifteen days' ordeal. Third Officer Mr R. Atkinson: 'Many of the crew drank salt water; although I threatened to stop their fresh water if they continued to do so, many of the men used to drink it at night; I could always tell when a man had been drinking salt water because the guilty ones suffered from hallucinations. During the tenth day the Second Cook became insane, probably through drinking seawater.'

Whaleboat from Whaleship Essex. *South Pacific. December*
Twenty-fifth day. Owen Chase, First Mate: 'Our thirst had now become incessantly more intolerable than hunger. . . . In vain was every expedient tried to relieve the raging fever of the throat by drinking salt water and by holding small quantities of it in the mouth. By that means, the thirst was increased to such a degree as even to drive us to despairing—in vain—relief from our own urine.'

Liferaft from SS Lulworth Hill. *Doldrums (Atlantic). March–April*
A fifty days' ordeal. Fourteen men on raft at start. Ship's Carpenter Kenneth Cooke: 'After a while I noticed some of the survivors drinking salt water. Six of the survivors were boys under the age of eighteen, whom I found taking occasional drinks of salt water, so I warned them they would die a terrible death if they persisted. They obeyed me for a day or two, but I soon found them again taking surreptitious drinks of seawater. As they drank more and more they rapidly became delirious, imagining they could see rivers of water and snow. One man became very troublesome and had to be forcibly held down until he became too exhausted to struggle any more. I threw water over him with an empty biscuit tin to subdue him. Three of the men jumped overboard shortly after drinking salt water, until eventually by 21st April, after thirty-three days on the raft, all survivors had died except myself and Able Seaman Armitage.'

Seaweed

Balsa Raft Kon-Tiki. *South Pacific. June*
Thor Heyerdahl: 'There was food to be found in our kitchen garden of seaweed and barnacles that hung like garlands from all the logs

and from the steering oar. . . . The barnacles tasted fresh and delicate; we picked the seaweed as salad, and it was eatable, though not so good.'

Sailing Yacht Pagan. *South Pacific. August*
John Caldwell: 'I remembered a moss-like growth on *Pagan*'s leeward side that had grown during the long traverse from the Galapagos. . . . Its colour varied between light and dark green, and it was hairlike, growing about an inch long in several spots. I scraped off a fistful of it and squeezed out its salt water. I pushed a part of the salty grasslike weed into my mouth and chewed and swallowed it. It tasted the way grass should taste, sprinkled with salt. It didn't ease the hunger but it eased the mind.'

Sailing Boat Gilca. *Indian Ocean. August*
Near the end of a 127 days' voyage, C. O. Jennings recorded: 'The storm gave us more fresh water and two small flying fish and as it blew itself out we were overjoyed to find a small bunch of seaweed about the size of a wire scrubber and with the same springy texture; the important thing was that it was eatable. As the days rolled by seaweed became more plentiful and small boughs began to float past. All these things we pulled into the boat, and Hall developed a great liking for boughs, whilst I remained partial to seaweed. When I caught boughs I handed them over to him, and he reciprocated with seaweed.'

Snow and Ice

Kayak. Arctic. April
Dr Nansen: 'For melting water in the cooker it is better to use ice than snow, particularly if the latter be not old and granular. Newly fallen snow gives little water and requires much more heat to warm it. That part of salt-water ice which is above the surface of the sea, and, in particular, prominent pieces which have been exposed to the rays of the sun during a summer and are thus freed from the greater part of their salt, furnish excellent drinking water.'

Shipwrecked Survivors from HMS Endurance. *Weddell Sea. October–*
    April
Commander Frank Wild: 'Sea ice, although salt, has the peculiar property that if piled up for two or three days, either naturally as pressure ridges or artificially by heaping up a number of frozen slabs, the salt leaves the upper pieces, which can be melted down and freely used as drinking water. . . . In the height of summer, when the sun beats down strongly upon the ice, pools of water form on the surface of the floes. They are fresh and can be used for drinking. It is

necessary, however, if water is being taken from this source, to see that the floe is a good solid one, not "rotted" underneath, in which case it may be brackish.'

Ship's Boat from HMS Endurance. *Weddell Sea. April*
Commander F. A. Worsley: 'Our spirits rose as we sailed on while small lumps of glacier ice tinkled against our bows. I steered in, till we were twenty yards off shore, to secure some lumps of fresh-water ice. The men leant over and caught a number of chunks to the tune of crackled laughter. Chipping the salt off the ice with their knives, the men joyfully sucked until, parched tongues and mouths being moistured, they remembered their hunger.'

Research Ship Karluk. *Arctic. June*
It is reported of Sir Hubert Wilkins: 'The ice in the ocean is bitterly salt only at the start, getting fresher month by month until in a year it is fresh enough for strong coffee, while in two it will make excellent tea, and in three years it is fresher than almost any mountain brook. There are great ponds of fresh water on top of the Arctic ice in summer. One only needs to dip it up in buckets.'

Teredo Worm

Bamboo Raft Tahiti-Nui. *South Pacific. March*
On the 137th day at sea Eric de Bisschop reported that a piece of bamboo was 'badly eaten by the teredo borer worm. I broke a piece off; it was riddled with tunnels the size of your little finger, each one with its fat white worm. They have wicked heads with two curved plates at the business end. . . . I have seen natives, especially in Melanesia, revelling in these large white worms, which they eat raw. Here, now, is . . . something to add to the menu of those who are cast away at sea.'

Turtle

Dinghy from Sailing Yacht Mignonette. *South Atlantic. July*
Four men from a foundered yawl. A fair-sized turtle was found on the fourth day, asleep on the sea. It was easily brought aboard. Blood was drained off into the inner case of the chronometer and drunk and the flesh was eaten. The finding of the turtle improved morale. The last of the turtle was eaten on the twelfth day.

Liferaft from Transport Ship Skaubryn. *Indian Ocean. February*
Twelfth day. Ensio Tiira reported that a turtle 'came alongside, I reached over and seized it, and jerked it into the raft. It was a big effort. The turtle must have weighed 10 lbs and I was extremely weak. It started to move off clumsily across the ropes and I threw it

on its back.' Tiira broke a mirror for use as a knife. 'Ericsson held its front flippers while I tried to keep down the back ones with my knee. Its sharp nails ripped my trousers and cut my leg and left arm before I was even in a position to attack. The throat looked the most vulnerable part . . . but in ten minutes I did little more than scratch the surface of the hide. I tried to choke it but there was no strength in my hands and fingers.' Tiira finally cut through a vein. 'A stream of dark red blood gushed out and hit me in the face . . . instinctively I put my head down and gripped the vein with my mouth and felt the warm blood flow into me.' Ericsson also drank some blood. 'The blood was warm and sweet and sickly, refreshing at first. But now I felt my stomach turn at the sight of it. . . . I tasted a little of the meat and it wasn't bad.' There was a rain-storm and the two men had a drink and ate about 2 oz. of turtle flesh. 'I felt much stronger . . . but Ericsson hadn't improved at all.' Tiira continued eating parts of the flesh until the fifteenth day, but Ericsson would not eat any. 'On the afternoon of the fifteenth day I could no longer stand the stink of the rotting turtle. . . . I took the remains of the body, loaded them in the shell and heaved the lot into the water.'

Sailing Yacht Pagan. *Doldrums (Pacific). October*
John Caldwell: 'I had gaffed a great sea turtle. . . . I would have fresh meat for three days. After that I would have dried meat—sun dried after the style of Indian jerky—for the full passage to the Marquesas.'

Sailing Boat Gilca. *Indian Ocean. August*
One hundredth day. C. O. Jennings reported that a turtle came up astern of the boat. His companion Hall took 'the right hand and I the left hand flipper . . . in two shakes an 18-inch turtle was lying on its back in the bilge. . . . With one blow of the axe Hall decapitated it and then began chopping out the belly skin with the axe. . . . Hall got the "lid" off and exposed a quantity of grey spongy matter. The liver and other oddments we consumed immediately, but the grey "meat" we rationed, considering it should last for two full days, though we could easily have eaten the lot there and then. . . . The turtle was finished with the exception of the shell. . . . The hard belly-skin or shell of the turtle was chopped up; we sucked pieces of it, and tried chewing it, but found it impossible to swallow.'

Whaleboat from Whaler Cachalot. *Mozambique Channel*
F. T. Bullen reported that a turtle was found sleeping on the surface. 'One of the Portuguese slipped over the boat's side and diving deep came up underneath him, seizing with crossed hands the two hind flippers and, with a sudden dexterous twist, turned the

astonished creature over on his back. Thus rendered helpless, the turtle lay on the surface feebly waving his flippers, while his captor, gently treading water, held him in that position till the boat reached the pair and took them on board.'

Sailing Yacht Spray. *North Atlantic*
Joshua Slocum 'came upon a large turtle asleep on the sea. He awoke with my harpoon through his neck, if he awoke at all. I had much difficulty in landing him on deck, which I finally accomplished by hooking the throat-halyards to one of his flippers, for he was about as heavy as my boat. . . . The turtle steak was good.'

Whaleboat from Whaleship Essex. *South Pacific. November–December*
Eleventh day. Owen Chase, First Mate: 'A small fire was kindled in the shell of the turtle, and after dividing the blood, of which there was about a gill, among those of us who felt disposed to drink it, we cooked the remainder, entrails and all, and enjoyed from it an unspeakably fine repast. After this, I may say, exquisite banquet, our bodies were considerably recruited, and I felt my spirits now much higher than they had been at any time before.' Twenty-first day: 'We killed the only remaining turtle and enjoyed another luxuriant repast, which invigorated our bodies and gave a fresh flow to our spirits.'

Whales

Whaleboat from Whaler Cachalot. *North Pacific*
F. T. Bullen: 'When he [a sperm whale] rose, he was very close, and on his back with his jaw in the first biting position. . . . Finding us a little out of reach, he rolled right over towards us, presenting as he did so the great rotundity of his belly. We were not twenty feet away, and I snatched up the gun, levelled it, and fired the bomb point-blank into his bowels. Then all was blank. . . . There were all my poor fellows with me stranded on top of our late antagonist, but no sign of the boat to be seen. . . . We had only one harpoon with its still-fast line, to hold on by; but the side of the whale was somehow hollowed, so that in spite of the incessant movement imparted to the carcass by the swell, we sat fairly safe with our feet in the middle. . . . We were ravenously hungry & thirsty. Samuela and Polly set to work with their sheath knives, and soon excavated a space in the blubber to enable them to reach the meat. Then they cut off some good-sized chunks and divided it up. It was not half bad. . . . But eating soon heightened our thirst and our real suffering then began. . . . Hardly two hours had elapsed before one of big-bellied clouds . . . emptied out upon us a perfect torrent of rain. It filled the cavity

in the whale's side in the twinkling; and though the water was greasy, stained with blood and vilely flavoured, it was as welcome a drink as I have ever tasted.'

ADVICE TO MEN LIVING OFF THE SEA

Water

On no account should survivors drink seawater nor mix it with fresh water when rations are short. Seafarers with plenty of fresh water and good prospects of replenishing their supplies may use a little seawater in their cooking, but the amount of salt consumed in this way should not exceed that taken in normal life ashore.

Maintain all rain catchment areas and collecting utensils in a good state of cleanliness and free from salt. Use solar still and desalting apparatus if provided. Improvise a distilling plant if facilities are available. Collect dew at night. Hang clothes in the rigging; place them over the face and suck in the drops. Collect dew on cold surfaces in the boat.

In ice-regions, remember that icebergs, glaciers and old sea-ice consist of fresh water. Old sea-ice is distinguished from young sea-ice by its smooth corners, bluish colour, glossy surface and its ease of splintering when struck. Young sea-ice has angular corners, milky colour, tough texture and is difficult to splinter. Pieces of sea-ice piled up for two or three days lose their salt. The pools which form on ice in summer are fresh: select those which are remote from possible contamination by salt sea spray. Where heating apparatus is available, use ice rather than snow—it is more economical on heat.

Food

Foodstuffs available at sea, such as birds, turtles and fish, contain protein, but protein should be eaten only when at least two pints of fresh water are drunk on the same day. Nevertheless, there are many examples where the catching of a fish or a bird has given a dehydrated survivor renewed hope, enabling him to continue the struggle for existence. Other foodstuffs like plankton and seaweed cannot easily be cleaned of salt. Survivors should avoid salt at all costs.

156

Barnacles

Barnacles growing on the side of a boat, on a trailed line or on shore, are edible. The paint on the underside of the boat should be non-toxic.

Birds

All sea birds are edible. If a bird perches on the craft, wait until it folds its wings. If it is within arm's reach, grab it. Catch others by using a fishing line and floating a baited hook.

Drink the blood, provided fresh water is drunk the same day. Skin the bird. Eat the entrails first. Flesh which can be spared for another day should be dried.

Fish

Some fish are dangerous to handle and some are poisonous to eat. Some parts of otherwise edible fish are harmful.

Do *not* tempt large and voracious fish.

Do *not* handle fish until they are dead; kill them with a blow on the head.

Do *not* eat fish which have spines or bristles instead of scales, in particular the puffer fishes which blow themselves up into a bladder-like shape and make a considerable noise by grinding their teeth together; these puffer fish have a disagreeable odour.

Do *not* eat fish which smell 'off', are pallid at the gills or have been left in the sun for more than two hours.

Do *not* eat fish taken from water where planktonic blooms are present.

Do *not* eat fish liver, intestine or roe.

Do *not* eat shark's liver, nor the flesh of Greenland shark, hammerhead, white shark, six- or seven-gilled sharks, or black-tipped sand shark.

Do *not* eat tropical moray eels.

If in doubt, throw out.

Fish which are considered safe to eat should be gutted, the flesh cut into thin fillets, and soaked in several changes of water. Throw the water away—any poison in the flesh may have leached out into the water. Survivors should then hang the fillets to dry; they will keep well if kept dry. Cooking will not have much effect on any poison in the flesh, but if the flesh is boiled the water should always be thrown away.

VENOMOUS FISH
do not touch

Zebra Lion or Turkey Fish

Sting Ray

Porcupine Fish

Scorpion Fish

Stone Fish

Toad Fish

POISONOUS FISH
do not eat

Trigger Fish

File Fish

Puffer Fish (uninflated)

Puffer Fish (inflated)

Mammals

Seals, whales, etc., are edible. The liver and kidneys of polar bears are poisonous.

Molluscs

The small octopus and squid which come aboard rafts are edible.

Plankton

Besides being rich in protein and salt, plankton also contains chitin, a hard shell-like substance, which is not a good thing to eat under survival conditions.

Some plankton is toxic and even deadly, e.g. the hydroids and dinoflagellates; the normal seafarer is probably unable to detect the dangerous types. Do *not* eat plankton.

The dinoflagellates may be sufficiently numerous to give the sea a reddish-brown colour. Do *not* eat fish or shell fish taken from such coloured water, or whenever planktonic blooms are present.

Seaweed

Seaweed is edible, but fresh water should be taken at the same time.

Shellfish

Crab-meat is edible except for the loose, finger-like, yellow/ grey, spongy material around the periphery of the de-shelled crab and the stomach, which is found just below the head.

Avoid shellfish which look like a large ice-cream cone or cornet with a lid on it; these have a very venomous bite. The white meat of all other shellfish is safe to eat when freshly boiled; the dark meat, gills and siphon should not be eaten. The water in which the white meat is boiled should also be thrown away.

5

Psychological aspects of exposure afloat

The mental and emotional reactions of survivors immersed in the sea are described in Chapter 2. When on a survival craft the period of survival is much longer and the survivor may be one of a group. The psychological aspects are therefore very different.

In normal life men vary in their response to stress; they may become immobilized, disorganized, dazed but amenable to command, or very active in a purposeful way. Men at sea are at greater hazard and their responses are more marked. Abandoning ship presents a personal crisis to many; even long-experienced seafarers may fear jumping into the sea. Life in the cramped community of a survival craft, possibly with strangers, in a hostile environment, without the comforts of normal life, often leads to mental deterioration. Shortage of food and drink and exposure to the elements result in biological changes, which in turn affect mental and emotional stability. It is usual for signs of mental impairment to appear before the body becomes severely physically affected.

The body's immediate reaction to stress, as in abandoning ship, is usually a phase of heightened mental and physical activity. Sudden fear causes a release of the hormone adrenaline which alerts the body. The heart rate and blood pressure rise; the liver releases more sugar into the blood stream; blood vessels in the skin are constricted, thus providing more blood in the muscles and reducing heat loss; the muscles are more easily excited and less easily fatigued; mental activity is increased. Without confidence and training in survival techniques the survivor may panic during this phase of heightened activity, making wrong and possibly fatal mistakes.

This phase of activity lasts for a short while—perhaps thirty minutes, giving way to a period of adaptation where a very wide range of mental reactions occur. The survivor who adapts well to a change in his environment will set his mind to survival, work out the priorities of action, avoid panic, and make active and deliberate attempts to improve his morale by singing, conversation, prayer and preparations for his survival.

160

As stress continues, his powers of adaptation weaken and he may unconsciously escape from harsh reality by day-dreaming, indulging in fantasies or lapsing into a stupor. He is then less able to exert self-control and he becomes irritable, selfish or aggressive.

Complete mental exhaustion will eventually occur, accelerated by the physical effects of exposure, malnutrition, dehydration and loss of sleep. At this stage he may be confused, delirious or hallucinated. True psychosis (madness) is unusual, but it may occur as a toxic effect, e.g. as a result of drinking seawater, severe wound infection, typhoid or any fever.

Occasionally, in the extreme, the basic will for self-destruction or self-preservation may dominate his mental state, resulting in suicide or homicide, or, rarely, cannibalism.

No matter how much physical equipment the survivor has, his chances of survival are very much weakened if he does not have the right mental equipment with the power to adapt and the will to survive. Training in survival techniques, confidence in his equipment and in his own ability to survive are all essential. Men with a minimum of equipment, but with a strong will to live, have survived for long periods, whereas other men with ample equipment have succumbed in less.

The following accounts are arranged in alphabetical order, taking the main topic of each one as the heading.

Adaptability

Ice Box as Raft. West Coast of Australia. April–May
The *Canberra Times* of 13 May 1963: 'The prawning trawler *NOR 6* sank about 5 a.m. on April 24th. . . . As the trawler went down the 7 ft × 8 ft icebox tore loose and bobbed up beside the swimming skipper. . . . Jack Drinan, the skipper, broke a hole in one of the 3 ft deep compartments and stayed in it for the next twelve days. For water he licked the moisture from the icebox lid, spending the days bailing salt water from the craft with a shirt. His only tools were a shovel and an eighteen-inch hammer. With these he cut the lid in half and made a flimsy raft measuring 6 ft 9 inches by 2 ft 4 inches. The first time he set out for the shore aboard the insulating foam-covered lid he lost heart after one mile and returned to his icebox "mother ship". A day later he tried again and was on shore within twenty-four hours.'

Age

Raft. South Pacific
William Willis was sixty years old when he took the raft *The Seven Little Sisters* from Callao to Samoa in 1954. He left Peru on the raft *Age Unlimited* on 4 July 1963 and arrived at Tully, North Queensland, on 9 September 1964; he was then seventy-one. He made the voyage to prove to himself that age is no handicap in adventure. He attempted a solo crossing of the North Atlantic in an 11-foot boat in 1966 at the age of seventy-two, and was lost.

Sailing Yacht Gipsy Moth IV. *Circumnavigation*
Sir Francis Chichester celebrated his sixty-fifth birthday whilst sailing alone around the world in *Gipsy Moth IV*.

Abandoned Ship SS Andalucia Star. *South Atlantic. October*
Captain J. B. Hall: 'A. Wheeler, lamp-trimmer, dived into the water from his boat after abandoning ship to rescue a little girl of six who was floating about quite unperturbed. When rescued her only concern seemed to be for her doll which she was still clutching in the water but was nearly lost when being pulled into the boat.'

Liferaft from SS Zaafaran. *Arctic Ocean. July*
Captain C. K. McGowan: 'I would also like to pay tribute to the Galley boy (name unknown) who was just celebrating his sixteenth birthday. He was in a vessel which was torpedoed a short time before, in P.Q. 15, and on arriving home on leave, his mother asked him why he had come home. He told her he had been torpedoed and had come home on a month's leave. "A month's leave", retorted his mother, "I have no food for you here." So he immediately volunteered for sea again and was sent to my ship.' He had to abandon ship again following attack by enemy aircraft. 'While on the rafts, the men on his raft were joking and telling him that there were too many men on that raft and that he had better swim to another less crowded one. They told him he did not really need his lifejacket, so taking this off, this boy swam with a heaving line to another raft and secured the line, thus enabling the rafts to be pulled together.'

Lifeboat from MV Port Victor. *North Atlantic. April*
Captain W. G. Higgs: '. . . the gallant action of Apprentice Matthews. This boy is only eighteen years of age, but he took complete charge of No. 5 lifeboat, creating order out of chaos. He saw two men in the water who were unable to reach the oars of the boat which were extended to them, so he dived overboard and swam

about thirty feet to bring each man back in turn to the lifeboat, thereby undoubtedly saving their lives.'

Anger

Carley Float from the Yacht Reliance. *English Channel. May*
Ann Davison: 'A wave thundered down on the float, which should have been the end of me, but instead, woke me from oblivion to anger. A bitter impotent rage, so that I struck out, beating the air with my fists, fighting a tangible battle with an intangible foe.'

Inflatable Raft from Trimaran Yaksha. *North Atlantic. June*
Second day. Joan de Kat: 'I left the entrance of my tent half open for a little too long and a wave broke into my dwelling place and left 10 cm. of icy water on the floor. The curious thing was that so far from demoralizing me, this woke me up and pulled me out of my torpor. I swore, picked up the bucket, and bailed out almost all the water.'

Anxiety

Sailing Yacht Cardinal Vertue. *English Channel. June*
First day, following a return to Plymouth to have his mast repaired, Dr David Lewis reported: 'Midnight . . . found me anxiously going around the decks, checking over the halyards and the gear, and keeping a worried eye on the mast. I would try to rest, but soon worry would drive me on deck to inspect the mast and rigging yet again, before going below to lie down. I was too tired and excited to eat anything except some sweets and biscuits and to drink a little water, and later make a cup of coffee. I slept hardly at all that night.'

Apathy

Carley Float from the Yacht Reliance. *English Channel. May*
Ann Davison and her husband were on a Carley float in the Portland Race. 'Hours dragged out in immeasurable misery as the sea struck with a sledge-hammer to kill a pair of gnats. No longer buoyed by the slightest hope of rescue we sank into an apathy of endurance, huddled together, heads on the ring, hands grasping life-lines with the prehensile, immovable grip of the new-born. Or the dying.'

Lifeboat from MV Richmond Castle. *North Atlantic. August*
A seven-day ordeal, fourteen survivors, nine casualties. The Second Officer, Mr F. J. Pye: 'The men who died all became apathetic and their morale became very low. I could not get them to move in an

163

emergency or do anything to help themselves. They complained continually of thirst but I could not spare them any more water.'

Autogenic [Self-Hypnotic] Training

Collapsible Canoe Liberia III. *North Atlantic*

Dr Hannse Lindemann reported that six months before his voyage he 'had already begun to prepare my subconscious sympathetically with the aid of an autogenic training course. First of all I drove in the command "I can do it". I needed an optimism which was more than a grim form of humour and rather something which sprang up from the depths of my being. The second command which was aimed at giving me strength was "Do not give in". Its chief purpose was to protect me from giving in to the call of the more comfortable beyond in moments of exhaustion or stormy periods. The third command was "Westerly Course". As soon as my boat deviated from the westerly course I would hear the words "Westerly course". . . . And the last command was "Don't accept any help". I was able to learn from the trip which my French colleague [Dr Bombard] made, when he twice accepted food from passing steamers, although he declared afterwards that he had only done it once.

'The surprising success of these post-hypnotic commands was demonstrated by the way the trip turned out. I will describe it with reference to the "Westerly course" command.

'As soon as I reached the stage of illusions, in which my powers of judgment were greatly diminished, there sounded from the sea "Wescht"; as the waves broke they produced this onomatopoeic word "Wescht". This was immediately linked up with the idea of looking at the compass and checking the course. Even in the stage of hallucination this "Westerly course" came through. On the fifty-seventh day of my crossing I was hallucinating as I had never done before. Suddenly . . . I had the vision of a Negro. I asked him where we were going. And now comes the completely new phenomenon: "To the west" he answered. There the post-hypnotic command breaks through even in hallucination; without this "Westerly course" I should have finished up where all my predecessors had ended, along with the fishes.

'My gymnastic exercises for the blood vessels will be more difficult to explain to the layman than the formulated resolutions. For seventy-two days I was forced to sit in the boat; I could not stretch out even during sleep, and I was sitting in wet clothes on a hard, wet seat. I was sure I would get a magnificent decubital ulcer. However, when I landed after more than ten weeks, I could not discover even the faintest sign of a sore on my hinder parts. Why? During the trip

I had used the autogenic training to direct my blood into the vulnerable parts of my body several times a day.'

Boredom

Sailing Yacht Pagan. *South Pacific. June–September*
John Caldwell: 'I was never bored; it is impossible for a person with an active mind to be bored with his own company. The days went too quickly. I hadn't time to do all I set out to do each morning.'

Sailing Yacht Lively Lady. *North Atlantic. May–August*
Sir Alec Rose on the 1964 Single-handed Trans-Atlantic Race: 'My days were full. There is always a job to be done of some kind, and, far from being bored, I enjoyed every minute, and I didn't seem to have time to read books.'

Rowing-Boat Puffin. *North Atlantic. June–July*
Eleventh day. David Johnstone: 'Life on board is settling down but there are the various irritations of routine which are boring us both. . . . We can still not seem to get a meal in less than an hour including washing-up time, and it's very boring getting it.'

Sailing Yacht Les Quatre Vents de l'Aventure. *Circumnavigation*
Marcel Bardiaux: 'I am often asked "Don't you get bored, all alone for months on end?" Boredom? None of that aboard. Anyone who asks such questions can never have set foot on a boat, especially when that boat carries a crew of one. When at sea I have to be navigator, crew (sails don't set themselves), cook, cabin boy, etc. But in port it is even worse, for I have to be jack of all trades.'

Sailing Yacht Gipsy Moth IV. *May*
Sir Francis Chichester wrote, 113th day: 'I was kept busy sewing the genoa staysail, a job I disliked very much. It made my back ache, which I suppose was due to boredom, because I don't sew with my back!'

Comradeship

Whaleboats from Whaleship Essex. *Doldrums (Pacific)*
The crew of the wrecked whaleship *Essex* took to three boats. Owen Chase, First Mate: 'We agreed to keep together in our boats, as nearly as possible, to afford assistance in cases of accident and to render our reflections less melancholy by each other's presence. I found it on this occasion true that misery does indeed love company.'

Sailing Yacht Suhaili. *Circumnavigation*
Robin Knox-Johnston: 'I never caught an albatross; I never tried to kill one either. I think being alone in a vast and hostile environment

165

gave me a feeling of comradeship with any fellow animal—
although I would certainly have killed them if I had run short of
food.'

War Casualties from SS Laconia. *Doldrums (Atlantic). September*
The ship was carrying Service personnel, their families and prisoners-
of-war; it was torpedoed and abandoned. Survivors were taken
aboard a German submarine, their clothes were dried, they were
given hot drinks and food, medical treatment and cigarettes, the
German officers gave up their bunks to the women and many of the
crew gave theirs to the men. Nursing Sister Doris Hawkins recorded,
'The Germans treated us with great kindness and respect the whole
time; they were really very sorry for our plight.' The submarine
was attacked from the air and had to put the survivors back in the
boats before it could submerge. Doris Hawkins wrote, 'Even in the
midst of a war one must recognize gratefully the humanity shown to
us survivors by the personnel of the German submarine which
picked us up. I shall always feel grateful for it, even though I know
that the German captain who was so courteous and humane in his
treatment of us was also responsible for our plight.'

Conversation

Lifeboat from SS Trevessa. *Indian Ocean. June*
Captain Foster: 'The chief topic of conversation was still the
prospects of being picked up by another steamer.' Sixth day: 'All
our thoughts and most of our talk were about the chances of being
picked up.' Seventh day: 'One of the chief topics of conversation
amongst us for the first few days at sea was the nature of the accident
which could have happened to the ship.'

Lifeboat from SS Britannia. *South Atlantic. March–April*
Third day. Frank West: 'At the first opportunity after daybreak we
had a conference during which the main subject was the maintenance of discipline and the apportioning of duties amongst us. On all
important matters decisions were made at our daily conferences.'
Fifth day: 'We spent a good deal of time discussing what we shall do
when we get ashore and always, of course, what we shall drink. We all
agree on beer, in large quantities. Everyone is very cheerful and
hopeful.' Sixth day: 'Despite the dryness in our throats we continued
to talk amongst ourselves fairly freely, but increasingly only about
rescue and food and drink. We all agreed that never again would we
eat anything resembling a hard ship's-biscuit.' Seventh day: 'Our
conversation usually centres around what we shall drink when we
reach safety and today we all went firstly for grapefruit. The second

choice was a wide variety, but always a long cool drink. Very few are interested in alcohol. To eat we would all like fruit salad.' Fourteenth day: 'Very little talk now of the food and drink we should like—now we want medical treatment.'

Liferaft from SS Lulworth Hill. *Doldrums (Atlantic). March*
Eighth day. Kenneth Cooke: 'No one had bothered about conversation in the past forty-eight hours. Tongues were swollen and blackened and even cursing one another had become an effort.'

Rowing-Boat English Rose III. *North Atlantic. June–September*
Sergeant Chay Blyth wrote, forty-second day: 'I was not bored. Nor was John. We never ran out of conversation.' Seventy-second day, after receiving food from a passing ship: 'By this time we were responding to our improved diet. . . . Some conversation became possible again.'

Captain John Ridgway: 'We quickly found that our own conversation was the best tonic of all and helped to overcome the many disappointments. Food was a subject never far from our minds. . . . I think most of the conversation for the ninety-one days we were at sea turned on the subject of food.' Seventy-fifth day: '. . . our conversations ended in mid-stream.'

Antarctic Research Vessel Quest. *South Atlantic*
The *Quest*, 125 tons, experienced a number of troubles. Sir Hubert Wilkins: 'Through all this trouble Shackleton kept our spirits up. . . . When any difficulty arose, he would go to each man individually, and take him aside and say, "We're up against it. Now, you're the one man I think has some real ideas about this job, and I wish you would tell me how to go about it."

'The fellow would be pleased, and would give his ideas, and Shackleton would say, "Good! That's a splendid idea and I'll use it. Thanks a lot."

'Then he would go to the next fellow and tell him the same story. Each man thought he was the one upon whom Shackleton depended for advice and help. In a little while we all knew that Shackleton was flattering us, but we were influenced by it just the same. You can't get away from the fact that a word well spoken does have great influence.'

Delirium

Dug-out Canoe Liberia II. *North Atlantic*
Dr Lindemann: 'I got into a state which I called "sleep-deficiency delirium", in which I threw overboard items which I needed desperately later on.'

Liferaft from SS Lulworth Hill. *Doldrums (Atlantic). April*
Kenneth Cooke reported that by the twenty-second day several men
were suffering from delirium. 'The youngster who had been drinking
seawater all night was the worst offender. The more he drank the
more he seemed to want. His mind by that time had completely
gone.'

Lifeboat from SS Peterton. *North Atlantic. October*
A forty-nine days' ordeal. Second Officer Mr G. D. Howes: 'Six
of the crew became delirious during the heat of the day; the attacks
seemed to start on the thirty-fifth day.'

Dementia

Lifeboat from SS Roxby. *North Atlantic. November*
Fourth day. The Master, Captain G. Robison: 'The Senior
Operator went out of his mind. He had not been in good health
when we took to the boats. At daybreak I examined him and found
that he was dead.'

Raft from Transport Ship Skaubryn. *Indian Ocean. February–March*
Fourth day. Ensio Tiira reported that Ericsson showed signs of
madness, made strange gestures and jumped overboard. Twenty-
fifth day, following the disposal of Ericsson's body, Tiira reported:
'My hands and knees were sore and my whole body ached. But I
worked and worked with the force inside me making me go on. I
think the work kept me sane.'

Liferaft from SS Lulworth Hill. *Doldrums (Atlantic). April*
Kenneth Cooke reported that on the fourteenth day the First Officer
asked for a knife, they struggled and the First Officer was subdued—
he showed signs of insanity, and attempted suicide. On the fifteenth
day, the First Officer recovered his sanity and knew nothing of asking
for the knife, but he lost his senses again soon after. On the night of
the eighteenth day, he spent a very bad night, shouting and raving
incoherently nearly all the time. Twice he had tried to get over the
side, but had been so weak that the weight of a restraining hand
proved sufficient to hold him down. He recovered sanity at 4 p.m.
and asked for water. He died at 4.30 p.m.

Lifeboat from SS Britannia. *Doldrums (Atlantic). April*
Eleventh day. Lieutenant Frank West reported of a man who drank
much seawater: 'He kept leaping high into the air and then lying in
the bottom of the boat with his arms and legs threshing and kicking
all around him.' William MacVicar: 'The poor man's face was a
ghastly sight. His eyes protruded straight out of their sockets while

his lips were drawn back over his teeth in a bestial smile. His lips and teeth were covered with a thick white froth. His whole body shook periodically with great convulsions. Suddenly, as three or four men were trying to hold him down, the man, with seemingly great strength, threw them off and leapt for the side of the boat.'

Depression

Sailing Yacht Cardinal Vertue. *North Atlantic. June*
Sixth day. Dr David Lewis: 'Always in these calms a profound depression dominated me. Hour after hour the ship would wallow helplessly in the swell, rolling 20 degrees each way. There was a vicious brutality in the slap, slap, slap of the sails, something of the shock of a hand slapped to and fro across a face, and on it would go, on and on. . . . But until I started working, and this needed a great effort, it was impossible to overcome my depression.'

Sailing Yacht Jester. *North Atlantic. June*
Fifteenth day. H. G. Hasler: 'Depressed . . . all sorts of doubt about my rig [a Chinese lug sail], provisions and time needed to get to New York. I dispelled this feeling in the afternoon by doing some work aboard.'

Lifeboat from SS Britannia. *Doldrums (Atlantic). March–April*
Second day. A ship was sighted. Frank West: 'We altered course to westward to close the ship as much as possible. Soon we could clearly distinguish a tramp steamer and our excitement grew. . . . A white shirt was hastily tied by the sleeves to our longest oar and held high aloft as the steamer came nearer and nearer until it seemed she could not possibly miss seeing us. She steamed on unheedingly. . . . As we returned to our true course we were strangely silent, each man suffering his disappointment alone and with a heaviness on his heart.' Third day: 'About noon we sighted another ship and we estimated it to be seven to nine miles away, crossing our bows. We burned rags soaked in Colza lamp oil tied to the end of an oar held aloft in an effort to attract attention, but again failed to do so and suffered great disappointment.' Eighteenth day: 'During the night another ship passed us and we burnt two red flares but failed to attract attention. We do not seem to suffer such great disappointment as at first.'

Lifeboat from MV San Ernesto. *Indian Ocean. July*
Twenty-seventh day. Second Officer, Mr G. Taylor: 'At 1700 Ordinary Seaman —— died. I held a short service before burying him in the sea. The death made the rest of the crew rather depressed so I issued an extra ration of water and gave them another "lecture".'

Despair

Inflatable Boat L'Hérétique. *North Atlantic. October–December*
Dr Bombard, writing of his experience in crossing the Atlantic in an inflatable boat, stated that despair is the greatest killer of all in the survival situation.

Liferaft from Transport Ship Skaubryn. *Indian Ocean. March*
Fourteenth day. After failing to stop two ships Ensio Tiira reported: 'We sank down on the ropes full of misery and rage, hurling oaths at the departing ships.' Later the same day, they failed to stop another ship. 'I was beyond hope now. I knew it wouldn't do any good to wave and hardly felt any disappointment when it went on.' Fifteenth day. A small tanker bore down on the raft. SOS was flashed and Tiira shouted 'Hallo' and a voice came back to him. Further 'Halloes' from the raft brought no reply. 'A great rage of black despair descended upon me. I cursed the ship until I could curse no more. Ericsson took it all quietly. He wasn't upset at all.'

Deterioration

Liferaft from Transport Ship Skaubryn. *Indian Ocean. March*
Seventh day. Ensio Tiira: 'We tried to talk sometimes, but our thoughts, like our voices, tended to wander off. One of us would stop talking in the middle of a sentence and the other couldn't be bothered prompting him to go on.' Nineteenth day: 'My worst trouble was that I was so very tired that when I decided to do something the co-ordination took a long time. My legs and arms responded very slowly to instructions from my brain.'

Sailing Yacht Lively Lady. *Southern Ocean. February*
On the fourteenth day after leaving Bluff and experiencing bad weather and carbon monoxide poisoning, Sir Alec Rose wrote: 'It was blowing a gale and I had to turn out and lower the mainsail, but I was too weak even to think straight.'

Liferaft from SS Lulworth Hill. *Doldrums (Atlantic). April*
Twenty-first day. Kenneth Cooke: 'To think was agony, to move a whole inquisition of torture.'

Rowing-Boat English Rose III. *North Atlantic. June–August*
Fifth week. John Ridgway reported that he and Chay Blyth would row for hours not exchanging a word. 'Then when one of us did say something, it was so unexpected that the other took some time to react. . . . There would be a pause. A long pause. And the reaction of the other would be something like this with a half-second hesitation between every word. "I—didn't—quite—hear—what—you

—said. Say—it—again." There would be another long pause, perhaps several seconds, before the words were repeated. . . . We knew that our mental processes had taken a strange turn, that we were thinking and speaking and moving with an unusual deliberation.' Twelfth week: 'As each hour succeeded monotonous hour, we were getting progressively weaker, both mentally and physically. Everything was becoming more and more of an effort. . . . I found that the days seemed to merge into one another now. You lose any sense of time and the happenings get out of place.'

Sailing Yacht Pagan. *South Pacific. October*
John Caldwell: 'Forty-seven days since the hurricane . . . and the closest land an estimated ten days away. I tried to scribble it into the front pages of my Bible. . . . But I didn't put it in; I tried but I couldn't. My brain was foggy, the foggiest yet—I couldn't think in a suitable way so I pushed it aside, and stared out of the porthole.'

Sailing Yacht Gipsy Moth IV. *Circumnavigation*
Sir Francis Chichester took 107 days to sail from Plymouth to Sydney. Four days after arrival he wrote: 'I am at the lowest physical and mental ebb that I've ever been in my life. I weigh 10 stone against my normal 11 stone 4. I feel so emaciated and wizened up that I thought on the boat I had lost nearer 40 lb. . . . I am too tired even to sleep properly. My bedroom heaves in my sleep worse than the boat ever did.'

Dissociation

Balsa Raft Seven Little Sisters. *South Pacific. July*
Nineteenth day. William Willis: 'I was falling deeper and deeper into my detached state—into this strange severance of the mind from the world I had left. It had been noticeable almost from the first day at sea. . . . My mind, like my body, was adrift in space with no shore in sight.'

Rowing-Boat English Rose III. *North Atlantic. August*
Seventy-third day. Chay Blyth: 'It took more than three days, with regular doses of vitamin pills, to get back to normal [after having unaccustomed food on a passing ship] and during that time we lived in a dream-like state mid-way between waking and sleeping. Nothing we did seemed to be really happening. It was just as though we were sitting outside the boat watching two other blokes doing the work for us.'

Sailing Yacht Gipsy Moth IV. *Southern Ocean. November*
Eighty-first day out of Plymouth. Sir Francis Chichester: 'The sight

of the self-steering gear broken beyond repair acted like a catalyst. At first I turned cold inside and my feelings, my spirit, seemed to freeze and sink inside me. I had a strange feeling that my personality was split and that I was watching myself drop the sails efficiently and lift out the broken gear coolly.'

Sailing Boat Gilca. *Indian Ocean. August*
C. O. Jennings reported, 103rd day: 'We had no food but plenty of rusty-coloured water. . . . Again silence reigned between us and we sat just staring. . . . The end seemed near, and, in contrast to a fevered body, it seemed that an ice-cold calculator had replaced my brain, and this new contraption was detached and placed just out of reach above my head.'

Collapsible Canoe Liberia III. *North Atlantic. November*
Dr Lindemann reported that in the third week every libido disappeared and all his thoughts centred around food or a farm he would buy in the tropics. The most interesting food was sweets which his imagination served up to him in all possible shapes and quantities. Concentrating on nothing, being at one with Nature, and not even knowing his own name, he only accomplished in the last three stormy weeks of his voyage. Then it happened he wanted to speak but could not do so, he felt himself weightless, happy and contented as if in another world. He had no painful feelings, heard nothing of a howling storm and knew nothing of his desperate situation.

Dreams

Lifeboat from SS Trevessa. *Indian Ocean. June*
First Officer Smith, who was in a lifeboat for twenty-five days: 'No one ever slept soundly, they merely dozed, often tormented by a dream which occurred again and again, that they were just on the point of having a long cool drink of water; but they always woke up before the drink could be taken.'

Sailing Boat Gilca. *Indian Ocean. July*
Sixty-second day. C. O. Jennings: 'During the twenty days of enforced starving, I had had dreams of tables stretching away to infinity in long low buildings situated always in beautiful grassy meadows, and peopled with the most generously and kindly folk it was possible to meet. From tables piled high with luscious food these dream-folk would press upon me great pieces of cheese and steaming mugs of cocoa, which nearly made me choke as the pleasant aroma assailed my nostrils. Hall and I compared notes about our dreams and found they were practically identical. Always we were allowed

to select and handle any food we desired, but as soon as we lifted some tasty morsel to our lips the dream vanished and we awoke.'

Balsa Raft Seven Little Sisters. *South Pacific. September*
Seventy-first day. William Willis: 'I finally dozed off . . . for a full twenty minutes. . . . Suddenly I awoke, for it sounded as if we were among rocks and this was the end. . . . I had again dreamed that someone was at the wheel, looking after the raft. . . .'

Sailing Yacht Pagan. *South Pacific. October*
John Caldwell, in a state of semi-starvation and with his yacht dismasted, wrote on the 96th day: 'Then came the worst night of all. A night of food dreams. A night of ghosts in the form of chocolate cake and steak dinners. Through the long hours I writhed between waking and sleeping and at last wakened finally and found myself champing at my blanket.' 103rd day: 'Don't eat leather if you want pleasant dreams. For unending hours I writhed in the grip of nightmares about food. I was in a mammoth grocery store running berserk among corridors of food. I wakened in a labour of sweat only to drift back to my horror dreams.' 105th day: 'I dreamed I was wrecked on a beach, and I was happy. There was a huge grey whale stranded there. I grabbed him by the tail and started devouring him alive as I had done the flying fish. And I awakened clawing and growling at my bunk boards.'

Factions

Lifeboat from SS Britannia. *Doldrums (Atlantic). April*
Seventh day. Frank West: 'There were the inevitable quarrels between all the Lascars and all the Goanese. . . . While these men all seemed to have grievances against each other, they were of small account compared to their feeling of grievance against and hatred of the Sikhs. We never knew the real cause of the dissension, but feeling between the two groups was always bitter. . . . The Sikhs' own quarrels were often family ones, for it seemed many were related.'

Fantasy

Rowing-Boat English Rose III. *North Atlantic. July*
Fifth and sixth weeks. John Ridgway: 'The hunger pains got worse and we tried a kind of self-hypnosis to retard our mental state. We thought that if we tried to think of nothing, the senses would be numbed of the pains. . . . I began to dream even when I was awake. My mind produced the most superb fantasies. I would relive episodes from my schooldays. . . .'

Fear

Liferaft from Transport Ship Skaubryn. *Indian Ocean. March*
Eighteenth day. Ensio Tiira: 'I had a terror of getting water in my
ears. . . . I felt the fear before the storm caught me. When Ericsson
was alive it was bad enough; now I was terrified.'

Sailing Yacht Cardinal Vertue. *North Atlantic*
Writing after the transatlantic single-handed sailing race, 1960,
Dr David Lewis stated that there were two types of fear; an initial
tension and anxiety, lasting the first few days at sea, then replaced
by calm confidence and enjoyment; and when there was good reason
to be afraid, as in gales.

Sailing Yacht Gipsy Moth IV. *Tasman Sea. January*
Second day after leaving Sydney. Sir Francis Chichester: 'The boat
had heeled over to at least 41° below the horizontal before it righted
itself. It must have been a fantastic wave. I was frightened. I
thought, that if this can happen in an ordinary storm, what would
it be like if I ran into a real hurricane. . . . The capsize left me in low
spirits.'

Rescue Ship. North Atlantic
Dr MacBain reported on rescued survivors in the second World
War: 'Survivors for a varying period after being picked up are very
"lifeboat" and "raft" conscious. As I know from personal experience
and discussion with others, the alarm bell automatically brought
visions of impending disaster, and caused one to rehearse mentally
the action of abandoning ship. Therefore, to remain below was
difficult.'

Frustration

Inflatable Boat L'Hérétique. *North Atlantic. December*
Forty-seventh day. Dr Bombard: 'Am completely baffled, have no
idea where I am. If the dinghy is thrown up with me as a corpse, I
have only one request, and that is that someone goes and boxes the
ears of the author of this Castaways' Handbook. It only serves to
demoralize anyone who has been unfortunate enough to buy it. It
states in black and white, "A considerable number of frigate birds
means that the land is about a hundred miles away". I have seen
quite a number during the last week and have covered about three
hundred miles. The same applies to those who make assertions about
the trade wind. It is perfectly clear that they have never had to make
the journey themselves, or else they were in a ship with an engine. In
the area of the West Indies, in November and December, there are
two days of wind for every ten days of flat calm.'

Sailing Yacht Suhaili. *Southern Ocean. October–November*
Robin Knox-Johnston found the winds quite different from the favourable (westerly) winds he expected. On the 109th day after leaving Falmouth he wrote: 'I had a terrible job getting to sleep last night; I was feeling frustrated by our slow progress and this sort of thing causes me to tense up. I usually notice it in my legs; they feel as though they want exercise. . . .' 200th day: 'I feel very depressed at the moment and thoroughly frustrated. . . . The wind is still slightly south of east. . . . I'm not the sort of person that takes adverse conditions calmly and my mood at present is murderous. . . . Why the hell don't they mark this stretch of ocean as having variable winds instead of westerlies.'

Grumbling

Liferaft from SS Lulworth Hill. *Doldrums (Atlantic). March*
Fifth day. Kenneth Cooke: 'Some of the blokes, the Gunners particularly, were losing all hopes of ever being picked up. They were not to blame. They were not, and never likely to be, seamen— the continued moaning was having a bad effect on the youngsters. Five of our lads were around eighteen years of age—after a while they, too, began joining in the dismal chorus.'

Lifeboat from SS Trevessa. *Indian Ocean. June*
Twentieth day. Captain Foster: 'The reduction of the milk ration produced a growl from Gomez who . . . did not at first understand the reason for it, but he was quite satisfied when matters were explained to him.'

Lifeboat from SS Holmpark. *North Atlantic. October*
A sixteen days' ordeal. Captain A. Cromarty: 'All my crew (49) behaved extremely well throughout, with the exception of a Gunner. This man was shipped on board at Suez, and whilst in the ship was a nuisance to everybody. Several times I told him to "shut up" and on one occasion it became necessary to threaten him with an axe.'

Hallucination

Liferaft. North Atlantic
Second day: 'Already the minds of some of them began to be affected, and they saw visions of land or of rescuing ships which existed only in their imagination.' Third day: 'The survivors suffered from the most cruel delusions. Some thought that they were back on the frigate or in their homes; some stretched out their hands towards green fields and shady plantations; some saw sumptuous repasts spread before them; some hailed imaginary ships, or cried

out that they were close to a magnificent harbour and that the shore was beckoning.'

Liferaft from SS Britannia. *Doldrums (Atlantic). March*
Lieutenant A. H. Rowlandson RN reported, third day: 'Marx showed signs of exhaustion and it soon became clear that his mind was wandering. His mind seemed very clear but he was able to picture a scene of his own fishing village and carried on conversations with imaginary boatmen round him. He was very anxious to swim ashore which he said he had often done from there before and I had to use force to restrain him on several occasions. He became worse throughout the day and had to be pulled back on the raft several times.' Fourth day: 'My own mind was full of queer ideas, and I thought I could see two fellucas and signalled with our lamp on several occasions. We also imagined that an aircraft passed overhead, but could see nothing.'

Sailing Yacht Cardinal Vertue. *North Atlantic*
Dr David Lewis, reporting on his outward solo crossing in 1960 wrote, 'When I was very tired, and had spent monotonous hours at the helm in winds too light for the vane, I sometimes heard voices. . . . Hallucinations seemed to occur only when solitude and fatigue are accompanied by monotonous occupations. . . . I would think that varying tasks demanding physical and/or mental effort would be valuable in preserving emotional stability.'

Collapsible Canoe Liberia III. *North Atlantic. December*
Dr Lindemann reported that at the time of the eclipse in 1956 he came into a terrible storm in which aural hallucinations induced him to sleep. The spray cover said to him, 'Now lie down, we will keep watch in the meantime.' The feeling that he was not alone in the canoe was strong in the hallucinations whether he was asleep or awake. Auditory hallucinations were more frequent than visual ones. On the fifty-sixth day when the wind was force 8 with squalls force 9, the steamer *Eagledale* came up behind him unnoticed; it poured oil round the canoe to smooth the sea. He saw a man climb down from the bridge, put a megaphone to his mouth and say in German, 'My dear Lindemann, don't be such a fool . . .' but he could not hear the rest of the sentence because of the roaring of the sea. He immediately ascribed the voice to a Hamburg shipping expert who did not like small craft taking to the high seas. The voice was a genuine auditory hallucination. In the following weeks he had many visual and audible hallucinations. They began with the idea that the canoe was going eastward although the compass

pointed plainly to the west. However much he tried, pinched himself, put his hand in the water and followed the course of the waves, he never got out of this state by his own strength. He only saw clearly again when a large breaker broke over the deck and carried the canoe with it. The visible evidence of his error alone gave him no further help. The black boom seemed to be an African with whom an imaginary conversation began, 'Boy, where are we going?' 'To my Boss.' 'Where does your Boss live?' 'In the West.' On the word 'west' he immediately woke up. The word 'west' kept coming into his conscious mind and but for this word he considered that he would not have completed the voyage. Dr Lindemann reported, following his transatlantic voyages, 'I generally passed from the state of illusion into a sleep of exhaustion lasting for only a minute or two, or else I fell into a state of hallucination.' He also recorded: 'The first night many shipwrecked persons suffer from hallucinations, especially if they were very tired before the catastrophe.'

Sailing Yacht Spray. *North Atlantic. July*
Joshua Slocum, after living luxuriously at the Azores, wrote, 'Plums seemed the most plentiful on the *Spray* and these I ate without stint. I also had a Pico white cheese and of this I partook with the plums. Alas! by night time I was doubled up with cramps. . . . Then I went below, and threw myself on the cabin floor in great pain. How long I lay there I could not tell, for I became delirious. When I came to, as I thought, from my swoon, I realized that the sloop was plunging into a heavy sea, and looking out of the companionway, to my amazement I saw a tall man at the helm. One may imagine my astonishment. His rig was that of a foreign sailor. . . .' A conversation took place and Captain Slocum learnt that the man was one of Columbus's crew. 'I am the pilot of the *Pinta* came to aid you. Lie quiet, Senor Captain, you have a calentura, but you will be all right tomorrow.' The pilot appeared to Captain Slocum again, in a dream on the following night.

Hearing

Inflatable Raft. North Atlantic. June
Second day. Joan de Kat: 'The biggest waves made a noise exactly like an aircraft when they approached from the distance. Except that they did not continue. The breakers faded away and the noise stopped.' Third day: 'I went out to wait for the sound of aircraft but the waves kept up their noise—perhaps it became even louder—and it was almost impossible to tell the difference between them and the aircraft.'

Lifeboat from SS Trevessa. *Indian Ocean. June*
First Officer Smith: 'Noticed curious thing which had not struck me before. In a small boat the wind, however strong, can be felt but there is no noise except the creaking of the boat and breaking seas.'

Sailing Yacht Cardinal Vertue. *North Atlantic. July*
Forty-fourth day. Dr David Lewis: 'A deep throbbing sound became audible far off in the mist. I stood stock still, my scalp prickling with fear of the unknown. The noise was rapidly becoming louder and nearer. I ran back to the cockpit and sat clutching the useless tiller so tightly that my knuckles showed white, while my eyes strained fearfully into the mist. I was still sitting there when the rumble became an ear-splitting roar and a deluge of blinding rain thundered out of the sky. I made for the cabin, gasping, drenched and unable to breathe freely, thoroughly ashamed of my fear.'

Sailing Yacht Lively Lady. *Southern Ocean. October–November*
Sir Alec Rose: 'The cold chills you to the bone. The surface of the sea is grey. There is a deadness that no words can describe. But it is the shriek of the wind that depresses you most: a vicious whine that never completely disappears even on the very occasional calm day.'

Homicide

Raft from the Frigate Medusa. *North Atlantic. July*
Second day. J. B. Savigny: 'He who was armed with an axe, with which he even threatened an officer, was the first victim, and a blow with a sabre put an end to his existence. . . . Animated by despair, one of the mutineers lifted his sabre against an officer, but immediately fell, pierced with wounds.'

Ship's Boat from HMS Bounty. *South Pacific. May*
Thirty-second day. Following a serious quarrel with his men, Captain Bligh kept his cutlass immediately available. He logged: 'The Almighty has seemed pleased to give me sufficient strength to make use of it.'

Passenger Liner Titanic. *North Atlantic. April*
It is reported of the loss of the *Titanic*: 'Another wave of men rushed the boat. Seaman Scarrott beat them back with the tiller. This time Lowe pulled his gun and shouted, "If any one else tries that, this is what he'll get!" He fired three times along the side of the ship as the boat dropped down to the sea.'

Hope

Liferaft from SS Lulworth Hill. *Doldrums (Atlantic). April*
Fifteenth day. Kenneth Cooke: 'The hope and the constant lookout
for the chance to stab a fish kept me going and by the mere act of
giving one something to do and something to think about, did a lot
to keep hope and life in my body.'

Liferaft from Transport Ship Skaubryn. *Indian Ocean. March*
Twenty-third day. Ensio Tiira: 'Despite my resignation about the
future, hope never abandoned me for long.' Thirty-second day:
'Life returned when despair changed into hope and I came slowly
out of the gloom into reality. The change was spiritual, but my body
responded. My nerves produced a final effort, my muscles worked
and my mind co-ordinated. . . . Now I wanted to live. Everything
had changed now.'

Ship's Boat from HMS Bounty. *South Pacific. June*
Forty-fourth day. Captain Bligh: 'The hopes of being able to
accomplish the voyage, was our principal support.'

Humility

Rowing-Boat English Rose III. *North Atlantic. July*
Fifty-fifth day. John Ridgway: 'Tonight we lie and wait—nothing
could save us if we got into difficulties. No ship could get us off the
seas, even if it arrived in time. We are completely in God's hands, at
the mercy of the weather . . . and slowly we were overtaken by an
enormous feeling of humility and a desire to return and lead a better
life.' Chay Blyth: 'I noted a similar conclusion in my own log. . . .
A lot of humble pie can easily be eaten in a situation like this. . . .'

Sailing Boat Pagan. *Pacific Ocean. October*
John Caldwell, sailing single-handed from Panama to Australia in
the cutter *Pagan*, after running into serious trouble, being dismasted
and profaning the Almighty, wrote, 105th day: 'And now, lost,
foodless, without instruments, I humbly bent my knees to the deck
and laid my folded hands upon the cabin. With eyes raised I read
off a most heartfelt plea for forgiveness and piteous appeal to *Pagan*'s
real Captain.'

Hysteria

Bombed Troopship SS Lancastria. *English Channel. June*
'About three hundred troops packed the alleyway. They were cool
and unruffled. . . . Marshalled by an officer, the men filed quietly up
a companionway and on to the deck. . . . Soon the corridor was
almost clear. One soldier had become hysterical and been bundled

179

into a cabin to stop the mental infection spreading and developing into some disastrous stampede. But the youth soon recovered, and was helped by understanding companions on to the deck.'

Warship. Wartime
The ship was badly damaged and there was much smoke. Commander Peter Gretton: 'One man got very excited and was running around screaming, but luckily a flooding wheel spanner was handy and he was soon quiet. Otherwise the behaviour of the whole ship's company was admirable.'

Lifeboat from Trawler Noreen Mary. North Atlantic. July
Mr James Macalister, deckhand: 'I was able to pull the Second Engineer over to the damaged lifeboat and lay him over the top. He was very badly injured [by gunfire from a U-boat] and became hysterical: he shook hands with me and said he was going to jump overboard, so the only thing I could do to prevent him doing so was to hit him on the jaw to make him unconscious. After about ten minutes he recovered, and was much quieter. . . . I learned later that the Second Engineer had forty-eight shrapnel wounds and a piece of steel wire two and a half inches long embedded in his body.'

Liferaft from SS Lulworth Hill. Doldrums (Atlantic). April
Nineteenth day. Kenneth Cooke: 'Stewart became hysterical at the Mate's death. A hard slap on the face broke the hysteria.'

Illusion
Liferaft from Transport Ship Skaubryn. Indian Ocean. February
Third day. Ensio Tiira: 'I swallowed as if I were eating food and it was dry and hopeless, but somehow worthwhile. Again and again I swallowed and had the illusion I was eating.'

Liferaft from SS Lulworth Hill. Doldrums (Atlantic). April
Fourteenth day. Kenneth Cooke: 'Many and many a time, a delicious poached egg, or perhaps a plateful of homely fish and chips appeared before the eyes of one of us, only to become a cigarette tin when an eager hand stretched for it.'

Collapsible Canoe Liberia III. North Atlantic
Dr Lindemann: 'In the last three weeks the hallucinations occurred less often, while the illlusions and the Nirvana feeling (weightless, happy and content) came more frequently.'

Irritability

Rowing-Boat English Rose III. *North Atlantic. June*
Twenty-second day. Chay Blyth: 'Little things I found were the irritating ones, and I knew that I must keep strict control over my feelings of annoyance if I was to keep a stable approach to our row.'

Lifeboat from SS Laconia. *Doldrums (Atlantic). September–October*
Nursing Sister Doris M. Hawkins: 'It must not be imagined there was no trouble at all. In circumstances such as these, small things seemed important, and disputes arose over trifling incidents, and quite alarming things were sometimes said; no one who has not sat cramped in a small boat, with the sun beating mercilessly day after day, and tormented by thirst, can ever imagine the strain and tension through which these men went.'

Ship's Boat from HMS Endurance. *Scotia Sea. April–May*
Commander Worsley wrote of Shackleton's voyage from Elephant Island to South Georgia: 'As a rule, when a sea wets a sailor through, he swears at it, and comprehensively and impartially curses everything in sight, beginning with the ship and the "Old Man"— if he's not within hearing; but on this passage we said nothing when a sea hit us in the face. It was grin and bear it; for it was Sir Ernest's theory that by keeping our tempers and general cheeriness we each helped to keep one another up. We lived up to this to the best of our ability, but Macarty was a marvel.'

Lethargy

Lifeboat from SS Gairsoppa. *North Atlantic. February*
Second day. Second Officer R. H. Ayres: 'While working aboard the *Gairsoppa* they [the Lascars] were as active as monkeys. Now many of them were lethargic. The sinking of the ship seemed to have weighed them down with a sense of impending doom.'

Rowing-Boat English Rose III. *North Atlantic. July*
Forty-sixth day. John Ridgway: 'Our lack of nutriment was dulling us. Our eyes and our ears and our minds were being dulled by the poorness of our food and the lack of fresh vitamins. . . . Our minds may have been getting a little blank and lethargic.'

Sailing Dinghies
'Lethargy induced by heat and humidity. . . . Reactions were inevitably slowed down [at the pre-1968 Olympic regatta] and there was an inability to think clearly. . . . The leaders in the Flying Dutchman and Finn classes set off for the wrong mark. . . . A

competitor sailed slowly up to a mark, hit it, stared at it in bewilderment and then dived overboard for a swim.'

Lightheadedness

Lifeboats from MV Waiwera. *North Atlantic. June*
Captain C. M. Andrews: 'I noticed that after the third day a number of the men became lightheaded, one old sailor completely losing his head when the boat was swamped and we had to knock him out to avert serious trouble. The Chief Officer also remarked that a number of men in his boat became lightheaded and talked nonsense, but they gradually became normal after being rescued. This fact was more evident to us both than any of the other troubles and worries.'

Liferafts from SS Llanashe. *Indian Ocean. February*
A thirteen-day ordeal. Fourteen men died, two survived, the Chief Officer, Mr S. P. Lloyd, reported. 'The men appeared to think that there was no hope from the beginning and with the terrific heat during the day, intense cold at night, and very meagre rations, they soon became lightheaded. . . . To my certain knowledge twelve men actually died whilst on the rafts. . . . Without exception they were all affected mentally, but were apparently quite happy.'

Ship's Boats from HMS Endurance. *Weddell Sea. April*
Reporting on Shackleton's crew, escaping in three boats from an ice floe to Elephant Island, F. A. Worsley wrote: 'Some of our men were almost light-headed. When they landed they reeled about, laughing uproariously. Others sat on the shingle and "like harmless lunatics" let it run through their hands to reassure themselves that they really were on dry land at last.'

Loneliness

Liferaft from Transport Ship Skaubryn. *Indian Ocean. March*
Fifteenth day. Ensio Tiira: 'With Ericsson unconscious the loneliness was almost unbearable.'

Sailing Yacht Cardinal Vertue. *North Atlantic. June–October*
Writing of the 1960 single-handed race across the Atlantic and his return voyage to the UK Dr Lewis recorded: 'We [the transatlantic sailors] were rarely lonely in our voyage. Even during the long awe-inspiring night, illuminated by the Northern lights of the homeward voyage, I did not feel lonely.' Reporting the single-handed race of 1964, Dr Lewis wrote: 'As always, after I flipped off the [radio] switches, I seemed more than ever alone. I found it upset my peace of mind to talk to someone each day. This was the third passage alone over the Atlantic, but my first in company with a radio trans-

mitter, and it was the only one in which I never achieved a sense of well-being and sufficiency. I think the regular unsettling contact with the world ashore was to blame.'

Sailing Yacht Lively Lady. *Southern Ocean. October*
Sir Alec Rose: 'Before sailing into this sea I had often felt aloneness, but I had never felt really lonely. Now loneliness struck me for the first time in my life. It was worst at night. I would lay in my bunk listening to the sea drumming against the top sides, then I would go on deck into blackness even deeper than off the Newfoundland Banks. I felt, then, as well I knew, that the nearest human beings were several thousands of miles away.'

Sailing Yacht Gipsy Moth IV. *Southern Ocean. November*
Seventy-first day after leaving Plymouth. Sir Francis Chichester: 'I felt weak, thin and somehow wasted, and I had a sense of immense space empty of any spiritual—what? I didn't know. I only knew that it made for intense loneliness, and a feeling of hopelessness, as if faced with imminent doom. On November fifth I held a serious conference with myself.'

Melancholy

Whaleboats from Whaleship Essex. *South Pacific. November*
Three whaleboats were prepared for a long ocean voyage following the wreck of the whaleship *Essex*. Second day. Owen Chase, First Mate: 'Many little things preparatory to taking a final leave of the ship were necessary to be attended to, but evening came and put an end to our labours. . . . As the gloom of night approached and obliged us to desist from that employment, which, by occupying us, cheated us out of some of the realities of our situation, we all of us again became mute and desponding. The preceding day a considerable degree of alacrity had been manifested by many as their attention had been wholly engaged in scrutinizing the wreck and in constructing the sails and spars for the boats. But when they ceased to be occupied, they passed to a sudden fit of melancholy, and the miseries of their situation came upon them with such force as to produce spells of extreme debility, approaching almost to fainting.'

Monotony

Rowing-Boat English Rose III. *North Atlantic. July*
Forty-sixth day. John Ridgway: 'We were slowly becoming robots tied to a computer programme which said "Two hours labour, two hours sleep, two hours labour, two hours sleep." Our minds may have been getting a little blank and lethargic.'

N

Damaged Invasion Barge. North Atlantic. November
SS *Barberrys* was sunk by one torpedo. A damaged invasion barge
floated off and a man boarded it. Third Officer Mr A. S. Robertson:
'The man we saw on the after section of the invasion barge was Able
Seaman Henry E. Heinson. He existed on one 5-lb. cabbage and
two gallons of distilled water for eighteen days before he was rescued.'
He eked out his distilled water with snow, hailstones and rain
collected by means of a canvas door. He overcame monotony by
propping up in front of him a photograph of his wife and talking to it.

Steam Barque Jeannette. *Arctic. December*
The ship was frozen in the ice. 'The monotony of continually
expecting trouble with none of the excitement of actually seeing
things happening, had its own peculiar affect on us, making sound
sleep impossible, killing our appetites, and leaving us restless, listless
and haggard.'

Morale

Liferaft from SS Lulworth Hill. *Doldrums (Atlantic). March–April*
Tenth day. Kenneth Cooke: 'Gone was their pretence of being
cheerful.' Fourteenth day: 'Morale was low after the Mate's out-
burst [attempted suicide].' Fifteenth day: 'Most of the hands were
extremely despondent and confidence was shrinking all round.'
Twenty-first day. 'All night I was obsessed with visions of the dead
Mate. The shock of his burial had left its mark on us all. We were
suffering bodily, mentally and spiritually.' Forty-ninth day. 'We
were liable and indeed likely to snap at any second just then and our
minds were incapable of clear and lucid thinking.'

Lifeboat from SS Trevessa. *Indian Ocean. June*
Twelfth day. Captain Foster: 'The effect produced by drinking
rainwater was very satisfactory and reviving, and it is almost
impossible to describe how much more cheerful it made everyone. It
would also be very hard to describe the eagerness with which the
crew looked on while an observation was being taken at noon, the
sextant put away in the box, and the few figures scribbled on a piece
of paper which would give us the latitude for that day; or the smile
which would greet the news that we were getting along alright. The
mere sight of the instrument seemed to give them added confidence,
and each day, after I had worked the latitude, I would smile as
though I was completely satisfied with the result, and nod to those
around. This would have the desired effect on the crew who were so
eagerly watching.' Nineteenth day: 'Rain easing off. All hands last
night and this morning got their fill of rain water and managed to

save some. Feel fit to carry on for a good while now. . . . Although after the rain there was a good deal of discomfort, due to the extra soaking we had got, no one minded it at all, for the effect of drinking the water we were all able to catch put renewed life and energy into everybody. It would produce a striking contrast to the quiet grimness of perhaps only a few hours earlier, when we had been waiting and hoping that something of the sort would come along.'

Lifeboat from SS Britannia. *Doldrums (Atlantic). April*
Twelfth day. Frank West: 'I found the hours of silent prayer and the complete solitude into which I was able to cast myself on these occasions, a source of strength, giving me renewed hope.'

Warship under Enemy Attack
Commander Peter Gretton wrote of the Battle of Narvik: 'How I blessed that morphia. The screams and moans of the wounded are ghastly to hear, and quickly destroy the best morale, but fortunately the drug had an immediate effect.'

Sailing Boat Kakugan. *Celebes and Arafura Seas. October–December*
A forty-seven days' voyage in wartime through enemy-occupied waters. Albert Klestadt: 'To boost morale we talked of what we should do when we reached Australia, as if that were a certainty.'

Collapsible Canoe Liberia III. *North Atlantic. October–December*
Dr Lindemann: 'When I sailed across the Atlantic in my standard collapsible canoe in seventy-two days, the main problem as far as I, personally, was concerned was that of morale and the capacity to keep my spirits up.'

War Casualty
'I was shipwrecked five times during the War. After being rescued on the third occasion I knew I was safe for the duration. . . . I have happy memories of my service afloat during the War.'

Mutiny

Sailing Boat Kakugan. *Arafura Sea. November*
Twelfth day. The crew considered that the leader had endangered their lives. Albert Klestadt: 'It had been decided that I was to be decapitated and the hour of execution was set for after sunset on that day. They drew lots who was to do it.'

Ship's Boat from HMS Bounty. *South Pacific. June*
Thirty-fourth day. Captain Bligh: 'Some of the people expressed their discontent at having worked harder than their companions, and declared that they would rather be without their dinner than go in

search of it. One person, in particular, went so far as to tell me, with a mutinous look, that he was as good a man as myself. It was not possible for me to judge where this might have an end, if not stopped in time; therefore to prevent such disputes in future, I determined either to preserve my command, or die in the attempt: and seizing a cutlass I ordered him to take hold of another and defend himself; on which he called out that I was going to kill him, and immediately made concessions. I did not allow this to interfere further with the harmony of the boat's crew, and everything soon became quiet.'

Other Presence

Liferaft from Transport Ship Skaubryn. *Indian Ocean. March*
Thirty-first day. Ensio Tiira: 'I'd lost all sense of a second person being on the raft. The guardian angel who had kept me company after Ericsson's death [on the seventeenth day] left the raft with my loss of hope.'

Balsa Raft Seven Little Sisters. *South Pacific. August*
Forty-sixth day. William Willis recorded that, during periods of weariness, 'Into my subconsciousness came the impression that somebody was busy on deck, handling the raft. I often had this impression. At times it seemed like Teddy [his wife] or someone from the distant past—my mother or sister. As I began to regain my senses, this impression became more definite and I felt relieved of all responsibility. Then I awoke fully.'

Panic

Troopship SS Yoma. *Mediterranean. June*
The ship was torpedoed. Mr A. Olding, Chief Officer: 'The native crew lowered and filled the two poop boats without orders, and altogether six boats were lowered, but two were capsized by the soldiers over-crowding them. I instructed one soldier to help me lower my lifeboat, and carefully showed him how to do it. Suddenly he let go the after fall, and the boat went down with a run and capsized. I learned later that the same sort of thing had happened to the Third Officer's boat. Lifeboat drill was practised everyday, everybody should have known what to do and all the troops and crew should have gone to their correct lifeboat stations within three to four minutes; there was no excuse for the panic which ensued.'

Merchant Ship SS Manaar. *Indian Ocean. April*
The ship was torpedoed. Captain R. Mallett: 'There was a very loud explosion. . . . The native crew in a sudden panic, rushed to

the boat deck and lowered Numbers 3 and 4 'midships boats; as the vessel was still steaming at full speed, they were both carried away and were lost. . . . All my crew behaved excellently throughout; and the natives, after their first fright, quickly calmed down and behaved very well for the rest of the time.'

Lifeboat from MV Kars. *North Atlantic. February*
A tanker carrying aviation spirit and oil fuel was torpedoed. Flames spread for about fifty feet around the ship. The Carpenter, Mr T. Black: 'Just as the boat got into the water the flames swept round the stern of the ship and caused the men in the boat to panic. In the scramble to get away from the flames the boat was capsized and all the occupants thrown into the water.'

Convoy Rescue Ship. Greenland Sea. July
'Each survivor was issued with a full set of clothing, given a tot of rum, food and cigarettes, and allocated a bunk. But it proved very difficult to keep men from staying on deck . . . and at every alarm there was a mad stampeding on to the upper deck.'

Sinking Warship HMS Warrior. *North Sea. June*
HMS *Warrior*, badly damaged and slowly sinking, was being towed by HMS *Engadine*. Flight Lieutenant Graham Donald in HMS *Engadine*: 'Just as we were about ready for "boarders" the *Warrior* gave a nasty little shudder which meant the end was near and for a brief moment there was almost a flicker of panic on some of the faces of the lads waiting to leap over to us—and the *Warrior*'s bugler sounded the "STILL". Every man-jack sprang to attention and stood stock-still. At that moment I knew exactly what Rudyard Kipling meant when he wrote: "To stand and be still, To the *Birkenhead* drill." If fully 600 lads had begun to scramble en masse over our port side they would almost certainly have capsized our extremely top-heavy and very small Carrier (which was only a converted cross-Channel steamer). As things were, however, we had no difficulty in helping aboard the entire 600-odd in three orderly queues and in shepherding 50% of them over to our starboard side to keep the ship trimmed.'

Passivity
Lifeboat from SS Britannia. *Doldrums (Atlantic). April*
Eighth day. Frank West: 'We began to feel how easy it would be to stop making the effort to live.'

Inflatable Boat L'Hérétique. *North Atlantic. November*
Twentieth day. Dr Bombard: 'Am always in a hurry for night to

fall, first of all because it means another day gone, secondly, because I can go to sleep trusting in Providence, and, finally, because I can see nothing to upset me. . . . This sort of passivity is typical of anyone who has been alone for a long time. He finishes by no longer dominating his surroundings, but bowing his head to whatever comes next.'

Persecution

Inflatable Boat L'Hérétique. *North Atlantic. November–December*
Twenty-fifth day. Dr Bombard: 'I began to believe in a confused sort of way, in the active hostility of inanimate objects. I would sit down with a pencil ready at hand, I only needed to turn round for ten seconds, and it found some means of disappearing. It was like a mild form of persecution mania, although, up till then, I had always been able to meet such annoyances with good humour.' Forty-seventh day: 'Everything seems to conspire against me. Since this morning I have literally been stewing in my own juice under a terrible sun. No shade, yet barely half a mile away the sky is covered with thick clouds. It is frightening to realize to what extent one can develop a persecution mania alone on the surface of the sea; it really seems as if one is the victim of a conspiracy which one will never defeat.'

Lifeboat from SS Britannia. *Doldrums (Atlantic). April*
Ninth day. Frank West: 'Emanuel [a Christian missionary who knew the Sikh language] gradually became completely obsessed with the belief that the Sikhs were going to kill him and said he often overheard them planning to do this.'

Prayer

Sailing Boat. Sulu Sea
Albert Klestadt, at the start of a single-handed voyage in enemy-occupied waters: 'Prayed in the morning and sailed out with the ebbing tide. Am alone now and in His hands, but cannot be better cared for!' When in the Arafura Sea on another voyage he was threatened with mutiny by some of his crew: 'I often prayed for Grace, for guidance and for my sense of humour not to desert me. Invariably my prayers were answered.'

Liferaft. North Pacific
Third day. An aircraft flew over. Ito Harcco: 'I started to pray. I called all the Japanese Gods. I called them by their names. I asked them to guide the plane to us.'

Inflatable Liferaft. Bay of Bengal
Seventh day. Following the suicide of the First Lieutenant, Lieutenant Ba Thaw reported: 'We all prayed for the Lieutenant. He was a Buddhist. Somebody chanted a piece of Buddhist scripture. After that we had prayers every day between 5 p.m. and 6 p.m.'

Liferaft from SS Lulworth Hill. *Doldrums (Atlantic). March*
Seventh day. Kenneth Cooke: 'One of us heard Little John praying. He humbly asked the apprentice to pray for us all. . . . All joined in the request and the day was finished with a heartfelt prayer from all aboard the two rafts. I realize now that it was a thing we had all wanted and each had been too shy to suggest—it was a good thing and every mind was easier the next morning because of it. I closed my eyes to pray for myself.'

Lifeboat from SS Britannia. *Doldrums (Atlantic). April*
Tenth day. Frank West: '. . . led the Sikhs in their daily devotions. They were carried out at great length, at no set time, but usually in the evening. . . . We certainly needed all the prayers.' Twelfth day: 'Praying seems to come easier when one is in trouble. It had become customary to have evening prayers. . . .'

Rowing-Boat English Rose III. *North Atlantic. June–July*
Eleventh day, during a hurricane, John Ridgway recorded: 'I was frightened all the time and so was Chay. Both of us prayed.' Fifty-sixth day. Chay Blyth: 'Sleep then prayer. God comes to you out there. You have three feet on each side of you then death.'

Liferaft from Transport Ship Skaubryn. *Indian Ocean. March*
Twentieth day. Ensio Tiira: 'I fell asleep praying that we would have another storm, and my prayers were answered.'

Lifeboat from SS Laconia. *Doldrums (Atlantic). September–November*
Twenty-seven days in lifeboat. Nursing Sister Doris M. Hawkins: 'During the time on the lifeboat there was a universal feeling after God, and a sense of dependence upon Him, and one or other of us used to lead "family prayers" at night. For the last ten days or so this was my privilege, and everyone joined in readily.'

Sailing Boat Gilca. *Indian Ocean. June*
Fifty-eighth day. It was decided to cut four feet off the mast to make the boat more manageable. The mast was unstepped, cut and shaped without difficulty, but could not be put back in place. C. O. Jennings: 'Sitting back, gasping and trembling, I thought of the previous eighteen days of starving and looked at my swollen-eyed friend's wasted body, cursed myself for all the fools in the world for

having agreed to unship the mast. . . . For three solid hours we tried to do the impossible. . . . His [Hall's] mouth opened and in a hardly audible voice he whispered "Why not say a prayer, Skipper?" Wondering if I understood right, I looked at him in dumb amazement while he nodded his head slowly to show he understood the peculiarity of his request. . . . I began to pray "Almighty God, help us and give us strength to restep this mast: we've done all we can, and now we ask for Divine assistance, for Jesus Christ's sake, Amen." . . . I looked at the rising sea and silently supplemented my spoken appeal to the Divine Creator for his help. The prayer lasted about half a minute, and with a "Now let's try" to my companion, we picked up the mast as though it weighed ounces instead of pounds and restepped it. Hall's red beard opened in an unbelieving smile, and my grey one followed suit, as we automatically turned to face the wide expanse of ocean to mutter our very grateful thanks.'

Quarrelling

Liferaft from Transport Ship Skaubryn. *Indian Ocean. February*
Two men on the raft. Ensio Tiira reported that there were quarrels on the first and fourth days as to the course which should be taken, and a second quarrel on the fourth day when one wanted to paddle and the other one did not.

Lifeboat from SS Trevessa. *Indian Ocean. June*
Tenth day. Captain Foster: 'When the natives were under cover for the night they were inclined to chatter and squabble with each other the whole night through. This was quite understandable, as owing to their cramped position all huddled together between the thwarts; the least move made by one would cause agony to those around him.'

Rowing-Boat English Rose III. *North Atlantic. July*
During a period of what they termed 'mental plonk' on about the thirty-fifth day, John Ridgway and Chay Blyth had a difference of opinion about fixing the rudder. John Ridgway: 'Chay leapt from his seat. He shouted, "If you can't fix the rudder properly, I'll do the damn thing myself." Those were the first strong words that had passed between us. For several minutes I continued to lay there while I pondered on this rift that had suddenly come between us. The whole thing was my fault and I was desperately sorry. Another few seconds silence. Then both of us spoke together. "I'm sorry John", said Chay. "I'm sorry Chay", said I. Our first and only row was over. I turned over and slept, happier than I had been at any time that day.'

Rowing-Boat Puffin. *North Atlantic. July*

Fiftieth day. David Johnstone: 'My nerves are not very far below the surface at the moment. There was a ridiculous and short shouting match which left me very weak and shaky, and I am sad and depressed more than ever and very unhappy, and I only want to be with my friends and family again, somewhere where the social and physical environment shows a fragment of sympathy and understanding for the normal frailties.' Sixty-third day, David Johnstone and John Hoare failed to attract the attention of a passing ship. 'Depressions set in and in a second we were arguing violently about how far away he had been. Tempers flared, the binoculars flew the length of the boat at speed, a clenched fist glanced off a stubbly cheek, swearing and insults rang across the now empty horizon. We settled down sullenly to sleep and row, immersed in our separate depressions—at the ship and at our angry senseless outbursts. Within the hour apologies were made and life was resumed on board.'

Sailing Boat Gilca. *Indian Ocean. July*

Eighty-fifth day. C. O. Jennings: 'Birds were the cause of the only friction that Hall and I ever had on the boat.' Two birds perched on the boat, Jennings caught his a second or two before Hall was ready, the screams frightened Hall's bird away. 'Hall and I said some unkind things about each other, so unkind that for quite a time afterwards neither of us spoke. . . . There was one skipper on the boat, and that was me. Any more nonsense and I would show him. I had already made the decision when he started ranting again. Without speaking, I put my right hand behind me, my fingers closing over the shaft of the axe, and I pulled, but the blade was wedged downwards between the seat and the planking of the boat. Hall saw what I was trying to do and pounced on top of me, and, with his extra weight, bore me down on the seat, while his fingers tightened steadily around my throat. . . . Panting and gasping, I released my hold on the axe, and just then, as though the storm was giving its last dying kick, *Gilca* shipped a wave, drenching both of us. Hall immediately let go of my throat; we automatically picked up the bailing things, and, in an ashamed silence, we began the work of getting the boat dry. When this was accomplished, we both apologized for our actions and shook hands, sinking our differences whilst eating the smallest bird we had ever caught.'

Religious Faith

Lifeboat from SS Britannia. *Doldrums (Atlantic). March–April*

Sixth day. Frank West: 'It is Sunday and we had a short service at

10.45. I said a prayer and then all sang the first and last verses of "Oh God our help in ages past" and said the Lord's Prayer. Afterwards we settled down to rest as well as we could.' Twelfth day: 'It would have been a great blessing to us had we had a prayer book or a Bible and it is most surprising that no one amongst us had brought one with him.' Fourteenth day: 'Have just had a short service of Remembrance for Harman and Beck [who died the day before] and Thanksgiving for rain.' Twentieth day: 'We had an Easter morning service after breakfast, but it was very short. It is hard to remember things, we sang the first verse of the only Easter hymn we could remember, "Christ the Lord is risen today". The Sikhs also carried out their Devotions. A very nice service conducted by McIntosh brought the Easter Sunday to a close.'

Raft. *Indian Ocean. April–May*
Jack Drinan, the skipper of a trawler wrecked off the west coast of Australia, who lived in an ice-box as a raft for sixteen days, licking water from the ice-box lid, with only twenty oranges and nine eggs as food, said: 'My faith in her [Our Lady of Fatima], knowing she would look after me, was the only thing that kept me going.'

Sailing Boat Kakugan. *Timor Sea. December*
Albert Klestadt, writing of men swimming in shark-infested water: 'I asked Sahibad whether he was not afraid of the sharks. . . . He pointed to the amulet around his forehead; it contained a powerful Moslem charm against sharks, in which he had complete trust.'

Sailing Yacht Pagan. *South Pacific. October*
John Caldwell, former atheist, dismasted, lost, beset with hunger, wrote, 119th day: 'Each day I read the Bible more assiduously; found more and more solace in prayer and gave more time to it. I learned the 23rd Psalm by heart and spoke it every rising and sleeping, and often in the night, as I heaved at the pump. As well, I learned the Ten Commandments and many other Scriptures. My Bible—a gift of my Grandpa when I was a boy—I had never read a chapter of. Aboard *Pagan* I read it cover to cover twice, devouring its words, searching out its comforts. I should have gone insane had I not had the comforting solace of my Baptist teaching. Men who sail small boats know the verity of the Good Captain who piloted my boat.'

Security
Rowing-Boat English Rose III. *North Atlantic. July*
Twenty-eighth day. John Ridgway: 'I took over the oars and Chay went under cover. It was the first time either of us felt the "ostrich

effect". When our heads were under the canopy we somehow felt safe, no matter what kind of hell was breaking loose two feet away.'

Collapsible Canoe Liberia III. *North Atlantic. October–December*
Dr Lindemann: 'I never suffered anxiety . . . in fact I felt very secure under my spray shelter. I think that a feeling of security . . . is quite significant because even the most courageous person needs this security which is, of course, only relative.'

Balsa Raft Kon-Tiki. *South Pacific. April–August*
Thor Heyerdahl wrote that after leaving the *Kon-Tiki* in the rubber boat: 'We rowed back and crept on board and felt that we had come home again to our own world, on board and yet on firm safe ground. . . . It was most remarkable what a psychological effect the shaky bamboo cabin had on our minds. This primitive lair gave a greater feeling of security than white-painted bulkheads and closed portholes could have given in the same circumstances.'

Selfishness

Whaleboat from Whaleship Essex. *South Pacific. January*
Nineteenth day in boat, after being on a deserted island for eight days preceded by thirty days in boat. Owen Chase: 'I had lain down in the boat without taking the usual precaution of securing the lid of the provision chest, as I was accustomed to do, when one of the men awoke me and informed me that one of his companions had taken some bread from it. . . . I immediately took my pistol in my hand and charged the man, if he had taken bread, to give it up without the least hesitation or I should instantly shoot him! He became at once very much alarmed and, trembling, confessed the fact, pleading the hard necessity that urged him to it. He appeared to be very penitent for his crime and earnestly swore that he would never be guilty of it again. . . . He was permitted to escape with the solemn injunction that a repetition of the same offence would cost him his life.'

Shock

Survivors from SS Melmore Head. *North Atlantic. December*
Captain W. J. Leinster: 'The ship sank within three minutes (the men were picked up over a period of about two hours). The Gunner died shortly after. . . . He had apparently not been injured in any way, but he was not a robust man, I think he lacked the stamina necessary to bring him through this ordeal.'

Lifeboat from SS Ocean Might. *Doldrums (Atlantic). September*
Captain W. J. Park: 'One of the firemen died during the morning of the second day. He had received no injuries, and I think his death

was due to shock, as he collapsed shortly after getting into the life-boat.'

Singing

Lifeboat from SS Starbank. *North Atlantic. May*
Eighth day. Captain G. A. Niddrie: 'In the evening we had a concert. I started off by singing a solo which I don't think was very much appreciated. Anyway, the concert was a great success and the next day the men were quite happy planning another concert for the evening. I found that these concerts helped considerably in keeping up the morale of the men.'

Balsa Raft Seven Little Sisters. *South Pacific. August*
Forty-eighth day. William Willis: 'There was a void, and then one day I started singing and realized that my soul had been hungering for this. What a joy to discover singing again. I knew that I had mastered the last big obstacle on my voyage.'

Rowing-Boat English Rose III. *North Atlantic. August*
Eighty-fourth day. Morale was low and the two rowers were tempted to request rescue by pulling the handle of their SARBE (emergency radio equipment); they decided to continue. John Ridgway: 'We were still wet and cold. But there seemed to be a new sense of purpose. . . . As if Chay sensed this, he burst into song, and this time he outdid everything he had done before. The songs fairly rolled out, Scots ballads, marching songs, even "Strangers in the Night".'

Solitude

Inflatable Boat L'Hérétique. *North Atlantic. October–November*
Ninth day. Dr Bombard: 'I was experiencing the first general effects of solitude and fatigue.' Twelfth day: 'I had begun to understand the difference between solitude and isolation. Moments of isolation in ordinary life can soon be ended. Isolation is merely a matter of isolating oneself, but total solitude is an oppressive thing and wears down its lonely victim. It seemed sometimes as if the immense and absolute solitude of the ocean's expanse was concentrated right on top of me. Solitude was a vast presence which engulfed me. Its spell could not be broken. And if from time to time I talked aloud to hear my own voice, I only felt more alone, a hostage to silence.'

Balsa Raft Seven Little Sisters. *South Pacific. July–August*
Thirty-fifth day. William Willis: 'The solitude continued to affect me. It had a sort of fascination that grew and grew. I began to feel more and more at home in it, and had no desire for a change. I am content with the sea and the sky. It is easy to see how men who have

lived in solitude seek it always and resent any intrusion of human beings. But there are moments of suffering too; a vague uneasiness which comes when one realizes that he lives on the edge of an abyss. Man must talk to someone and hear the sound of human voices.' Forty-eighth day: 'Then one day I started singing . . . singing was a miracle that worked for me at all times. . . . People do fear the solitude.'

Sailing Yacht Spray. *Circumnavigation*
Of an experience in the North Atlantic, in the early part of his single-handed voyage round the world, Joshua Slocum wrote: 'The acute pain of solitude experienced at first never returned. I had penetrated a mystery, and by the way I had sailed through a fog.'

After disposing of a goat at Ascension he wrote: 'I was destined to sail once more into the depths of solitude, but these experiences had no bad effect upon me; on the contrary, a spirit of charity and even benevolence grew stronger in my nature through meditations of these supreme hours on the sea. In the loneliness of the dreary country about Cape Horn I found myself in no mood to make one life less in the world, except in self-defence and, as I sailed, this trait of the hermit character grew till the mention of killing food—animals—was revolting to me.'

Speechlessness

Liferaft from Transport Ship Skaubryn. *Indian Ocean. February–March*
Thirty-first day. Ensio Tiira: 'The black sides of the ship slid along beside me. . . . I screamed a great shout to tell them and no sound came out. Even to me the shout was soundless. . . . My mouth made the right movement but no sound came out. . . . My lips formed the words "I'm not a Russian" and nothing came out.'

Liferaft from SS Lulworth Hill. *Doldrums (Atlantic). April–May*
Nineteenth day. Kenneth Cooke: 'Morning Prayers—fourteen scarecrows with tattered clothing, salt grimed and beards, thin gaunt faces and bodies, swollen tongues and red-rimmed eyes—some too far gone to speak—but joining in silently.' Fiftieth day. A ship appeared. Excitement struck the survivors dumb.

Open Boat. Indian Ocean
Sixteen people (one dead) adrift for thirty-three days, thirty-one days without food and little water. 'Their lips were severely parched and they were speechless from exhaustion and hunger.'

Balsa Raft Seven Little Sisters. *South Pacific. October*
On coming ashore after one hundred and fifteen days on his raft,

William Willis reported: 'I stood speechless, overcome by the unbroken silence.'

Stress

Sailing Yacht Spray. *Circumnavigation*
Joshua Slocum wrote of his experience of a big wave off Patagonia: 'The mountain of water submerged my vessel. . . . It may have been a minute that from my hold on the rigging, I could see no part of the *Spray*'s hull. Perhaps it was even less time than that, but it seemed a long while, for under great excitement one lives fast, and in a few seconds one may think a good deal of one's past life. Not only did the past, with electric speed, flash before me, but I had time while in my hazardous position for resolutions for the future that would take a long time to fulfil.'

Sailing Yacht Moana. *South Pacific. July*
Bernard Gorsky: 'A white wall of sea, immense, rose behind us and broke over us. We were drowned. I hugged the mast. My eyes and throat full of water, my shoulders crushed. Thank Heaven, nobody had been swept overboard. And then an upsurge of new nervous energy took possession of us. A reserve was turned on. The instinct of self-preservation began to act. We were lucidity itself, knowing clearly just what was to be done. In such moments one's understanding is heightened. Thought becomes ultra rapid. All fatigue vanishes.'

Sailing Vessel Fat-el-Rahman. *Red Sea*
Henry de Monfreid: 'The ship was now moving backwards, and we were all in the stern, bending over the sea with boat hooks held ready, to give ourselves the illusion that we could do something if we hit a rock. This mental tension is preferable to the passive anguish of the condemned man awaiting his end.'

Stupor

Ship's Boat from HMS Endurance. *Weddell Sea. April*
Commander F. A. Worsley wrote of the passage from the ice floe to Elephant Island, fourth day: 'I had not slept for eighty hours. . . . In the afternoon I had been steering for nine hours while leading the other boats and found it almost impossible to keep awake. Green-street—a fine seaman—continually urged me to hand over the tiller and have a nap. I had, however, become so obsessed with steering for the Island and maintaining the utmost speed that I kept on when I should have handed over to him. The consequence was that at intervals I fell asleep for a few seconds and the *Docker*, with the *Wills* in tow, sheered off her course. Everyone through fatigue and loss of sleep had slightly lost his judgment.'

Lifeboat from SS Trevessa. *Indian Ocean. June*
Seventh day. Captain Foster: 'Sailing this small boat day after day it was not so much the man who was steering actually went to sleep, as that he was inclined to sink into a semi-comatose state, steering the boat automatically, and at times erratically. That this could happen became apparent quite early in the voyage when we were all comparatively fresh. After the first few days, a sort of coma appears to have settled on to many of the crew and whatever was done was done, more or less, automatically and without thought.'

Suicide

Inflatable Raft. Bay of Bengal
Seventh day. Lieutenant Ba Thaw: 'On the seventh night the First Lieutenant, Saw Oo, died. He had a gastric ulcer and had gradually been getting worse. He was in fearful pain. The skin was stretched tight across his face and chest. He was retching nearly all the time. He had nothing to throw up. He was my old shipmate. We joined the Navy together nine years ago. He whispered to me, "Let me go. Let me go. It's better to go than suffer more." I nodded. He slipped over the side.' Eighth day: 'Two men died on the eighth day. One of them went mad. I think he had been drinking seawater. . . . The other man flopped over the side without making a sound. Before he went he just looked at me. I think he meant to say goodbye.' Ninth day: 'Two more died this day. One of them was lying on his stomach on one of the lifebuoys. His hands and legs were lolling in the water. The lifebuoy was under his middle. Suddenly it drifted clear of the line. Maybe he untied the line. Maybe the lifebuoy just broke free. The last we saw of him was his figure, still spread-eagled face down, on the bobbing lifebuoy. The other man who died went overboard. It was suicide. He could have stood no more.' Tenth and eleventh days: 'Another man died on the tenth day and another on the eleventh. They were both only skin and bone. Incredibly they did not die where they were. They found a sudden strength to go overboard. None of the others seemed to register any emotion. They were beyond that.'

Liferaft from SS Llanashe. *Indian Ocean. February*
Chief Officer Mr S. P. Lloyd: 'The last I clearly remember was on the eleventh day when the Steward went over the side, after which we must have fallen into unconsciousness.'

Lifeboat from SS Laconia. *Doldrums (Atlantic). September*
Nursing Sister Doris M. Hawkins: 'Doctor Purslow developed a deep infection of his left hand and arm and of his right foot and leg.

I used a razor blade to open his finger, and this discharged well, but nothing came from his foot. His glands began to swell and red lines streaked his arm and leg. He felt ill, and we were anxious. His condition did not improve at all, and as he became weaker, he relinquished his self-appointed task of handing out the water ration, and lay day and night, only moving when necessary, and scarcely speaking at all. More septic places appeared, and it became evident that he was suffering from blood poisoning.

'One morning, about nineteen weary days after the ship was torpedoed, I heard voices, and after a while realized that one was his, although I could not hear exactly what was being said. I gathered that, realizing that he was a potential source of infection to the rest of us, Doctor Purslow had come to a great decision.

'I stumbled to where he was sitting, and tried to speak to him; but no words came. He was quite conscious, and in a voice stronger than I had heard from him for many days, he said: "As I cannot be of any further help, and if I am now a source of danger to you all, it is better that I should go." As he heaved himself painfully up the side of the boat, I found my voice, and said: "Greater love hath no man than this, that a man lay down his life for his friends." He said: "Goodbye", and with a long look, he took that final step backward. The sea closed over him.'

Liferaft from SS Lulworth Hill. *Doldrums (Atlantic). April*
Twenty-fourth day. Kenneth Cooke: 'The youngster who had drunk seawater to excess jumped overboard at 11 p.m.'

Taste
Liferaft from Transport Ship Skaubryn. *Indian Ocean. February*
Third day. Ensio Tiira: 'Cigarettes only made us thirstier, their taste was vile. . . .' Fourth day: 'We agree they [the cigarettes] tasted like wood. . . . I'd lost my sense of taste.' Later on he found the taste of an unlit cigarette between his lips agreeable.

Lifeboat from MV Peisander. *North Atlantic. May*
A nine days' ordeal. Captain A. Shaw: 'The pemmican tasted somewhat like Stockholm tar and sawdust.'

Rowing-Boat English Rose III. *North Atlantic. July*
Thirty-ninth day. Chay Blyth: 'Our palate was now quite acute. We were really tasting the difference between foods. I had never liked sardines before. Now we both pronounced them great.'

Unselfishness

Troopship SS Yoma. *Mediterranean. June*
The ship was torpedoed. Chief Officer Mr A. Olding: 'Immediately after the explosion RAMC Staff Sergeant Cook went to the ship's hospital and got out the three patients, who were suffering from malaria, and put them over the ship's side. He then jumped overboard and hung on to all three men until they were finally rescued by a minesweeper about an hour later. They were all wearing lifejackets. He stayed with them and attended to them whilst on board the rescue vessel, and on arrival at Derna he accompanied them to hospital.

'Whilst in the water Fourth Officer Muir observed Senior Medical Officer David Cathie, who was stunned and in a semi-conscious condition. Muir went to his assistance, supported him and towed him for about half an hour toward the minesweeper, which subsequently picked them up.'

Merchant Ship SS Britannia. *North Atlantic. March*
SS *Britannia* was struck by gunfire and had to be abandoned. Frank West: 'A Naval Lieutenant, RNVR, named Strong, who had assisted nobly to control the flow of Indians into our boat, would not join us, saying we were already overloaded. He threw his gun and binoculars into the hands of Wheater, standing amidships in the lifeboat, shouting at the same time that they might be of more use to us than to him. Our last sight of him was as he jumped into the water and swam away towards a raft.'

Vision

Rowing-Boat English Rose III. *North Atlantic. July*
Forty-fourth day. Chay Blyth: 'We were using the stars to steer by too. This is particularly tricky when stars on the horizon are used. They often shrink suddenly when seen by the weary eyes of a tired oarsman.'

Sailing Boat Gilca. *Indian Ocean*
A 127 days' ordeal. C. O. Jennings: 'The only book we had on board was the Bible and it became our practice at 2 o'clock each afternoon to read a chapter from the New Testament. Unfortunately my sight had deteriorated to such an extent that I could not see the print, and the reading therefore devolved totally upon Hall.'

Sailing Yacht Cardinal Vertue. *North Atlantic. June–October*
Dr David Lewis, reporting on his outward solo crossing in 1960: 'For one whole day in fog the sea appeared to slope uphill; during

o

a foggy night I had seemed to be sailing on a height with the lights of two passing steamers on a plain far below.'

Sailing Yacht Gipsy Moth IV. *South Pacific. December*
Sir Francis Chichester reported, 102nd day after leaving Plymouth: 'I was coming up from Gabo Island, off the Australian coast. It was a fine day with a steady breeze and moderate seas. I was repairing the navigation light on the stern which should be nearly five feet above the waterline. Suddenly the light appeared to be about eighteen inches above the sea. I looked aft: the stern also appeared to be nearly under water. She seemed to be sinking, nearly awash.... I ran below to check how deep she was flooded. The bilge was completely dry.'

Sailing Yacht Gipsy Moth IV. *Doldrums (Atlantic). April*
On the eighty-eighth day after leaving Sydney, Sir Francis Chichester wrote: 'Sometimes I saw strange things. Just before crossing the Line the boat appeared to be sailing up a gently sloping sea surface, in other words, uphill. At the time I was a little worried, but when I was two hundred and forty miles north of the Line I noticed the same thing again. This time the sea appeared uphill in every direction, as if I were sailing in a shallow saucer.'

Sailing Yacht Spray. *South Atlantic*
On nearing the Strait of Magellan, Joshua Slocum wrote: 'The phenomenon of mirage frequently occurred. An albatross sitting on the water one day loomed up like a large ship; two fur seals asleep on the surface of the sea appeared like great whales, and a bank of haze I could have sworn was high land. The kaleidoscope then changed, and on the following day I sailed in a world peopled by dwarfs.'

Weeping

Liferaft. Indian Ocean
A six days' ordeal. 'When I was picked up I was in such a weak condition that I cried for an hour.'

Sailing Yacht Felicity Ann. *North Atlantic. January*
Ann Davison: 'I don't know what to do about this nervousness. I feel dizzy most of the time and am completely at the mercy of uncontrollable emotional impulses. The least little thing can delight or distress me beyond measure. Mostly it is distress and I have wept more in these last few days than I have ever done in my whole life and for such trivial reasons as failing to light the stove with one match.'

Sailing Boat Gilca. *Indian Ocean. July*
Seventy-second day. C. O. Jennings: 'That night was one of the most horrible we experienced; one moment we could have cried with joy, and the next we literally cried with grief and despair.' A bird appeared, it was shot with the last round of ammunition, but fell too far from the boat to be grasped. 'We had had food within our grasp and missed it. That night we cried ourselves to sleep. . . . We had no more ammunition.'

Will-Power

Liferaft from SS San Gerardo. *North Atlantic. March*
A forty hours' ordeal. The Bosun, Mr Karl Olin: 'There were seven of us on the raft but the Third Officer died about two hours before we were picked up. He was very despondent and toward the end he lost heart and gave up and died.'

Lifeboat. North Atlantic. November
A twenty-one days' ordeal. Fifteen men died. Third Officer Mr J. A. Scott: 'I think a number of the men became dispirited and despondent and it seemed to me they lost the will to live.'

Lifeboat. Indian Ocean
A twenty-eight days' ordeal. Second Officer, Mr G. Taylor: 'On the nineteenth day Ordinary Seaman —— showed signs of weakening and was losing heart, so I gave him brandy, but he simply did not have the will to live. On the twenty-fourth day, he showed further signs of weakness and despair, refusing to eat anything, so I had to spoon-feed him on brandy and water, with a paste of biscuits and chocolates. The morale of the remainder of the men was quite good, on the whole, but they required an occasional lecture on the subject of not giving up hope. At 1700 on the twenty-seventh day Ordinary Seaman —— died.' The remaining eleven men were rescued on the following day.

Sailing Boat Gilca. *Indian Ocean. June*
About the sixtieth day, C. O. Jennings reported: 'Logic was the standard by which we measured our decreasing reserve of energy; to climb from my bed into the tiller cockpit required a tremendous effort of will-power, but the reverse direction was comparatively easy because the watch was over and I savoured the thought of rolling up into my blanket with the hope of glorious oblivion.'

Withdrawal

Sailing Yacht. Circumnavigation

Bernard Moitessier threw away a certain second place in the 1968–9 *Sunday Times* round-the-world yacht race by beginning a second circumnavigation. On arriving at Tahiti he said: 'Talking of records is stupid, an insult to the sea. The thought of a competition is grotesque. You have to understand that when one is months and months alone, he evolves; some say people go nuts. I went crazy in my own fashion. For four months all I saw were the stars. I didn't hear an unnatural sound. A purity grows out of that kind of solitude. I said to myself: What the hell am I going to do in Europe? I told myself I'd be crazy to go on to France. . . . I feel impeccable.'

Sailing Yacht Moana. *South Pacific*

Bernard Gorsky, sailing with three companions in the forty-foot cutter *Moana*: 'For sailing across oceans the key is reading. You can expect absolutely nothing from your companions—you see them all the time, you see them too much. Meditate? Well, you have the night watches for doing that in. Work? Out of the question, except from sheer necessity or in calm weather.'

ADVICE ON THE PSYCHOLOGY OF SURVIVAL

The Solitary Survivor

The solitary survivor is in the worst position. He is a tiny speck, alone in the immensity of the sea. He will hang on for a time, expecting rescue, but as the days pass he may become despondent and even contemplate suicide; he may become confused and delirious, tempted to consume all his food and water quickly instead of rationing himself. On the other hand, he may have complete faith in other seafarers finding him and, remembering the rules of survival and adhering strictly to them, settle down to await rescue. If he is a religious man he may pray for guidance and deliverance. Prayer relieves stress and liberates energy. There are many instances where survivors have felt an Unseen Presence, helping and comforting them, even telling them what to do. The survivor may have illusions and hallucinations, but his training will put him on guard about swimming to palm trees and such like which he imagines he can see.

The longest period of solitary survival at sea is 131 days,

achieved by the Chinese steward, Poon Lim, who was adrift on a raft with provisions appropriate for 50 days only.

Survivors in a small Group

Survivors in a small group will have many of the reactions of the solitary survivor and some of the reactions of those in a large group. They have a greater chance of survival than the lonely man as they can help one another, and a dominant personality who has resolved to stay alive, come what may, will influence his companions to do the same. Small groups have experienced the phenomenon of the Unseen Presence.

Survivors in a large Group

A large number of survivors congregated together are subjected to group reactions. Good leadership is essential for the maintenance of morale and for remedial action in the event of emotional disturbances occurring.

The good leader will:

face the facts, and explain the situation as fully as possible;

appoint look-outs and assign duties as necessary so that all share the responsibility of keeping in a state of efficiency; determine the rations and time of issue, ensure that all rations are equal, make a ritual of meal-time so as to mark the passage of time in a pleasant way;

keep a brave face, encourage cheerful conversation;

watch for anti-social behaviour, settle disputes;

watch for any attempts to drink seawater and deal firmly with any who are so tempted;

encourage good hygiene;

collect any lethal weapons or anything else which would be injurious to man or dangerous to the raft in a quarrel; secure such items or throw them overboard;

lead the survivors in prayer;

hand over to a worthy successor if necessary.

The problems of leadership are increased where the group consists of men of various nationalities, religions and cultures. The good leader will encourage each to practise his separate faith and he will maintain scrupulous fairness in all respects.

A survivor who is not a leader should remain calm and cheerful and do what he is told.

Never Say Die

Resolve to hang on to life and never give up hope of rescue, the chances of which are far greater than ever before. Many men who have succumbed would have been rescued had they held on for just another day.

6

Search and rescue

Merchant Ship British Monarch. *North Pacific. June*
Douglas Wardrop: 'I climbed on top of the solid bulwark [at the stern, to inspect a faulty log clock]. While leaning outboard the ship lurched slightly and I lost my balance. A desperate grab at the bulwark missed and I fell into the ocean. When I came up gasping to the surface the *Monarch*'s sternlights were disappearing into the darkness [it was 0400, 9 June 1957]. I shouted but no one heard me. . . . Hours passed. . . . I saw two masts on the horizon. With all my strength I started swimming towards them. Then I stopped. Swimming was pointless. I tried to wave my arms, but they weighed a ton each. . . . And then they were lowering a boat. It was the *Monarch*. . . . I was in the water for nine hours. The *Monarch* covered a hundred miles before she found me.'

Merchant Ship. North Atlantic. September
Franz Maria Streycharczyk: 'After over fourteen hours naked in water, signalled ship vigorously with undershorts held in hand, and after being brought alongside, climbed cargo net unassisted but then collapsed on deck.'

Warship. North Sea
Peter Gretton: 'I went over the side with the other three, but I was lucky enough to be washed back through the midships guard-rails by the next wave, being picked up by the captain of the pom-pom who jumped down very quickly. I was shocked and badly bruised but had nothing broken.'

Warship HMS Cheviot. *Indian Ocean*
A seaman, fully dressed and wearing oilskins, shoes and a partially inflated lifejacket, was washed overboard from HMS *Cheviot* during replenishment-at-sea operations. He struck his head in falling. He was in the water for seven to ten minutes, and he was submerged for about half of the time, each swell passing right over him. His attitude in the water was nearly vertical, being slightly tilted on his back. HMS *Chichester* went full astern hard a-starboard. The whaler, which was already swung outboard, starboard side, as a seaboat, was lowered when near the survivor. *Chichester* continued to turn, making a lee. The whaler made two passes before picking up the survivor. There was a sick-berth attendant in the whaler. He draped the

survivor over a thwart and attempted resuscitation without success. The survivor was not deeply unconscious and he was brought aboard *Chichester*. The ship's doctor gave artificial respiration and oxygen for twenty minutes and the survivor recovered. Several stitches were put in his face.

Stranded Trawler Jeanne Gougy. *Land's End, England. November*
'Five hours after trawler *Jeanne Gougy* had been practically submerged, six men were rescued alive from her. At noon, a woman watching from the cliff top saw a man's hand waving inside the wheelhouse, then his voice could be heard calling. Coastguards fired a rocket line over the ship and a man, clinging to the edge of the wheelhouse doorway, which was then facing the sky as the ship lay completely on her side, struggled to grasp it but was deluged in heavy waves. At last he succeeded and a breeches buoy was hauled from the cliff top down to the ship. The man could not use it, but four others on the foc'sle could and they were hauled to safety. Then the helicopter, recalled from Chivenor, hovered over the ship and a crewman, lowered by wire rope, rescued two more seamen. It is now known that the trawler had a crew of eighteen. Twelve are missing, including the skipper, M. Jo Paenner.' [Later] 'The six men rescued had survived by breathing air trapped in pockets in the wheelhouse and forecastle. None of the men was seriously injured. All were taken to hospital at Penzance after first-aid treatment. Four bodies have so far been recovered, leaving eight men missing. Flight Sergeant Eric Smith, who had winched down to the wrecked ship, said: "I found two men in the wheelhouse. Water was up to their chins. They were breathing from pockets of air trapped in the ship. The ship lay completely on her side and had been under water for several hours before I reached her." '

Inflatable Liferaft. North Atlantic. February
Captain of the Rescue Ship (a Destroyer): 'In the bad conditions of the trial it was found best to approach the raft, to recover it, beam on to wind and sea, aiming for a point about 20 yards to windward of the raft and at the lowest speed which would make it possible to stop the ship heading up into the wind. This was found to be about 10 knots. It is important to let the backwash develop on the leeward side before the raft is alongside, it makes a most effective fender. Hence also the rather large aim-off to windward.

'The method to recover men from the raft was remarkably safe and effective. The recovery line was rove through a block at the head of the torpedo davit which was turned about 3 feet outboard. It was led through a leading block on deck and kept in hand by about some twelve seamen. This gave the maximum flexibility in control of the helicopter rescue strop which was at the outboard end of the recovery line. There were sufficient effectives amongst the survivors to see all the others safely into the strop and out of the raft. If this was not the case it would be necessary to order two fit men from the ship into the raft to place the strop over the ineffective bodies.'

Lifeboat from SS Sirius. *North Atlantic. July*
Tenth day. Chief Officer T. A. Buckney: 'We were eventually picked up by the corvette HMS *Jonquil*. She first sighted our red sail and at once altered course towards us. . . . They drew alongside, put nets over the side of the ship and we all (twenty-eight) climbed up on to the deck without help, but on reaching the deck many of us found we could not stand. We all quickly recovered once we had been rescued.'

Survivors in Water from SS Corinaldo. *North Atlantic. October*
The Master, Captain W. Anderson: 'No. 1 boat was capsized by the heavy sea as it came alongside and twenty of the twenty-four occupants were saved. These men were saved by the bravery of some of the crew of HMS *Cowslip*, who were lowered into the oil-covered water with ropes tied round them and hauled the men in the water to safety.'

Survivors in Water from SS Lerwick. *North Sea. January*
Captain J. Robison: 'A trawler and HMS *Winchester* rescued the men from the water and, with the exception of one man who was not wearing a lifejacket, the whole of these men were saved. The Destroyer had rubber floats alongside and put a net over the side so that we could all climb on board very easily. They also used a contrivance like a paravane, consisting of pieces of wood on a rope, which was towed at an angle from the ship's side and swept the men towards the ship. I am of the opinion that the lifejackets, which were fitted with lights, were responsible for so many of the crew being saved; they kept the men well up in the water.'

Liferafts
Captain J. M. Walters USCG: 'USS *Saufley* had arrived at the scene and picked up thirty-seven survivors [from liferafts]. The thirty-eighth was not so fortunate. When the ship was only thirty yards away, he jumped into the water and attempted to swim to the ship. A large mako shark started for him, but sailors along the rail of the ship opened up with rifle fire and the shark turned away. But a

few seconds later it turned quickly, and bit the unfortunate man, taking off an arm and a shoulder. Men from the *Saufley* courageously leapt into the water to help, but it was too late. He died shortly after being brought aboard.'

Fishing Boat. South China Sea

Four men and a boy clinging to the pilot house of their swamped fishing boat survived without food and water for eight days; they were picked up by the American steamer *Pioneer Main*. A fifth man lost his life in attempting to swim to the rescue ship before the lifeboat was lowered.

Cargo Ship Ambassador. North Atlantic. February

United States Coast Guard: 'On 18 February, the US Atlantic SAR [Search and Rescue] Co-ordinator (Commander Eastern Area) received an urgent message from the British MV *Ambassador* stating that the ship was listing heavily and that her engine was broken down. Shortly thereafter, the foundering vessel broadcast an SOS. *Ambassador* with thirty-five persons on board was located about 400 miles south-southeast of Cape Race, Newfoundland. Commander Eastern Area (Coast Guard, New York) directed the Coast Guard Cutter *Coos Bay*, then 370 miles north of *Ambassador*, to divert to the scene, and forwarded an AMVER [Automated Merchant Vessel Report] Surface Picture to the cutter for relay to the stricken freighter.

'Vessels arriving at the scene included the Italian SS *Leonardo da Vinci*/ICLN and MV *Vulcania*/ICOF, the French MV *Caraibe*/FNUQ, the Norwegian MV *Fruen*/JXPD, the American SS *City of Alma*/KEDU, and USCG *Coos Bay*/NBPG.

'The wind was very strong and seas were running high, with the large vessels already on scene yawing wildly, when the *Coos Bay* arrived on the morning of 19 February. None of the rescue vessels were able to successfully launch lifeboats. The port boat of the *Ambassador* had been crushed by the heavy seas and the heavy port list prevented launching the starboard boat. Aircraft had dropped rubber liferafts for use by the crew of the *Ambassador*.

'*Coos Bay* recovered a deflated liferaft which had been sighted by a lookout just before arrival on the scene. The previous day, the crew of *Ambassador* had entered the liferafts, but two rafts had immediately upset spilling the men into the water. Eleven were lost but twenty-one reached safety back on board the *Ambassador*, where they spent the night huddled in the lee of the bulwarks on the bow of the heavily listing ship.

'When *Coos Bay* arrived, *Fruen* was lying about 200 yards to leeward of *Ambassador*. *Fruen* passed a line by means of a line-throwing gun and removed five men before the line parted. A total of nine men were rescued before the third and last available line parted. Meanwhile, *Coos Bay* co-ordinated the search of the other vessels on scene for the crewmen lost from the liferafts. United States Air Force and Coast Guard and Canadian aircraft also participated in the search, but no survivors were found, although the water was warmed by the Gulf Stream.

'The question of how much longer the ship would stay afloat was a big one. Already she had lasted much longer than the crew had thought possible the previous day, and there were still twelve men on board *Ambassador*. The ship listed so steeply that men could not walk on the decks but had to climb from handhold to handhold. The lee deck was awash and seas broke heavily on the hatch covers.

'*Coos Bay* relieved *Fruen*, who stood off ready to assist, and manœuvred into position close to the bow of *Ambassador*. The two vessels drifted at very different rates and rough weather and heavy seas still made launching of the ship's boats out of the question. A rubber raft was passed to *Ambassador*, but the personnel who attempted to utilize the raft failed to crawl under the protective canopy and into the bottom of the raft and were washed overboard. Fortunately, two of the men were recovered by swimmers from the cutter, while the remainder were able to reach *Ambassador*.

'Since darkness was approaching, *Coos Bay* decided to put a line aboard the freighter for the men to secure around themselves, so that they could be pulled to the cutter through the warm water. After making several approaches, passing a line each time, eleven survivors and one body were brought aboard *Coos Bay* with the assistance of swimmers in rubber "wet" suits.

'*Coos Bay* with the help of various merchant vessels and aircraft then searched until dark on 20 February in an effort to locate additional survivors, but with the weather worsening, and search visibility almost nil, active search was discontinued. Although the Dutch salvage tug *Elbe* took *Ambassador* in tow and set course for the Azores, the foundering merchantman sank before they were able to to reach port.'

Warships. North Atlantic. October
Gales hindered the return of the British Fleet from the Battle of Trafalgar. Admiral Collingwood: '. . . the bad weather continuing, determined me to destroy all the leewardmost that could be cleared of the men, considering that keeping possession of the ships was a matter of little consequence, compared with the chance of their falling again into the hands of the enemy.'

SEARCH AND RESCUE: ORGANIZATION

Radio is the most important aid in search and rescue (SAR) operations. Ships keep watch on the international distress frequencies, details of which are given in *Reed's Nautical Almanac*. As a further precaution ships observe 'silence periods' on 500 Hz, when no transmissions are made except distress calls, messages arising therefrom and urgency and safety signals; the silence periods are of 3 minutes duration at 15 to 18 minutes and 45 to 48 minutes past each hour for W/T and at every hour and half-hour for R/T.

A ship which receives a distress message from another ship or aircraft in its vicinity acknowledges receipt immediately. If not in the vicinity of the casualty a short interval of time is allowed before acknowledging receipt so that ships which are nearer can acknowledge and answer without interference. The ship's radio officer reports distress calls immediately to the Master. British Masters are obliged by law, and it is the long-accepted tradition of the brotherhood of the sea, to proceed with all speed to vessels in distress and render assistance, provided it can be done without danger to their own ships and the personnel aboard. They report promptly the sighting of wreckage or the recovery of survivors so that the search plan can be updated.

An aircraft which receives a distress call answers it immediately and relays the information on other frequencies to the Oceanic Control Centre and/or broadcasts it on other distress frequencies. Unlike ships, aircraft do not normally attempt to locate a distressed vessel because of the high altitudes at which they fly; going down to look for a ship and climbing back again would involve crossing the flight levels of other aircraft and a severe expenditure of fuel.

Coast Radio Stations guard the international distress frequencies, alert ships in the vicinity of the casualty, and inform the relevant shore authorities. The shore authorities in the UK are HM Coastguard, the Royal Navy, the Royal Air Force, the Air Traffic Control Centres, the Fisheries Department, the Meteorological Office, Lloyd's, and the Royal National Lifeboat Institution.

In this section is described the SAR organization in the UK. Other maritime countries have a similar organization for casualties in their region. The USA operates an oceanic system with a world-wide capability—this is described on page 214.

Coast Radio Stations

The Post Office operates eleven medium-range coast radio stations (CRS). All these stations, except that at Oban, keep continuous watch. The daylight ranges of these stations are about 300 miles on W/T and 150 on R/T; much greater ranges sometimes occur, particularly at night. The Post Office also has a long-distance CRS, with almost a world-wide range, at Burnham/Portishead in Somerset.

On receipt of a ship's distress signal a CRS transmits the appropriate alarm signal and then retransmits the distress message to ships at sea. The distress message is also passed by telephone or teleprinter to HM Coastguard, the Naval Commander in Chief of the area in which the CRS is situated, and to Lloyd's. The CRS controls all radio signalling in the area, informs the ship nearest to the scene of distress and requests the Master's intention as to rendering assistance, maintains communications with the casualty and rescue vessels, keeps the Coastguard informed of all relevant signals received, and acts as a communications link between Coastguard Stations and RNLI lifeboats. In the event of communications with the casualty ceasing the CRS informs all authorities to whom the distress message was sent.

Where the casualty is beyond the normal MF range of the CRS and there is doubt as to whether it is within range of other European Coast Stations, the distress signal is also retransmitted on HF by Portishead. The message is broadcast and is repeated as necessary until it is certain that assistance is being rendered or another CRS is dealing with the traffic.

An aircraft distress signal is routed to the Rescue Co-ordination Centre and the Coastguard. A ship in UK waters requiring medical assistance informs the CRS who routes the request to the Coastguard District HQ.

HM Coastguard

The Coastguard consists of some 550 full-time and 7,000

auxiliary personnel who maintain an extensive watch from a number of coastal stations. The Coastguard warns off ships standing into danger, renders all possible assistance in the preservation of life, initiates the appropriate search and rescue facilities for ships in distress and fishing vessels which are overdue, and keeps in close touch with all relevant authorities throughout the incident. Shipping casualties further off shore referred by the CRS, and aircraft casualties referred by the Rescue Co-ordination Centres (RCC), are also dealt with.

Depending on the nature of the casualty, the Coastguard musters the local company of the Coast Lifesaving Corps, informs the Royal National Lifeboat Institution (RNLI) and requests a lifeboat, informs the Royal Navy and requests advice, or ship or aircraft assistance and informs the RCC and requests aircraft assistance. The Coastguard is also empowered to request tug owners to provide assistance.

Royal Navy

Naval Commanders-in-Chief give assistance by ships and aircraft at the request of HM Coastguard or the RCC. Naval helicopters have proved a valuable aid in SAR missions. The Fishing Protection Squadron, many of whose ships carry doctors, take special care of fishing vessels in need of assistance.

Royal Air Force

The RAF is responsible for providing rescue facilities for Service aircraft and for ensuring that SAR aircraft are available for civilian planes. The RAF also provides coast helicopter detachments and has a number of marine craft with SAR capability.

Rescue Co-ordination Centres

Two RCCs, at Edinburgh and Plymouth, are administered by the RAF. They initiate and co-ordinate SAR operations for aircraft in distress around the coasts of the UK, they may call on Naval Cs-in-C for assistance, though the Coastguard requests the RNLI to dispatch a lifeboat, and though the ATCC requests an Ocean Station Vessel to stand by. At the request of HM Coastguard the RCCs dispatch aircraft to help with shipping casualties off-shore.

Air Traffic Control Centres

The ATCC is notified of aircraft missing or overdue by the destination aerodrome. If it is a transatlantic incident the ATCC initiates the action for SAR; for all other incidents, and where a distress signal is received from an aircraft, the ATCC informs the RCC who will initiate the action, and also informs other aircraft, Master Radar Stations, Air Traffic Control Radar Units and Ocean Station Vessels as appropriate. For shipping incidents the ATCC informs the RCC for the Coastguard.

Fisheries Department

The District Office of the Fisheries Department is informed of fishing vessels missing or overdue by the owners, and calls on HM Coastguard to undertake SAR duties as necessary.

Ocean Station Vessels

In collaboration with other European maritime countries Britain provides ocean station vessels (OSV) for four of the nine weather stations in the North Atlantic. The ships are administered by the Meteorological Office, as their prime function is weather reporting. Like any other ship, however, they are obliged to come to the assistance of ships or aircraft in distress, a task for which they are well fitted on account of their extensive radio equipment.

Lloyd's

On receipt of information about a shipping casualty from Agents, wireless stations, Coastguard Stations, etc., Lloyd's Intelligence Department, which maintains a 24-hour staff, relays the report immediately to those tug and salvage companies requiring information in the area of the vessel in casualty. It is then the decision of the tug company to decide on whether to act on the information and send a tug to the scene of the casualty.

Owners or interested parties can contact the Department if they are concerned for the safety of a vessel, either because it has sent no radio communication or because it has not arrived in port at the scheduled time. The Department has facilities for making broadcasts to shipping in most parts of the world requesting vessels in the area for later news.

Royal National Lifeboat Institution

The RNLI is a private organization supported entirely by voluntary contributions. It has about 140 seagoing lifeboats stationed around the coasts of the British Isles, and a large number of small rescue craft for incidents inshore. The seagoing lifeboats have ranges up to 175 miles, are fitted with radio equipment and have a towing as well as rescue capability. Two recent 70 foot lifeboats have a range of 560 miles.

RNLI lifeboats work in close association with the Coastguard. Where radio communication between the two is difficult during a SAR mission, messages are passed via the CRS. All district headquarters of RNLI are fitted with either M/F or VHF radio equipment, or both.

Radar Units

Radar units are administered by Ministry of Defence. Distress messages from aircraft are routed to the ATCC and from ships to Coastguard or the RCC.

Lighthouses and Lightships

Lighthouses and lightships are administered by Trinity House. They pass to the Coastguard distress messages received from aircraft and ships.

Police

The police route distress messages from aircraft to the ATCC and from ships to the Coastguard or to RCC.

Public

A member of the public seeing or hearing a ship or aircraft in distress should telephone 999 and ask for the Coastguard; failing this, inform the Police.

AUTOMATED MERCHANT VESSEL REPORT SYSTEM

The Automated Merchant Vessel Report (AMVER) System provides rescue co-ordination centres throughout the world with essential information about merchant ships at sea who may be requested to undertake a SAR mission. It eliminates the search phase of the mission.

AMVER is operated by the United States Coast Guard at their centre in New York. Co-operating parties are a network of radio stations, rescue co-ordination centres and merchant ships of all nations departing on off-shore passages of 24 hours or longer.

Merchant Ships

Merchant ships participating in the system give their sail plan (place, date and time of departure, route, destination, average speed) to the Ship Plot Centre, either direct or through specified coastal island or ocean-station vessel radio stations. The ships should have long-range two-way communications. AMVER encourages them to give a position report at every 15-degree change of longitude or latitude. The success of the system depends on the accuracy of the information, and on the sail plan being strictly followed, or, in the event of departure from it, on AMVER being informed promptly. Participation is free of cost.

Amver Computer

The information received in the Centre is manually checked and evaluated as appropriate and punched into tabulation cards. The cards are checked and then put into the computer. The information about merchant-ship voyages is also supplemented with relevant data about their SAR capability, taken from such publications as *Lloyds Register of Ships*. The computer produces a sail plan for each ship, or corrects a plan already on the plot, and stores it on a magnetic memory disc for immediate use in the event of an emergency.

Surpic

The Controller of a rescue co-ordination centre dealing with a distress incident at sea requests the AMVER Centre by teletape to produce a Surface Picture (SURPIC) for a specified area. His request may be for all ships on the plot, or only those with a doctor on board, or just those which are east-bound or west-bound. The Centre can produce, within about two minutes, all essential data for every participating ship in the area, including ship's name; international call sign; predicted position by latitude and longitude; time of position; course; speed;

P

radio-watch schedule; availability of radar, doctor and radio-telephone; and estimated date of arrival at destination.

The US Coast Guard make SURPICS available to a SAR agency of any country engaged on a SAR mission. They are not available for commercial exploitation. If it is not possible to make contact with ships on the SURPIC through normal procedures, the Traffic List of a Commercial Radio Station should be used. The Traffic List is a regularly scheduled marine broadcast made on high frequency every two hours. A phone call from the RCC Controller to the Station Manager will ensure that the name or call sign of a ship is added to the next Traffic List.

Various types of SURPIC are available. The *Radius* SURPIC gives information on ships within a desired distance of the specified spot and is a useful tool for finding the source of an SOS; the *Hi-Lo* SURPIC is used when a large area of the ocean has to be covered; the *Trackline* SURPIC is a precautionary measure in cases of aircraft alert; the *Precautionary* SURPIC is provided when Heads of State make flights over water. SURPICS are also produced to cover the area surrounding an embryonic storm or hurricane.

Medical Cases

Help may be obtained from AMVER in cases where the treatment of a seafarer's illness or injury is beyond the immediate resources of the ship. Messages sent from a ship should be signed by the Master and prefixed with 'DH MEDICO', thus ensuring that no charge will be made by the receiving station for relaying the message. If the prescribing doctor considers that the patient should be evacuated, and this course is decided on, then the term 'MEDEVAC' is used whenever referring to the MEDICO. When a doctor is badly needed well out at sea a *Radius* SURPIC of at least 500 miles should be requested. If the vessel is passing within a reasonable distance of port, a *Radius* SURPIC of all ships within that distance is required. Although none of the ships may have a doctor on board it is very likely that one of them is bound for the port, in which case a rendezvous can be arranged and the patient be transferred.

Ships like the RMS *Queen Elizabeth II*, T/S *Bremen*, SS *France* and SS *United States*, which carry medical staff and are well fitted for surgical treatment, report their positions to AMVER at regular intervals. Unfortunately all ships do not participate in the AMVER system, but they all have equal obligations to assist. As a last resort, therefore, a ship can broadcast an inquiry as to whether any nearby ships have a doctor on board. Radio medical services are also available through most coastal stations. Stations which specialize in this work include IRM (Rome), PCH (Scheveningen) and the US Public Health Service.

A radio message requiring medical help is given priority over all others with the exception of distress signals.

Vessels Missing or Overdue

Ships at sea usually have a routine of radio communication with their shore bases, and vessels in a fleet, when fishing, for example, also maintain contact with one another.

British fishing vessels which are missing or overdue should be reported to the District Inspector of Fisheries (the Inspector of Sea Fisheries or the Fishery Officer in Scotland) or, failing this, direct to the District Officer of Coastguard. Responsibility for initiating the search and rescue measures is vested in the Coastguard.

Any other British vessels which are missing or overdue should be reported to the Intelligence Department at Lloyds, who may request a broadcast message to shipping by one or more of the UK Coast Radio Stations and who will inform the appropriate Coastguard Liaison Station or Stations of the action being taken. Lloyds may also seek the advice of Naval Commanders-in-Chief with a view to arranging further broadcasts to shipping and making a search by Naval aircraft and vessels.

As a safeguard, yacht skippers about to make a voyage should complete a Coastguard Form CG 66 (it can be done by telephone) giving the name and details of the yacht, the route and the estimated times of arrival. HM Coastguard relays this information to the next Coastguard Station along the line of the planned voyage, including French stations. The yacht's progress is thus checked all the way to its destination. To aid identification the Coastguard recommend that the yacht's name be marked in black on a white canvas dodger.

A vessel which participates in the AMVER scheme is at great

advantage in the event of becoming missing or overdue. AMVER can quickly provide the intended sail plan to those searching for her, thus permitting concentration of search units along the trackline of most probable detection.

DISTRESS SIGNALS

Ships

Details of distress signals are given in the *Handbook for Radio Operators* (HMSO), the *International Convention for the Safety of Life at Sea* (HMSO) and in *Reed's Nautical Almanac*. Radio communication is the most important means of making distress known. Warning to other ships or the Coast Radio Stations of the impending distress call is given by making radio alarm signals. An automatic keying device is fitted to radio equipment for use by unskilled personnel in the event of the Radio Officer being incapacitated; it gives the Alarm Signal followed by the Distress Call.

Aircraft

An aircraft indicates urgency by repeatedly switching on and off the landing lights, or at irregular intervals its navigation lights, or by firing a succession of white pyrotechnics. The flashing of landing lights may also indicate intention to ditch.

An aircraft indicates distress by firing red pyrotechnics either singly or in succession. It transmits a distress signal on the designated air/ground route frequency in use at the time between the aircraft and the appropriate ground station, normally an Air Traffic Control Centre. If unable to contact the ground station on the route frequency, any other available frequency may be used.

An aircraft finding another aircraft in distress at sea may notify ships in the vicinity by using a signalling lamp to pass a message in plain language. It may also guide a ship to the casualty or survivors by flying low round the ship, or crossing the bows close ahead at a low altitude, opening and closing the throttle or changing the propeller pitch. It may also fire a succession of green pyrotechnic lights or make a series of green flashes, or the aircraft may be rocked laterally. It will then fly off in the direction of the casualty. The ship should acknowledge receipt of the signal and messages by a succession of Ts in Morse Code on the signalling lamp; then follow the aircraft, or if it is unable to comply, inform the aircraft by hoisting the international code flag NOVEMBER. If the aircraft has to cancel the instructions it will cross the wake of the ship close astern at low altitude and open and close the throttle or change the propeller pitch or rock laterally.

Survival Craft

Various signal devices are carried on survival craft, depending on the type of craft. They include pyrotechnic distress signals (red flares, orange smokes and parachute signals), heliograph signal mirror, electric torch and whistles. Some carry radio equipment; see page 251. Lifeboats have red sails and may lift an oar with clothing or a smoke signal at the end; the crew can shout if close enough. Inflatable liferafts have a canopy of conspicuous colour (yellow or orange-red) and they may have also a fluorescine dye marker giving a bright conspicuous colour to the sea.

AIRCRAFT IN DISTRESS

An aircraft in distress at sea may seek assistance from its air-ground station, from other aircraft *en route* and from ships. Assistance from other aircraft is usually the most immediate; assistance from ships, particularly if they are Ocean Station Vessels, is the most advantageous. A pilot unable to inform a ship in his vicinity by normal communications of his intention to ditch will flash the landing lights, lower and raise the landing gear, or jettison cargo.

Assistance by Aircraft

The pilot of a nearby aircraft may act on his own initiative or at the request of a RCC through his air-ground station, but the decision to assist is his entirely. Most SAR authorities provide an intercept aircraft on request.

The best position for an escort is 1,000 feet above the disabled aircraft and behind it, but the pilot will move clear in the event of the disabled aircraft jettisoning fuel as so to avoid the fuel-air mixture. The escort gives a continuous position of the disabled aircraft thereby eliminating the search phase of the SAR operation should ditching or bailing-out occur.

An aircraft intercepting a distress call by radio takes a bearing on the transmission, plots the position given, listens on the frequency, retransmits the distress message on behalf of the distressed aircraft if necessary and listens for the ground station.

Assistance by Ships

A ship who receives an SOS direct from an aircraft informs the nearest coast radio station and passes all relevant information, e.g. identity, position and intended action by ship, call-sign of aircraft, time of message and bearing at which the distress message ceased.

If the ship is some way off and it is decided to make a rendezvous the ship gives help firstly by transmitting homing bearings to the aircraft, or, when requested to do so, transmitting signals on which the aircraft can take its own bearings. Visual aids to attract the pilot to the ship in darkness or bad visibility are the switching on of all deck lights and pointing searchlights or Aldis lamps vertically and/or sweeping them round the horizon; in daytime the ship makes black smoke. The ship ultimately tracks the aircraft on the radar and gives the pilot his heading and range to the ship.

The ship informs the aircraft of the wind speed and direction, visibility, state of sea and swell, the barometric pressure, and, if the pilot so requests, a recommended ditch heading. Preparations are made to guide the aircraft on its ditching heading and to rescue and receive the survivors; the sea boat is put ready, boarding-nets rigged over the side and manned.

Ditching

On airliners, the Captain notifies passengers of the emergency over the Passenger Address System. 'No smoking' and 'Fasten seat-belt' lights are switched on and the Cabin attendants instruct the passengers. There is a ditching procedure for each type of aircraft. Aircrew receive frequent training in the procedure. As a precaution, the Cabin crew demonstrate the use of the lifejacket prior to take-off on a trans-ocean flight and draw attention to the emergency-procedure pamphlet or card which is given to each passenger. Flight Deck crew procedure is given in the relevant Operator's *Flying Manual*.

Typical instructions for passengers are:

Loosen neckwear. Put on warm clothing. Remove glasses, dentures and chewing gum. Remove high-heeled shoes and any other sharp footwear which is likely to damage a rubber raft. Empty pockets of pens, pencils and other sharp objects. Extinguish cigarettes; do not use lighters or matches.

Don lifejacket by pulling it over the head; do *not* inflate it. Secure it to the body in accordance with the instructions given in the emergency-procedure pamphlet. A baby or very small child for whom the lifejacket is not suitable is put into an inflatable life-cot and taken care of by a Stewardess. A special child's lifejacket is now available.

Ensure seat is in vertical position. Fasten seat-belt tightly.

Pair off 'buddie' fashion, to help one another if in difficulty. Pair elderly people and children with able-bodied men.

Take ditching posture:
Forward-facing passengers bend forward with one arm across knees, place pillow, blanket or coat on lap, hold the head on the pillow with the other arm. Place legs well forward and brace them. Tall passengers unable to bend fully forward push the backrest of the seat in front forward and rest the folded arms on it, holding the head firmly.

Backward-facing passengers lean back against seat.

Passengers on floor protect head with pillows, blankets, or coats.

The Cabin crew take the following precautions:

Stow and secure loose equipment (normally put it in the toilets). Move heavy baggage aft. Switch on personal electric torches at night, and lifejacket lights if possible. Check survival equipment.

Remove certain overwing emergency-exit windows (after the aircraft has been depressurized) so that liferafts may be launched quickly. This is a precaution against pressure build-up in the event of water entering the ditching aircraft

—such pressure would prevent the windows being opened. If there is a fire, say on one wing, then the exits on that side would not be opened.

The Captain gives early warning over the Passenger Address System when approaching the water and some 20–30 seconds before alighting will call, 'Brace, brace!' He will touch down at the lowest speed and rate of descent which permits safe handling and optimum nose-up attitude on impact.

After the second or subsequent impact, as soon as the aircraft has settled on the water, the Cabin crew launch some liferafts, jerk the retaining cord (which operates a CO_2 cylinder) and thus inflate each raft. An escape rope from the exit windows is secured to a wing attachment point and serves as a guide line.

The passengers are herded out of the aircraft, able-bodied men being stationed at the exits to assist as necessary. Exit is usually by first placing one leg out of the window, followed by the head and shoulder and then the other leg. The lifejacket is then inflated in accordance with the safety instructions, usually by pulling a knob, or knobs, at the bottom of the lifejacket smartly downwards. In most cases passengers are able to walk along the wings and board the liferafts without getting wet. The first few liferafts are overloaded in case the aircraft sinks before the remaining rafts are launched. The loading between rafts is adjusted later.

As each raft is loaded it is pushed clear of the aircraft and the cord retaining it to the aircraft is cut. All rafts are connected together by a line and sea-anchors or drogues are streamed— the object is that the survivors should remain near the scene of the disaster as the position has been given by radio.

Other Cabin attendants collect and take off water containers, portable radio beacons and first-aid kits.

Each raft is under the command of a member of the Flight Deck, or failing this, a Steward. Throughout the incident the aircrew exercise firm leadership in order to overcome any emotional disturbances.

Ditched aircraft usually stay afloat for about twenty minutes, but they may sink in about three minutes. Speedy, but orderly, evacuation is therefore essential.

SEARCH AND ASSISTANCE BY AIRCRAFT

In seeking a casualty at sea aircraft search an area which is calculated to include the most probable position of the incident, allowing for drift. Search is usually by the 'creeping-line ahead' method, the spacing between the tracks depending on the visibility, the size and conspicuity of the casualty, and the type of any radio aids carried.

Searching aircraft fitted with M/F radio maintain W/T silence during the periods of 15 to 18 minutes and 45 to 48 minutes past each hour, and listen for distress calls. During the night search aircraft use one green pyrotechnic light every 5 to 10 minutes as a call to survivors to fire red pyrotechnics.

When co-operating with a rescue ship at night the aircraft drops two lights to define the search area and a creeping-line ahead search is started from one light to the other. The aircraft drops flares over the rescue vessel at intervals of about one mile along the line of search.

On locating the casualty the aircraft immediately informs the RCC and keeps the casualty in sight, fixes the position by radio, and/or marks it with smoke floats, sea markers, flame markers or buoyant electric lights. Gear such as pumps is dropped to help keep a vessel afloat and other equipment is dropped to aid survivors in the water or in rafts. RAF search-and-rescue aircraft carry the Lindholme droppable survival gear comprising three cylinders secured in line on a buoyant rope about 800 feet long. A 9-man inflatable liferaft is packed in one of the containers (the largest) and supplies in the others. The gear is dropped in relation to the survivors so that one drifts down on to the other. The aircraft may also drop other containers as circumstances require. In general, when dropping a single item aircraft fly into the wind and for multiple items across the wind.

RESCUE BY TUG

Preparations by Disabled Ship

Bring a bower anchor inboard, or jettison it, to enable the towing wire to be passed up the hawse-pipe for connecting the eye to a plain link in the anchor cable with a 'pin and pellet' cable shackle with an oval sectional bolt. Alternatively, secure the anchor in the hawse pipe, disconnect the cable and pass it through a fairlead. Another alternative is to make the towing wire fast to the first long link next to the anchor connecting shackle and let the anchor act as a weight to keep the towing wire in the water.

If the foregoing is not possible, use a length of cable around strong points, e.g. windlass, gun-mounting, deckhouse or hatch coaming; bring the two ends together for securing the towing wire in an inboard position. One leg should be in line with the fairlead and the other joining at an angle of about 45° to prevent unnecessary yaw in the event of the fairlead carrying away.

Failing all else, arrange to lead the tow wire around as many bollards or strong points as possible.

Prepare wood slats, platform of soft wood and burlap (coarse canvas) for fitting to all chafing areas, e.g. bitts, fairlead and stem bar. If the ship's stability is suspect, remove or reduce all 'free surfaces', jettison top-weight, lower and secure derricks, slip anchor, drain fresh-water and sanitary gravity tanks, flood double bottom tanks if this can be done quickly and without large 'free surface' effect.

Spread oil as the tug approaches; use a length of punctured canvas hose filled with vegetable oil secured along the leeside of forecastle head.

Approach by Tug

The rescue tug approaches a disabled ship from windward and circles at close range to determine the angle of rest at which the ship lies to the weather. The tug also stops to determine her own angle of rest. Should a boarding party be required the tug prepares a boat for lowering, runs downs into the lee of the disabled ship and lowers the boat quickly; the ship then drifts down on to the boat. The final approach of the tug to pass the tow depends on the behaviour of the ship, but usually she moves slowly ahead to position herself just ahead and to leeward of the ship's lee bow.

Connecting the Tow

Ships are normally towed bow first, but if trimmed heavily by the head, open to the sea, with forward bulkheads in a weak state, they are towed stern first.

The tug throws a heaving line of about 45 fathoms' length, with a monkey's fist at the throwing-end and a long eye splice at the retaining-end. This is followed by a 3 in. or $3\frac{1}{2}$ in. manilla rope for use as a messenger, and finally the towing-wire. A line-throwing apparatus, buoyant line, or line with float, are sometimes used to messenger a tow line.

The towing wire is connected to the ship's cable or structure, as described above. The ship takes sufficient wire inboard to allow for paying out when freshening the nip (slackening off the wire) to avoid chafe. When connecting a towing wire to a cable with a shackle, ensure that the wire and cable are snug in the bow and on the pin of the shackle and not on its two legs.

Commencing the Tow

The tug runs down to leeward, paying out her towing gear, then gets the tow underway; when the full weight of the tow is taken and the gear is stretched, the tug comes on to her required course by easy degrees.

Pay out cable from the towed vessel as necessary in order to provide the right catenary.

The Tow

The following precautions should be taken: Maintain constant watch on the towing gear, both on the tug and on the disabled vessel. Lubricate frequently and regularly all bearing surfaces of the towing gear inboard. Inspection by the Officer of the Watch at the end of each watch. Maintain constant watch between the tug and the vessel, by Aldis lamp or R/T. The disabled vessel should make a report to the tug twice daily. The tug should reduce speed at 24-hour intervals to allow the disabled vessel to pay out a few links of cable to freshen the nip. Self-aligning swivelling fairleads which dispense with the need to freshen the nip are now available.

Watch the weather, and dodge any bad weather. If bad weather develops, the tug passes oil through the waste pipes of forward WCs or washbasins on port and starboard sides. Where the disabled vessel yaws a lot an 'oil bag' with recovery line attached is slid down the tow line to a point about three-quarters of the distance from the tug to the ship. The tugmaster may request the Master of the disabled ship to flood up (to flood his ballast tanks) to reduce yaw.

Sinking of Disabled Ship

Where there is any danger of a disabled vessel sinking, the crew and boarding party are taken off by the tug. The tugmaster endeavours to ensure that the vessel does not sink where it would be a danger to navigation. He determines the navigational position, leaves a wreck buoy and informs the appropriate Hydrographic authority. In the event of a wreck buoy being unavailable, he marks the wreck as best he can and may remain in the vicinity to warn shipping until the wreck is properly marked.

RESCUE SHIPS

The following information is based on experience with convoy rescue ships in time of war. The arrangements for the rescue, accommodation and treatment of survivors are necessarily scaled down for peace-time conditions.

Function

To proceed quickly to a distressed ship through all types of weather; to launch and recover their own rescue boats and to take on board men from lifeboats, liferafts and the water; to feed, clothe and accommodate survivors and to give medical care and treatment where necessary; to extinguish fires and pump out water from distressed ships; to tow disabled ships.

Hull Features

High-speed performance under adverse sea and weather conditions, since many casualties occur in heavy weather; good seakeeping properties; ability to ballast as necessary to provide the best trim for particular conditions; slow rolling characteristics—a tank stabilizer system is advantageous. (When rolling there is considerable surge close alongside, particularly on the lee-side, which may draw a swimmer under the ship.) Good manœuvrability at low speeds—a bow thruster or active rudder is advantageous. Adequate stability, to include a reserve against exceptional weather conditions, e.g. accumulation of ice on upperworks.

Parallel body, wall-sided for as much of the ship's length as possible, particularly at and near the rescue stations. (Pronounced flare and counter render boat work difficult and boarding by scrambling net dangerous.) Low freeboard at rescue stations; hospital; helicopter hangar and deck.

Rescue Stations

A main station on each side of the ship, in good view of the bridge, fitted with: recovery davit, safe working load of about $\frac{1}{4}$ ton (a man's saturated clothing may weigh as much as 300 lb.), outreach of about 3 feet clear of ship's side, fitted with block at head to take a line attached to a survivor; boarding net, to stand off from ship's side and reach at least 4 feet below the water in the worst condition of roll and waveslope—the bottom of the net to be weighted as necessary; boom and net (about 12 feet wide), rigged at right angles to the ship's side, at the after end of the rescue station—useful when the ship proceeds slowly through a group of survivors in the water, also useful for stopping boats and rafts from drifting past and for holding them alongside whilst exhausted men are taken off; buoyant mat secured alongside; good lighting overall; easy access to hospital and accommodation.

A secondary rescue station should be provided abaft the main station for the recovery of weak survivors who may drift past the main station. A small hinged platform, right aft, is useful.

Sand should be available at rescue stations to provide a good foothold, especially when oil-covered survivors are brought aboard.

Clean-up Area

Sited close to the rescue station, with easy access to hospital and accommodation spaces, and with supplies of rags and cleansing oils (diesel oil and kerosene will do).

Equipment

Search and rescue equipment, sited close to the rescue station; salvage equipment store, sited close to the work boats; searchlights to illuminate the water at night; loud-hailers for communicating with distressed ships and men in boats, rafts or in the water.

Rescue boats, work boats and surf boats, stowed in mechanically operated davits. Sited over a straight, wall-sided part of ship, well clear of flare and counter, so as to facilitate manœuvring alongside. One rescue boat on each side of ship, to obviate turning the ship to make a lee.

Sufficient survival craft to accommodate the full ship's complement and all survivors. (The Rescue Ship might become a casualty.)

Helicopter, fuel storage and crane for rescuing a ditched helicopter.

Long bamboo poles with three-pronged hook at end for drawing men in the water alongside; square green flag with white diagonal bar, to fly when effecting rescue; electronic datum marker buoy, to determine the rate of drift in the search area; Neil-Robertson and Paraguard stretchers.

Survivors' Accommodation and Stores

Wartime survivors prefer large accommodation spaces, not small cabins, with easy access to the open deck. A common arrangement is for the crew to give up their accommodation to survivors, working from forward to aft. Stores of clothing, toilet outfits, books and games for survivors and containers for survivors' valuables are required.

Hospital

The hospital should have six or eight cots and should allow the rapid evacuation of stretcher cases in the event of an emergency. A bathroom and lavatory should be sited adjacent to the hospital. A small store and dispensary should be sited close by, or, if space does not permit, combined with the hospital and operating theatre.

The operating theatre should be fitted and equipped with: an operating table suitable for use in rough weather and for undertaking plaster work; anaesthetic apparatus; sterilizers; main and auxiliary lighting; instruments for major surgery; library of medical and surgical books; splints and plaster of Paris.

Organization

When proceeding on a rescue mission all rescue equipment, cleaning gear and medical facilities are put in a state of readiness, blankets and bunks are got ready, and hot drinks and food prepared.

RESCUE BY SHIP

Ship-to-Ship Rescue

Various methods are used, depending on the facilities available and the prevailing circumstances, for getting people off a disabled ship. The rescue ship can:

launch a boat;

drift an inflatable liferaft down to the disabled vessel, with a line attached to haul in the survivors who board it. If necessary, add another line so that the raft may be shuttled back and forth until all the survivors are taken off;

pass a line to the vessel; the survivor, wearing a lifejacket, secures the line round him and jumps overboard; the rescue ship hauls him in carefully, but as quickly as possible, so that he does not drown;

use a light jackstay rig;

come alongside the distressed vessel so that the men jump from one to the other; or

come close to the distressed vessel and improvise its forederrick to effect the transfer.

Rescue in rough seas is facilitated by laying an oil slick to windward, but fuel oil should not be spread if there are survivors in the water. Vegetable, animal and fish oils are the most suitable; if these are unavailable use lubricating oil; these oils are less harmful to men in the water.

Men on boats or small craft alongside a ship should avoid walking along the side nearer the ship. There is the danger of falling between the boat and the ship. There is also the hazard of a heavy roll—a deck house can crush the head and chest of a man against the ship's side and cause instant death. Walk along the side remote from the ship and head fore or aft according to the position of the Jacob's ladder or scrambling net.

Rescue from Survival Craft

Recovery is usually effected by the ship drifting down on to the survival craft and making a lee for it. Exact procedure depends on the ship's handling qualities and the prevailing conditions of sea and weather.

Where the survival craft drifts faster than the ship, the ship must be manœuvred down-wind and the craft allowed to drift down on to it. The recovery may be hazardous and the rescue party must work very quickly.

If the survivors are active and the conditions favourable, they come aboard without assistance by rescue net or ladder. If they are distressed, or if conditions are unfavourable, two fit men with lifelines attached and wearing lifejackets board the survival craft from the rescue ship. They place a helicopter rescue strop, with line attached, round the survivor. The line is passed through the block at the head of the recovery davit fitted at the rescue station, and thence through a leading-block on deck, and is kept in hand by a few men. Injured survivors should be handled with great care.

Some lifejackets, as used by the Armed Services, are fitted with a lifting becket to which the recovery line may be secured, thus dispensing with the use of a rescue strop. The use of a bowline knotted loop around the survivor should be avoided, for in the event of the survivor becoming unconscious he may slip through the loop and be lost.

Rescue from Water

Where there are survivors in the water and in survival craft, those in the water are rescued first. Give priority to those who are in greatest need.

The ship is placed slightly upwind of the survivors, the engines stopped, and allowed to drift down on the men. Under bad conditions of sea and wind, the weather is kept on the quarter and the survivors on the lee bow. Care is taken that the ship does not get way-on from a following sea. Keeping the sea on the quarter prevents heavy rolling and therefore reduces the hazards to the rescue party and the chance of men in the water being sucked under the ship.

If the survivors are active, the rescue ship will toss them heaving lines, for making a bowline-knotted loop round the body or, where the lifejacket is so fitted, for securing to the lifting becket.

Immersion, particularly in cold water, quickly saps the survivor's strength, and he may be unable to help himself or may perish in making the attempt. Many men were lost in the second World War because they could not climb up a rescue net or ladder, or even put a line around themselves. Rescue stations therefore include a rescue party wearing protective clothing and with lifelines attached, who work over the ship's side or in the water alongside, actively assisting the survivors to safety. The preferred method of recovering weak and distressed men from the sea is by hoisting them on board by the recovery davit; it is much quicker and less exhausting on the rescue party. Assisting an oil-covered survivor up the scramble net to the deck of a ship with only 8 feet freeboard will exhaust five active rescuers.

Active survivors are taken from the rescue station to the clean-up area, stripped of their oil-soaked clothing and cleaned by the use of kerosene or other suitable oil-remover. Distressed survivors are taken straight below from the rescue station. Injured survivors must be handled with extreme care.

MAN-OVERBOARD

Wherever practicable, men in danger of falling or being swept overboard should wear a safety belt or harness, and a lifejacket and highly visible survival suit as appropriate.

Powered Ships

The method of rescuing a man who falls overboard depends on the characteristics of the ship and the prevailing circumstances, in particular the speed of the ship at the time of the accident. The following paragraphs are based on the typical advice given to Trawler Officers of the Watch at Sea, by the Hull Steam Trawlers' Mutual Insurance and Protection Co.

If the man is seen to go overboard, stop the engines, order the wheel to be put over towards the side from which the man fell, and throw a lifebuoy and marker over the side as close to the man as possible. Smoke markers by day and light markers at night are preferred to combined day and night markers as their smoke obscures the light.

Do not take eyes off the man or, failing that, the lifebuoy. Call for assistance and get the first man who arrives to act as look-out. Appoint the second man to arrive as look-out also and, weather permitting, send him aloft. The look-outs must not take their eyes off the man or the marker, until the man is recovered.

Get the ship round on the return course at full speed. Sound the signal 'O' on the whistle even if no other ship is in company; it will rouse the crew and bring the seamen within call. Fly the flag 'O' to explain the manœuvres to approaching vessels and cause them to keep a special look-out.

(The speed of warships is usually such that a man-overboard is quickly astern of the vessel. British Naval practice, generally, is to bring the ship round to rest just to windward of the man.)

Order arrangements to receive the man.

Ideally, if the ship is close enough, cast a heaving-line with a circular lifebuoy, rescue quoit or other handy buoyant item attached. Turn the ship so that the line encircles the man and stop for pick-up. Alternatively swing the ship out of the wind, keep the man in the lee forward of amidships, and cast the line. If the man is beyond heaving-line distance and is judged active enough to handle a line, use the line-throwing gun. Fire it upwind of the man so that the projectile misses him and the line drifts down to him.

If it is necessary to use a sea boat or inflatable liferaft, do not lower it until the ship is near the man, as the ship is more manœuvrable than the boat. If a boat is used, put it in the water to windward of the man, and pick up the boat to leeward. If a liferaft is used, veer it from the ship on its painter and point the ship according to the weather, so that the raft or the bight of its tow-line drifts down on to the man. Alternatively, if it is better to get the ship to windward, launch the raft on the lee side, put a bow and stern line on the raft and two men in it. As the ship drifts on to the man, adjust the raft so that it comes between the man and the ship. The man is then pulled into the raft and passed on deck.

Some Naval vessels carry swimmers and man-overboard squads, equipped with wet suits, gas-inflated lifejackets, belts with knives, buoyant lines and snap hooks. If the man is uninjured the swimmer places a bowline round him or bends the line to the lifting becket on the lifejacket after making sure that the lifejacket is properly secured. Alternatives to the bowline are a line with snap hooks sewn in, and a canvas/leather belt large enough to go round a man wearing a lifejacket— this belt is less likely to cause injury. An injured man is best secured to a buoyant stretcher. The swimmer accompanies the man as he is hauled to the ship.

An uninjured man may climb a Jacob's ladder or scramble net unaided or be brought aboard on the bowline rove through the block of a recovery davit. A bosun's chair can be used for an injured or helpless man; the chair is lowered into the water and a swimmer helps the man into the chair and secures him there. A Stoke's or similar stretcher with single point suspension is best for a badly injured man.

Sailing Vessels

Throw the man something buoyant to grab hold of; a lifejacket, lifebuoy, oar, grating or anything else that will float. Order a look-out to keep his eyes on the man. Get boathooks and lines ready for grappling. Manœuvre the boat alongside the man, according to the sailing point at the time of the accident, as follows:

Beating or Reaching
Wear the boat round so as to bring her to leeward of the man, then approach close-hauled. Never approach from windward, as you may blow over the man or run him down.

Running
Run on a short distance, bring the boat round close-hauled on the same tack, go about so as to come up just to leeward of the man, then luff up alongside him.

In a strong wind it may be necessary to sail a 'figure-of-eight' and then tack up to the man.

Bring the man aboard over the stern, never over the side in a small boat.

233

RESCUE BY HELICOPTER

Survivor in Water

Guide the helicopter by use of pyrotechnics, radio beacons, tracer ammunition or heliograph signal mirror if available. Stop using the heliograph when the helicopter is approaching on course—it may dazzle the pilot.

If the survivor is able to help himself the helicopter will lower a rescue strop, dunk it (to discharge the static electricity) and trail it up to the survivor. The survivor should grasp the looped strop, slip one arm and the head through the loop, then slip the other arm through; arrange the strop round the upper part of body under the armpits, with the hook and D ring in front; pull the toggle or webbing loop down towards the chest to prevent the strop from slipping; and give the 'thumbs up' sign to the helicopter crew.

On his arrival in the helicopter the survivor should be treated for hypothermia, if necessary, as described on page 271.

If the survivor is unable to help himself a helicopter crew man is lowered into the sea to effect the rescue.

A diver may be necessary where the survivor is submerged. British Naval divers who jump from helicopters on search-and-rescue missions wear a swimmer mask and carry a special self-contained breathing apparatus, named BASAR, which comprises two cylinders containing compressed air which passes through a reducer and demand valve to a free mouthpiece according to the user's requirements. The apparatus is effective for about 30 minutes under conditions of hard work at the surface and progressively less with depth, as when making rescues from ditched aircraft or sunken ships.

Survivor on Liferaft, Dinghy or Small Boat

Use pyrotechnic signals or heliograph as necessary to guide the helicopter. Keep one pyrotechnic smoking to give the helicopter pilot indication of wind direction.

Lower the canopy of a raft or sit on it to collapse it. If the survivor takes to the water he should have a lifeline attached to regain the raft in the event of the rescue attempt being abortive. Lower the mast and sails of a boat. If in a power-assisted boat, steam into wind at slow speed and do not stop the boat for the transfer.

Casualty on Ship

Give the Rescue authority all relevant information (type of vessel, radio frequencies, position, time, speed, course, wind direction and speed, sea conditions, nature of casualty). Maintain radio guard. RN helicopters guard 243·0 MHz and RAF helicopters 121·5 MHz (which is used by RNLI lifeboats). A very few helicopters carry 500 kHz. It is particularly useful to make radio contact with helicopter when the visibility is poor, as the pilot can home on to the ship's transmissions. Continue contact with the helicopter throughout the operation.

Check whether it is practicable for the helicopter to effect a transfer direct from the ship. The length of the helicopter winch wire is about 70 feet. If it is impossible to clear away a transfer area due to rigging, superstructure or other obstructions higher than 70 feet, put the casualty into a powered boat and steam it clear of the ship into wind at low speed. The casualty should be tagged, as described below.

If a direct transfer is practicable, prepare a hoist area on deck or hatchcover of minimum 50-foot radius, clear of all obstructions, preferably right aft (in which case strike the flag-staff). Trice running-rigging and secure all loose items likely to be affected by the helicopter downwash. The rotor blades are very susceptible to damage from objects like caps, canvas covers, and plastic buckets which easily become airborne in the downwash, and such incidents may well cause the pilot to lose control of his machine. The majority of helicopters are powered with gas turbines which suck in large volumes of air. When hovering over a ship it only needs an object the size of a drawing-pin to be sucked into the compressor to cause engine failure and almost certain loss of life.

Usually the hoist area is obvious to the pilot on arrival over the ship by the number of people congregated there, but if any doubt is likely to exist mark a large white letter 'H' to indicate the hoist area.

Prepare the casualty. Tag him to show the medical treatment he has received. Put a lifejacket on him and place him as close as possible to the hoist area. If he is too ill to be lifted on a rescue strop, secure him in a Neil-Robertson stretcher. The helicopter may lower a Stoke's litter; this is a large wire stretcher into which the Neil-Robertson stretcher fits snugly.

Guide the helicopter to the ship. By day, use an orange smoke signal or a heliograph signal mirror if the sunshine is suitable, but stop using the heliograph as soon as it is obvious that the ship has been identified. At night, point a searchlight vertically upwards, then illuminate the ship as much as possible as the approach to the hoist area is the most hazardous for the pilot.

A 3-inch helicopter reconnaissance flare, of 250,000 candle power, burning for two minutes, has been used successfully for rescue at night.

Remember that the pilot sits on the starboard side of his machine. If the hoist area is on the foc'sle steam the ship so that the relative wind is Green 150° at about 15 knots. If the hoist area is on the quarter deck, steam so that the relative wind is Red 30° also at about 15 knots. In rough weather it may be necessary to steam the ship downwind and sea to lessen the ship movement. If the ship is on fire and making smoke, head the ship so that the wind is two points off the bow. Fly a pennant or flag to give the helicopter pilot indication of wind direction.

It is most important that all the foregoing preparations be made before the arrival of the helicopter, as it has limited range and may be able to remain over the ship for a very short time only.

Show a green flag or light to show that the ship is ready for the transfer, or a red flag or light if not ready. Flags are preferred to lights.

When the helicopter winch wire is lowered, do *not* secure it to any part of the ship or allow it to become entangled with any rigging or fixtures. If the helicopter lowers a crewman he is to take charge of the rescue and ship's personnel should give him assistance only if asked to do so.

Some helicopters lower a basket or litter; do *not* touch it before it has made contact with the deck; it will have gained a static charge during flight. Sometimes there is a trailing line with a padded weight at the end suspended from the basket; this may be handled before contact with the ship, take hold of it and guide the basket to the ship. Place casualty in the basket, sitting with hands clear of the side. When all is ready for the hoist give the 'thumbs up' sign. Keep the trailing line free of all obstructions.

RECOMMENDED READING

Rescue by Shore Lifesaving Apparatus

Details of the arrangements and signals used in the UK by the Shore Lifesaving Stations for guiding small craft in distress to a safe landing and in rescuing the crews of distressed ships by means of a breeches buoy can be found in the following publications:

Merchant Ship Search and Rescue Manual (MERSAR): Inter-Governmental Maritime Consultative Organization

Reed's Nautical Almanac: Thomas Reed Publications

Trawlermen's Handbook, by R. C. Oliver: Fishing News (Books), 110 Fleet Street, London E.C.4

General

In addition to the above, the following publications on search and rescue procedure are recommended:

International Convention for the Safety of Life at Sea: HMSO

Handbook for Radio Operators: HMSO

Notices to Ship Wireless Stations: HMSO (obtainable free of charge from Mercantile Marine Offices and Custom Houses and by application in writing to ETS (Wireless Telegraphy Section), Union House, St Martin's-le-Grand, London E.C.1)

Aircraft Emergency Procedures over Water (obtainable from the Superintendent of Documents, US Government Printing Office, Washington DC, 20402, USA. Price $1.00)

Annual Summary of Admiralty Notices to Mariners: HMSO

Lloyd's Calendar

AERAD Flight Guide: International Aeradio

Notices to Airmen (NOTAMS)

Radio Regulations, promulgated by the International Telecommunications Union

International Code of Signals, adopted by IMCO

ICAO Search and Rescue Manual (Doc. 7333; International Civil Aviation Organization)

7

Safety and survival equipment

Man is a terrestrial animal unsuited for life in the water, where he can drown in a matter of seconds, die from hypothermia in minutes or hours, from dehydration in days and from hunger in weeks. He may also be the prey of man-eating sharks and other dangerous creatures. Equipment and drink or the means of making seawater potable are necessary in order to ensure survival; food is of minor importance.

Drowning is prevented by wearing a lifejacket or using some other means of support in the water, death from cold is delayed by protective clothing or an adequate shelter, and death from dehydration by rations designed to keep the survivor in an acceptable state of health until rescue is effected.

The individual survivor in the water, or a group on a raft or in a boat, is a very small object in the immensity of the sea and if the sea is rough or visibility bad detection becomes even more difficult. An active survivor sees a ship or hears an aircraft before the look-outs observe him, so he is provided with means to draw attention to himself. When unable to help himself at the last extremity of survival, detection devices are available which are independent of human activity.

The requirements and recommendations concerning safety and survival equipment carried on shipboard are given in the International Convention for the Safety of Life at Sea (SOLAS) 1960. Implementation in the UK is given by the Merchant Shipping (Lifesaving Appliances) Rules 1965, which are administered by the Department of Trade and Industry.

Certain items which affect the safety of life, such as lifting appliances, are tested in accordance with the Dock Regulations. Test certificates are obtained and the safe working load is marked on each item. The tests are made at prescribed intervals.

The safety and survival equipment carried in aircraft flying over water derive from the Convention on International Civil Aviation (ICAO) 1963. The body concerned with these matters in the UK is the Air Registration Board.

LIFEBUOYS AND JACKETS

Lifebuoys

The familiar ship's lifebuoy is of circular shape, with inside diameter of 18 inches and outside diameter of 30 inches. A man-overboard is able to pass his head and shoulders through the buoy and, whilst still active, keep his face above water. Beckets (loops of rope) are fitted and securely seized to the buoy and at least one lifebuoy on each side of the ship is fitted with a buoyant lifeline of length not less than 15 fathoms. Lifebuoys are sited at easily accessible positions and are capable of being rapidly cast over the side. At least two of them are sited where they can be quickly released from the navigating bridge; these lifebuoys are fitted with light and smoke markers.

Lifebuoys are strong enough to be hoisted without damage when taking the weight of a man wearing waterlogged clothing. When fitted with canvas breeches suitable for holding a person they are used for transferring personnel from vessels wrecked close inshore.

Rescue Strop

The rescue strop consists of a length of heavy flax webbing, a D-ring at each end, with the centre portion padded with expanded rubber. The two ends of the strop pass through a sliding toggle. The survivor puts his head, shoulders and arms through the loop, with the padded central portion at his back and the sliding toggle in front of him. He adjusts the toggle so that the strop fits close to the body. The free end of a single rope fall led over a davit head is bent to the D-rings and the inboard end is kept in hand by a few men. If there is any severe motion on the water, the right moment must be chosen for commencing to haul in.

Lifejacket

There are many types of lifejacket, lifebelt and buoyancy aid which will support a man in the water, but not all of them will prevent death from drowning. Some are intended for certain circumstances and may be unsuitable for others; for example, an aid with a buoyancy of only a few pounds may be adequate for a person who falls in the water uninjured and within easy reach of a refuge or under the eye of rescuers, but it would be of little or no value to a man-overboard in high seas, or to one who is injured or unconscious.

The ideal lifejacket, better named a lifepreserver, provides sufficient buoyancy high on the chest to cause an unconscious wearer to turn quickly from the face-down to the face-up position with his mouth and nostrils clear above the water, and to keep him in this position regardless of wave motion. It also provides sufficient support around the head and neck to prevent the head from drooping, as would otherwise occur when the survivor is exhausted or unconscious, with possible immersion of the mouth and nostrils. The part round the neck also keeps the back of the head relatively warm and dry, and so has an important effect on the temperature control of the body. The buoyancy of the neck support is kept as small as possible as it reduces the righting effect. A completely immersed life-preserver has a buoyancy force of about 35 pounds.

A lifepreserver with the essential characteristics of adequate and well-placed buoyancy, self-righting ability and head support causes the inert wearer to float with his face upwards and to windward and with his body at an angle of about 45° to the surface of the sea. As wind and waves are usually in the same direction, this means that the survivor faces the oncoming waves. The lifepreserver is therefore so shaped and constructed that moving water does not seep over the jacket or up channels on to the face. When facing oncoming waves the survivor is able to time his breathing to best advantage; a survivor whose lifejacket causes him to float with his back to the waves might inhale water from an unexpected breaker.

The lifepreserver is also undamaged and remains firmly in place when the wearer falls or jumps from a height, as when abandoning ship, and it does not cause injury on impact with the water or discomfort through prolonged wearing. In order to aid detection the lifejacket is of conspicuous colour, usually traffic-yellow which shows up distinctly against sea water, and is generally fitted with a two-tone whistle and an electric lamp.

The general service lifepreserver used in the Royal Navy consists of an inflatable stole fitted for oral inflation only and a belt and harness incorporating a lifting becket. The deflated stole is packed in a pouch which includes a toggle and line and a battery for the lamp. With the pouch worn in the small of the back the sailor is completely unimpeded and can pass through the escape scuttles and hatches. On standing into danger the pouch is swung round to the front of the body, and the stole is withdrawn and passed over the head. A few exhalations are sufficient to inflate the stole; the whole operation takes but a few seconds. The Royal Navy also has a special gas-inflated lifepreserver which incorporates a 34-gram CO_2 cylinder activated by sponges which expand immediately on immersion. The sponges are protected from spray and rain to prevent unwanted inflation. In addition, the gas inflation can be made manually by a twist-and-pull motion on the operating head; an oral inflation tube is also fitted. The lifepreserver worn by submariners consists of an inflatable stole which is integral with the submarine escape and immersion suit. It includes two pressure relief valves to take account of varying pressure as the submariner rises to the surface. The stole is inflated from the submarine's compressed-air line.

When operating in shark-infested water a packet of shark repellent is carried with RN lifejackets.

Lifejackets provided on Merchant Ships are usually of the inherently buoyant type containing a closed-cell plastic or plastic bags containing kapok. Illustrated posters giving full instructions for donning and securing are exhibited in cabins and other passenger spaces, and all passengers on long voyages have lifejacket drill shortly after leaving port.

Aircrew lifejackets consist of a gas-inflated stole which is generally mounted on a waistcoat; some are an integral part of an underwater ejection escape system and others are blast resistant for when ejecting at high speed.

Specially designed lifejackets are available for particular military, industrial and other uses. Some have a dual purpose, such as the canoeist's and diver's lifejacket, which permits of unimpeded movement when canoeing and, by adjustment of the stole, accommodates the diving lung.

SHIPS' LIFEBOATS AND RAFTS

The boats are designed to have good seakeeping qualities and to remain afloat with positive stability when open to the sea.

They are made of rigid materials and are of sufficient strength to enable them to be lowered in the fully laden condition to the water. Arrangements such as air cases and buoyant materials are provided inside the boat to limit the effect of swamping.

Lifeboats are carried on each side of a ship. Their aggregate capacity, taking into consideration any rafts carried, is governed by the SOLAS regulations. The DTI requires certificated lifeboatmen for each lifeboat on every sea-going passenger ship, the number depending on the boat's complement.

Motor Lifeboats

Boats carrying more than 100 persons must be motor boats; those which carry more than 60 but not more than 100 must either be motor boats or be fitted with a mechanical propulsion system. The number and speed of motor boats depend on the size and service of the ship, but in general at least one motor lifeboat is carried in cargo ships and two (one on each side) in passenger ships. Fuel is carried for 24 hours' continuous operation. The engine is of the compression-ignition type, kept in a state of readiness, protected from the weather and provided with a fire-resisting cover. At least two portable foam-type or dry powder fire extinguishers suitable for oil fires are carried in the boat plus a sand box and scoop.

Motor lifeboats with a radio cabin have a dynamo fitted to the engine for recharging the radio battery; the dynamo must not be wired to any other equipment. The radio battery must not be used for engine starting or for any other purpose.

Mechanically Propelled Lifeboats

The mechanical gear is capable of being operated manually by persons untrained in its use and is fitted with a device whereby the helmsman can put the boat astern when the gear is in operation. The gear is adequate for getting the boat clear of the ship's side and keeping its heading under adverse weather conditions.

Tanker Lifeboats

Special arrangements are available for tanker lifeboats to take account of the greater possibility of fire at sea. Ideally, personnel should be able to board the boats safely, launch them through fire, cast off and get safely away, and the boat should still be suitable as a normal lifeboat.

A totally enclosed lifeboat approved by the DTI is constructed of glass-reinforced plastic; the hull is pigmented white and the canopy international orange. Water sprinklers are fitted to spray water over the outside of the boat, all external surfaces being shaped to ensure maximum coverage. Embarkation is through two inward-opening doors in the canopy amidships. Propulsion is by a diesel engine with a closed fresh water cooling system which allows the engine to be run up and warmed through whilst the boat is still at the davits. A large capacity compressed-air cylinder in the bottom of the boat supplies air to the occupants and the engine, and drives a pump for delivering water to the sprinkler system. The coxswain's position is forward, provided with a large viewing port, steering wheel, controls for the engine and the Mills release gear. A slight positive pressure inside the hull prevents fumes from entering.

The totally enclosed boat without the sprinkler system, providing maximum protection from exposure and fumes, is available for ships other than tankers.

Stowage

Every lifeboat is attached to its own set of davits by the sling hook or release gear at each end of the boat engaging a ring or link on the underside of the lower fall block. In general, all davits are sited on one deck, high enough to be clear of the sea in rough weather and sited at positions from which launching can take place with the maximum degree of safety. They are clear of any discharges which may foul the boat during launching and embarkation.

Davits are of two kinds, the luffing type for boats weighing not more than $2\frac{1}{4}$ tons in the light condition (namely boat, equipment, stores and two crew members only) and the gravity type for all other lifeboats.

Launching

The arrangements are such that a lifeboat can be launched with the ship listed 15 degrees either way and at a trim of 10 degrees. Skates are provided to facilitate launching against a list of 15 degrees.

The boat is served with wire falls and a winch. A span between the two davits carries two or more lifelines of sufficient length to reach the water under the most adverse condition of draught and list. To launch the boat the operator releases the hand brake on the winch and holds it in the 'off' position. In the event of the operator losing control the boat will be stopped in its descent until control is recovered. A built-in centrifugal brake controls the rotation of the winch drum paying out the falls, thus ensuring a safe and steady speed of descent of between 60 and 120 feet per minute.

On gravity davits automatic tricing pendants bring the boat against the ship's side. Bowsing-in tackles or lines are used to hold the boat while the passengers embark. The tricing pendants are cast off *before* the passengers are embarked.

Frapping lines passed around the falls above the lower block are used to prevent swaying when the ship rolls. To prevent swinging when the ship pitches the frapping lines are given a fore and aft lead or painters at bow and stern are held taut.

Embarkation

Ladders or other means of embarkation are also provided; there is at least one ladder down each side of the ship for embarking on a water-borne boat. There is special illumination in the form of electric lighting for the launching position and the embarkation area.

Fittings and Equipment

Items for handling and navigating the boat include buoyant oars and steering oar, thole pins or crutches, boat hook, rudder and tiller, mast or masts with orange-coloured sails, magnetic compass in binnacle, sea anchor and associated vessel containing a gallon of oil, an oil lamp with oil sufficient for 12 hours and two boxes of matches.

Cordage includes a lifeline becketed around the outside of the boat, two painters (one secured to the forward end of the boat with strop and toggle so that it may be released, and the other firmly secured to the stem and ready for use), grab lines secured from gunwale to gunwale under the boat and two light heaving lines. A hatchet is provided at each end of the boat.

Signalling equipment comprises four parachute signals

giving a bright red light at high altitude, six hand flares giving a red light, two buoyant smoke signals (giving an orange-coloured smoke, for daytime use), electric torch (with spare batteries and bulb), daylight signalling mirror and whistle.

Fresh-water rations are six pints (or three litres) per person the boat is designed to carry, or four pints (or two litres) plus a desalting apparatus capable of producing two pints (or one litre) of drinking-water per person. A dipper and three drinking-vessels (one graduated) are provided for dispensing the rations. Food rations are determined by each Administration adopting the SOLAS regulations; for UK ships the ration per person is 16 oz. of biscuits, 16 oz. of barley sugar and 16 oz. of sweetened condensed milk of first quality. A jack-knife with tin-opener and one set of fishing tackle is provided.

A manual pump, bailer and two buckets are provided for keeping the boat dry. Boats fitted with plug holes have two plugs for each hole. A waterproof fabric cover of a highly visible colour and fittings for rigging it is provided to give protection from exposure. The cover extends to about two-thirds the length of the boat and is left open at the after end to permit the occupants to escape in the event of a capsize. A searchlight is fitted in motor boats carried on passenger ships and some other types of ship; it has a lamp of at least 80 watts, a reflector and a source of power.

Inflatable Liferafts

The inflatable liferaft offers the best conditions for survival at sea except when there is fire on the water, where the totally enclosed fire-resistant lifeboat gives the only effective protection.

Stowage

The inflatable liferaft packed in its deflated state in a valise or rigid container occupies very little stowage space on shipboard and requires the minimum of launching arrangements. It is readily portable, can be manhandled to the most favourable position for launching, is buoyant and can be inflated within a minute, when it is immediately available for use.

The lashing of a liferaft at its stowage position may incorporate a hydrostatic release gear which can also be operated manually. The gear is set so that it does not operate hydrostatically under a head of water of less than about six feet, which prevents unwanted release should a green sea swamp the stowage. In the event of a ship sinking before the gear can be operated manually, release occurs when the unit sinks below six feet: the retaining cord, the free end of which is secured to a strong point on the ship, uncoils, and when it becomes taut the tension caused by the buoyancy of the packed raft is sufficient to operate the gas cylinders and inflate the raft. The buoyancy of the inflated raft produces a tension which breaks the retaining cord, and the raft floats free on the surface.

Launching and Boarding
Normally the inflatable liferaft is launched over the side, either thrown or dropped manually, or released from a ramp. The retaining cord uncoils and when tugged inflates the raft. Boarding is by side-ladder, man ropes or canvas hoses improvised for the purpose; failing these, the survivors jump on to the raft or as close to it as possible and board from the water. The raft may be jumped on from a moderate height without damage to the fabric or injury to the jumper, but any survivors already aboard should move clear.

Passenger ships are fitted with special davits, usually of single-arm type, for launching loaded liferafts. The liferaft is inflated, held outboard at deck level on the davit and is bowsed temporarily to the ship's side until boarding is completed. It is then lowered to the water by the centrifugal brake on the davit winch. The davit hook is automatically detached when the raft becomes waterborne, recovered up the ship's side and used for succeeding rafts. The stowage, launching and embarkation positions are provided with special illumination and are clear of ship's side discharges which may foul the rafts.

Thermal Properties
The greatest advantage of the inflatable raft is that its buoyancy tube, double floor and double tent provide a complete thermal barrier against the elements. The air inside the raft is warmed by the body-heat of the occupants and the barrier prevents this heat being lost to the surrounding air and water. The smaller the airspace in a raft the quicker will it be warmed by the

occupants; for this reason it is better in cold climates to herd together, filling a raft to capacity, than to occupy a number of rafts to undercapacity.

Raft Equipment

SOLAS 1960 requires that inflatable rafts carried on shipboard be fitted with arrangements for towing, righting and for boarding from the water, a painter, one lifeline all round the outside of the raft and one round the inside, and a marker lamp mounted on top of the tent powered by a sea-activated cell.

SOLAS 1960 also requires that the following equipment be provided: a buoyant quoit and rescue line, floating knife, bailer, two sponges, two sea anchors, two paddles, repair outfit, hand air pump or bellows, three tin-openers, first-aid outfit, graduated drinking-vessel, waterproof torch with spare batteries and bulb, two parachute distress signals, six hand flares, fishing-tackle, food rations, water rations (three pints or one and a half litres for each occupant, one third of which may be replaced by a desalting apparatus capable of producing an equal amount of fresh water), six anti-seasickness tablets for each occupant, survival book and information on lifesaving signals.

Inflatable rafts carried on hovercraft and aircraft that fly over water are generally similar to those carried on ships, but are not so heavy; they are usually made of lightweight proofed synthetic fabrics and some have air-induction devices in order to reduce the weight of the gas cylinder.

Rigid Liferafts

Rigid liferafts are of substantial construction, capable of being dropped into the water from a height without damage to the raft or its equipment. The rafts are stowed clear of overhanging obstructions so as to float free in the event of the ship sinking before they can be launched. They are fitted with a cover of conspicuous colour which can be rigged whichever way the raft floats. Cordage includes a painter and a lifeline becketed around the outside of the raft and there are arrangements for towing the raft and boarding from the water. A buoyant light is attached to the raft by lanyard.

The equipment and rations are the same as for inflatable liferafts.

R

COMMUNICATIONS

Distress Signals

SOLAS 1960 requires that ships be provided with the means of making effective distress signals by day and by night. They are to include at least twelve parachute signals capable of giving a bright red light at a high altitude. British yachts of 45 feet in length and over coming within the regulations of the DTI are required to carry on board six approved rocket parachute signals or six approved red stars. Signal packs suitable for sailing dinghies, off-shore and deep-water cruisers are available from manufacturers.

Day signals consist of orange-coloured smokes. A hand-held type burns for 20 seconds and a buoyant one for 3 to 4 minutes. They are most effective in calm weather; in windy weather the smoke is dispersed and is difficult to detect at sea level, but is still seen fairly easily from the air. It is seldom visible from sea level for more than 2 or 3 miles.

Night signals include rocket parachute red flares, red hand flares and red star signals. The parachute signals are hand-held and eject a suspended flare at a height greater than 1,000 feet, making it visible on a clear night for 35 to 40 miles; even in daylight it is visible for 6 to 7 miles. The red hand-flares have a candle-power in excess of 15,000, but as they burn near the surface they are unlikely to be seen at distances of more than about 5 miles although from the air they can be seen at distances up to about 30 miles. There are various types of red star signal and these are mainly used in boats; they include hand-held types which eject two, three or four stars, rockets which eject stars to a high altitude, and stars fired from a Very pistol.

Of special use in survival craft and small boats is the combined day and night signal, consisting of a smoke at one end and a flare at the other. For the potential man-overboard there is a pocket-size signal comprising a pen-type projector and eight screw-on red cartridges all in a plastic container.

A radar reflective signal is available for use in fog or other conditions of poor visibility. It consists of a rocket which carries some 300,000 radar reflective dipoles and two free-falling red stars to a height of 1,250 feet. The radar echo can be detected by aircraft at ranges of 20 miles and by ships at 10 miles and it persists for up to 15 minutes or more dependent on wind conditions.

Pyrotechnic signals are stowed carefully, in a readily accessible position and clear of heat and dampness. They are replaced at regular intervals, according to the manufacturers' recommendations or Government regulation; replacement is usually three years after date of manufacture. They must be handled with care and pointed clear of the survival craft; flares must be held downwind. Time-expired signals should be weighted and dumped in deep water.

Training in the use of distress signals, particularly at night, is most desirable and the plan of action in an emergency should be carefully prepared. It is of no use firing an orange smoke if there is no potential rescuer within the 2- or 3-mile visibility range, nor firing a hand flare if there is no obvious help within 5 miles. A parachute flare or red signal should first be fired. On the assumption that the Coastguard have seen the signal, allow sufficient time for a rescue craft to begin its search. If the rescue craft is seen or heard (those in distress will almost certainly detect the rescue craft before the rescuers see them) fire a flare or smoke signal. If there is no sign of a rescue craft fire another parachute flare or red star, and repeat the procedure. Endeavour to retain one smoke or flare to aid the rescuer in his final run-in.

Aircraft parachutes flares must be dropped from such a height that they will burn out before touching the water, otherwise any fuel on the water may be set alight.

Radio Equipment

Ships

The radio-operating room is located at the highest possible (and therefore safest) place in the ship, clear of noise and close to the bridge. It is sound-proofed and provided with a two-way system for calling and communication with the navigating position independent of the ship's main communicating system. A clock with dial not less than 5 inches in diameter, with concentric seconds hand marked to indicate the silence periods, is mounted where it is in full view of the radio operator from the positions of operating the radio and testing the auto-alarm. Emergency lighting and essential spare parts are provided.

The radio-telegraph station includes a main and a reserve installation electrically separate and independent of each other, each comprising a transmitter, receiver, source of energy and an aerial. The equipment is capable of transmitting and receiving on the distress frequencies.

A radio-telegraph auto-alarm is actuated by alarm signals transmitted on the distress frequency by coast radio station, ship's emergency or survival craft transmitter. A continuous audible warning is given in the radio room, the radio officer's accommodation and on the bridge. Only one switch, in the radio room, is provided for stopping the warning. The efficiency of the auto-alarm is tested by a radio-officer at least once every 24 hours, usually between his watches, when the auto-alarm is switched on and turned off.

A radio direction finder receives signals for the purposes of distress and direction finding and from maritime distress beacons. It is calibrated on first installation and is checked at yearly intervals. A two-way means of calling and voice communication is provided between the direction finder and the bridge. When not in use the D/F apparatus is tuned to a distress frequency and linked with the ship's auto-alarm receiver; the bearing of the distress transmission is thus available when the alarm sounds.

The radio-telephone station also comprises a transmitter, receiver, source of energy and aerial. A device is incorporated in the transmitter which automatically generates the radio-telephone alarm signal; it is capable of being taken out of operation to permit the immediate transmission of a distress message. The transmitter and receiver both operate on the distress frequency of 2,182 KHz and at least one other frequency in the bands between 1,605 KHz and 2,850 KHz.

Motor Lifeboats

Radio-telegraph apparatus is installed in every motor lifeboat of a ship carrying 1,500 or more persons on a long international voyage. Only one motor lifeboat need be so fitted when the number of persons is less than 1,500 but more than 199.

The apparatus is installed in a radio cabin and is capable

of being operated by an unskilled person. It comprises a transmitter, receiver and an accumulator battery of sufficient capacity to give 4 hours' continuous transmission. Facilities for re-charging the battery, by a dynamo on the engine, are provided where necessary.

The transmitter and receiver operate on the distress frequencies of 500 KHz and 8,364 KHz and in addition transmissions can be made in the bands between 4,000 KHz and 27,500 KHz. The transmitter has a key for manual transmission and an automatic device for the transmission of alarm and distress signals; its minimum normal range on the distress frequency is 25 miles. The transmitter is tested at weekly intervals, and the battery is brought up to full charge if it is a type which requires re-charging.

Survival Craft

A portable radio apparatus, normally kept in the chartroom or other suitable place, is provided on all ships except those which carry on each side of the ship a motor lifeboat fitted with a radio-telegraph installation. It comprises a transmitter, receiver, source of energy and an aerial, all in a compact watertight container, readily portable, buoyant and sufficiently robust to withstand impact with the sea when dropped from a height. An unskilled person is able to transmit a distress signal merely by setting the auto-key and turning the handles which operate the electric generator.

A well-known portable radio equipment is the Clifford and Snell 'Lifeline' Type 610. One of these, manufactured in 1964, was used by Robin Bunker on *Vanda Caela* in the 1964 Single-handed Transatlantic race, and he was able to operate it with a broken wrist. It was then carried by John Ridgway and Chay Blyth on *English Rose III* for their transatlantic row in 1966, by John Ridgway in his attempted circumnavigation in *English Rose IV*, and by Trooper Tom McLean in his transatlantic row in 1969. After each of these voyages the set fully met the required performance specifications without adjustment. It is now (1970) being carried by Chay Blyth on *British Steel* in his attempt to circumnavigate non-stop single-handed from east to west. Another 'Lifeline' was loaned to Eric Shipton for his mountaineering in South America, and then to David Lewis for his circumnavigation in *Rehu Moana*. This set was likewise found to meet full performance specifications on return to the manufacturers. It is now with David Lewis on *Isbjorn*.

There are also available for survival craft various types of radio beacon which transmit homing signals on the aeronautical distress frequencies of 121·5 MHz (international) and 243 MHz (military); some transmit on both frequencies simultaneously. They comprise a transmitter and a battery with a life of 48 hours and most of them have a self-erecting aerial. Some types are buoyant for streaming from survival craft, others are held or are attached to the craft. A special type is available for mounting on inflatable liferafts and lifejackets, the inflation of which releases the aerial and switches on the beacon, thus producing a signal immediately and automatically. A microphone/speaker unit is available for permitting two-way speech between the survivor and the rescue party.

Radio beacon signals are received at distances of up to 200 miles by aircraft at 40,000 feet and up to 60 miles when at 10,000 feet. Ships receive the signals from beacons mounted in survival craft at distances up to 10–12 miles and from the buoyant beacon up to about 25 miles.

Heliograph

The heliograph is used by survivors to flash signals during hours of sunlight. It consists of a metal mirror with a hole at the centre and a foresight attached by a short cord. The foresight is held in one hand about six inches from the eye and in line with the target. The mirror is held in the other hand and the back of the mirror is brought close to the eye. The mirror is tilted until crosslines appear on the foresight and the black spot centralizes on the foresight hole. The reflected sunlight is then 'on target'. Slight movements of the mirror with returns to 'on target' appear as flashes to the observer. In a newer type of heliograph, made by BCB Ltd of Cardiff, an improved foresight carries a strip mirror on the side facing the survivor.

A heliograph may be improvised from a flat piece of bright metal such as the lid of a ration tin, tobacco tin or first-aid container. Punch a small hole in the middle, hold the metal a few inches from the face and sight the searching ship or aircraft through the hole. The sun's rays will pass through the hole on to the face or clothing and be reflected on to the back of the metal. Tilt the metal until the reflected spot disappears through the hole; the sun's reflection from the metal will then be directed to the searcher.

Flash the mirror at the sound of an aircraft even if it cannot be seen—the pilot may see the flash. Also flash along the horizon even if an aircraft cannot be heard nor a ship be seen. Stop flashing as soon as the pilot has acknowledged the signal, otherwise he may be blinded.

Aircraft at 30,000–35,000 feet have observed heliograph flashes. The sunlight reflected from a tobacco tin (Ticklers) at a height of 50 feet has been seen 14 miles away.

Signalling Torch

The signalling torch, as provided in survival craft, has a pre-focused bulb, folding rubber sleeve, plastic lens and is fitted for morse signalling. It is buoyant, waterproof and shockproof and can be operated under water.

Sea Marker

The fluorescine sea marker is a chemical dye which gives a patch of bright conspicuous colour to the surface of the sea. It is of particular value to lone survivors in the water who present a very small target to search forces, but it is ineffective during hours of darkness.

The dye is contained in a waterproof pack fitted with tabs which are pulled apart, exposing the chemical, when the marker is required for use. It is attached to the lifejacket by a short cord which is adjusted for length so that the marker streams just below the surface of the water. When used from a raft the marker should be streamed down wind.

Signalling Lamp

The daylight signalling lamp is an item of ship's safety equipment. It is obligatory on all ships of more than 150 Gross Registered Tonnage when engaged on international voyages, and it must not be solely dependent on the ship's main source of electrical power.

SOFAR Signals

United States aircraft operating over the Pacific carry small devices which when dropped into the sea detonate at a prescribed depth. The sound is received and interpreted by a chain of US Navy Sound Fixing and Ranging (SOFAR) stations. The position data thus obtained is used for search and rescue purposes.

Line-throwing Apparatus

A form of apparatus in general use comprises a 41 mm. rocket pistol with cleaning materials and brush, four 41 mm. line rockets, four 300-yard buoyant polyolefin lines $\frac{1}{2}$ inch circumference and five ignition cartridges.

DRINKING WATER

Solar Still

The solar still consists of a spherical envelope 33 in. (85 cm.) diameter made from transparent plastic sheet (polyvinyl chloride, toxic free). A black cloth is suspended inside the sphere, a water ballast chamber is fitted at the bottom to ensure stability when the still is put in the water, and a funnel is fitted at the top. Seawater is poured into the funnel and its level is maintained between two marks. The still is streamed from the liferaft on a short line.

The heat from the sun is absorbed by the black cloth. Water which drips from the funnel on to the cloth is vaporized, salt is left on the cloth and the vapour condenses on the inside of the plastic sphere. The condensate runs down the sphere into a drain tube in the bottom and finally into a plastic container which is graduated in ounces. Under normal conditions of solar radiation about 0·75 litre of fresh water is obtained each day, or 1·0 litre under good conditions.

Care is necessary in operating the still and full instructions are provided. The still is packed into a small parcel for economy of stowage and is inflated when put to use. Inflation is made orally or by means of the air bellows in the raft.

The still has an indefinitely long shelf-life and a working life of about two months, by which time the accumulation of salt on the black cloth reduces its efficiency. The knowledge that drinking water can be produced for this period is a great aid to morale.

The mirror effect of the condensed water on the inside of the still provides an important secondary use; it has been seen from aircraft long before the liferaft to which it is attached.

Chemical Desalters

The solids dissolved in seawater, which amount to about 3·7%, may be separated out by ion exchange leaving a water fit to drink. The desalting kit comprises a purifier bag made of rubberized fabric containing an integral filter, a storage bag also of rubberized fabric and chemical charges. The chemical charges consist of mixed silver barium zeolite, silver ion exchange resin as a disrupter for the charge, a small amount of graphite and activated carbon. Seawater is measured into the purifier bag to an indicator line, and a chemical charge is added which, after its integration, is shaken for 30 minutes. The water is then squeezed out of the purifier bag through the filter to obtain clear treated drinking-water.

Electro-Dialytic Desalter

Desalting apparatus based on the electro-dialytic process is available for use in lifeboats. The apparatus comprises: one membrane stack, consisting of pairs of ion-exchange membranes providing a number of dialysation and concentration cells which form parts of separate circulation systems; two manually operated circulating pumps; one manually operated direct current generator, with handles for operation by two men simultaneously; one dialysate tank, of capacity about 12 litres; associated piping, valves and fittings.

Fishing Kit

A typical fishing kit, as supplied by BCB Ltd, Cardiff, for survival craft, comprises a length of nylon twine, six hooks and a one ounce pear-shaped weight. A shaped spoon, cut from a water can, silver paper or any shiny object such as a coin or button, is used as bait. After the first catch the scaly skin and entrails can be used. Bright pieces of cloth, feathers, etc., make useful lures.

Do not secure the fishing line to the person or the craft. Take special care of fish-hooks in an inflatable craft.

Use a mirror to reflect moonlight in the water to lure fish. Rig rubber sheeting to reflect moonlight and snare leaping or flying fish. The torch may be used very sparingly at night to lure fish, but only if battery-power is plentiful.

MEDICAL KIT AND FIRST-AID PACKS

Ships

British ships, with certain exceptions, carry medicines and medical stores in accordance with *Merchant Shipping Medical Scales*, copies of which are obtainable from Her Majesty's Stationery Office. Scale I applies to ships which are obliged by law to carry a qualified medical practitioner; Scales II and III apply to other ships, the actual scale depending on the area in which the ship trades. In ships which do not carry a doctor, the Master, or a nominated member of the crew, should have a knowledge of first aid in advance of that of the normal first-aider ashore.

A copy of the *Ship Captain's Medical Guide*, which is also obtainable from HMSO, is carried on British ships, and some ships also have a copy of *Radio-Medical Assistance*, published by the Centro Internazionale Radio-Medico, Rome, or *The International Medical Guide for Ships* (World Health Organization, 1967).

Yachts, Boats and Small Craft

All yachts, boats and small craft should carry at least one standard first-aid pack comprising standard dressings, scissors and antiseptic creams with the addition of anti-seasickness and analgesic tablets. It is also advisable to carry a good standard text-book on first aid, preferably one printed on water-proof paper.

A seafarer undertaking a long voyage should consult his medical adviser before setting out and equip himself with the medical supplies to deal with the illnesses and upsets that may arise, taking into account, for instance, the dangers of sailing near malarial coasts. Usually surprisingly little untoward occurs and the seafarer remains very fit.

The following kit for a lone seafarer is based on advice given by Dr David H. Lewis; the quantities should be assessed on the longest estimated time between successive ports of call. Morphine is excluded as its use may so impair judgement as to put the lone seafarer in jeopardy.

First-Aid Pack: Standard type, comprising standard dressings, scissors and antiseptic cream

Dressings: Waterproof adhesive bandages
Adhesive elastic bandages, 3 in.
Cotton wool
Gauze
Crepe bandages

Instruments: Dressing forceps
Splinter forceps

Medicaments: Anti-seasickness tablets, Hyoscine hydrobromide 0·3 mg.
Antibiotic tablets, Oxytetracycline 250 mg.
Phthalylsulphathiazole 500 mg.
Aspirin 500 mg.
Analgesic-compound tablets of aspirin 250 mg., paracetamol 250 mg. and codeine phosphate 9·58 mg.
Antiseptic cream, Dibromopropamidine 25 g. tubes
Anti-scurvy tablets, Ascorbic acid 50 mg.
Protective skin cream, Kerodex No. 78 (Total Spectrum)
Eye drops, Amethocaine hydrochloride 0·5%
Eye ointment, Neomycin and Hydrocorticone
Foot powder, 'Tineafax'

Where two or more persons are sailing together morphine injection ampoules of 15 mg. may be added to the above kit.

Survival Craft
Based on survivors' reports such as are included in this book two types of first-aid pack are recommended for provision in lifeboats and liferafts, namely a basic pack suitable for short-term exposure when rescue may be expected within three days and a supplementary pack for when exposure is likely to be of

long duration. The quantities suggested for each pack are relative to ten survivors.

Dressings	Basic Pack	Supplementary Pack
Standard medium dressing (No. 14 BPC) 6 in. x 4 in.	2	4
Standard large dressing (No. 15 BPC) 8 in. x 6 in	2	2
Waterproof adhesive dressings, assorted sizes	12	12
Waterproof adhesive plaster, 1 in. wide, reel of 5 yards	—	1
Cotton wool, 1 oz. packets, sterilized	2	2
Bandages, cotton, 3 in. wide	—	4
Triangular bandages, linen	2	2
Safety pins, rustproof	12	12
Instruments		
Scissors, rounded ends, 5 in.	—	1
Forceps, rounded ends, 5 in.	—	2
Medicaments		
Anti-seasickness tablets, Hyoscine Hydrobromide, 0·3 mg.	100	—
Antibiotic tablets, Oxytetracycline 250 mg.	40	40
Analgesic-compound tablets of aspirin 250 mg., paracetamol 250 mg. and codeine phosphate 9·58 mg.	—	24
Morphine injection capsules, 15 mg.	2	4
Antiseptic cream, Dibromopropamidine 25 g. tubes	1	2
Soft paraffin jelly, 50 g. tubes	1	2

The standard dressings, Nos. 14 and 15 BPC, consist of a cloth dressing with cotton-wool pad sewn on to a cotton bandage. The whole dressing is wrapped and sterilized. It is unwrapped and placed on the wound without the need for any cutting or adjustment.

The waterproof adhesive bandages are for use on small wounds, cuts and abrasions. They consist of a small medicated gauze pad in the centre of waterproof adhesive material; the adhesive effectively seals right round the wound.

The cotton wool should be in separate small packets, the unopen packets thereby remaining clean and dry.

The triangular bandage can be used as a sling or, when folded, to secure dressings or splints. Simple drawings should be printed on the bandage, showing its uses.

The scissors and forceps have blunt rounded ends to avoid accidental damage to the fabric of inflatable liferafts.

There are many kinds of anti-seasickness tablets and it is prudent for seafarers to establish by personal trial the type and strength which suits them best. In light of the many tests carried out by the Royal Navy hyoscine hydrobromide is recommended. The strength suggested is 0·3 mg. If at all possible two tablets should be taken about one hour before exposure to unusual motion and certainly immediately on boarding a survival craft. Subsequent dosage is one tablet every 6 hours for the next 48 hours.

The antibiotics should be chosen for their keeping qualities, their effectiveness in a wide range of infections and for minimal side effects. No single antibiotic is ideal and new ones frequently become available. At present 250 mg. tablets of oxytetracycline satisfy the conditions reasonably well; the dose is one tablet at six-hourly intervals for five days. The phthalylsulphathiazole 500 mg. tablets for the long-distance seafarer is for dysentery; the dosage is 10 tablets a day in divided doses.

The familiar aspirin is recommended for slight pains and discomforts and the compound tablets of aspirin, paracetamol and codeine phosphate for severe pain as from sprains, jellyfish stings, feverishness, diarrhoea and violent seasickness. The dosages are two tablets chewed up and swallowed, repeating if necessary every four hours, but not more than eight tablets should be taken in 24 hours. Morphine is used for extreme pain and for quieting mentally disturbed people whose behaviour might threaten the safety of their companions. It must *not* be used, however, in cases of unconsciousness, severe head injuries or other injuries causing impairment of breathing, or of alcoholic intoxication. It is supplied in 15 mg. ampoules fitted with a hypodermic needle ready for injection. Each ampoule should be packed in a separate waterproof container and clear instructions as to use and the contra-indications for morphine should be printed both on the outside and the inside of the container.

The antiseptic cream should have good antiseptic properties and not be likely to cause allergic reactions. Dibromopropamidine is recommended.

The soft paraffin jelly is used for removing oil contamination, especially around the eyelids, for softening hard, rough patches of skin, relieving inflammation of eyes caused by flashburn and tropical sun, and for applying to salt-water boils and to burns of face and neck.

The eye ointment is for treating inflammation of the eye and the eyedrops to relieve pain when removing foreign bodies. For the eyedrops Amethocaine hydrochloride 0·5% in single dose disposable units ('Minims', Smith and Nephew Pharmaceuticals Ltd) is recommended.

For long sea voyages, where the diet may be deficient in Vitamin C, one 50 mg. Ascorbic acid tablet should be taken daily.

Shark Repellent

The shark repellent in general use consists of nigrosine dye and an acid substance which irritates the shark's eyes. The type manufactured by BCB Ltd of Cardiff comprises a porous bag containing the repellent, packed in a light metal tube with closure.

In use, the bag is withdrawn from the tube and is kneaded in the water until a dark discoloration is obtained; the bag should then be replaced in the tube. The discoloration extends over a cylindrical volume of 8 feet diameter on the surface to 8 feet depth and is therefore ample to conceal a survivor. Two such repellents kneaded near the ends of a craft would conceal the submerged part of the craft. The discoloration lasts for 2 hours. The bag may be kneaded to give five discolorations, thereby providing a repellent effect for a total of 10 hours.

Not all sharks are man-eaters, and some are inquisitive only. Do not use the repellent needlessly, but when it is used, use it properly. A discoloration less than the full dark colour may well attract and not repel sharks.

CLOTHING

The body needs light clothing in hot climates to give protection from the sun and, by soaking with water during hours of sunlight, to reduce the rate of dehydration. The individual survivor is usually able to provide such clothing from his own resources and no arrangements are made for special supplies.

Warm, dry clothing is necessary in order to protect the body from exposure to cold. This clothing reduces the rate at which the body loses heat to the surrounding air or water by providing a thermal barrier, by keeping the body dry and shielding it from the wind. The insulation value of the clothing is reduced by wetting, either by perspiration on the inside or by moisture on the outside, by soiling or by compression of the material, as at the joints, the seat or under straps, belts or other constriction.

Cold-weather Clothing

Underwear should be loose fitting to provide an air barrier next to the skin during periods of inactivity and ventilation when active. A thick cotton vest holds the air in its mesh when the body is still but allows for air flow when the body moves; the fibre has a good wicking action, which picks up body moisture and distributes it throughout the garment; the fibre also dries out easily and completely.

A shirt or similar garment is necessary to contain the air gap created by the vest and it also has an insulating effect depending on the thickness and nature of the material. Then two or three thin woollen pullovers, or a thick knit sweater with or without a thin under pullover. Finally a windproof and waterproof jacket. A thick light-weight quilted jacket filled with nylon or terylene fibres, with elasticated cuffs, drawstring round the bottom and a detachable hood is available. When worn with woollen underclothes an electrostatic charge is built up sufficient to cause sparks; these are a very serious hazard in the presence of volatile fuels and certain explosives. When wearing such a jacket cotton underclothes should be worn and on removing the jacket the wearer should 'earth' himself, for example by touching the exposed metalwork of the ship's structure, to discharge the static electricity.

261

For the legs, woollen trousers over long pants or flannel pyjama trousers. Two pairs of socks, the inner pair thin and the outer one of thick knitted wool. Leather boots.

The face and hands should be well protected. The parka hood is effective and mittens are better than gloves for withstanding the cold.

Fishermen wear a two-piece suit, consisting of smock and trousers, made from a foamed material with a synthetic rubber outer surface, which usually has a conspicuous colour in order to aid detection in the event of the wearer being washed overboard. Heavy gloves are used for handling trawl gear, and lighter ones for gutting fish.

In extremely cold climates the Royal Navy uses sheepskin caps and duffel coats and showerproof, kapok-padded Arctic coats, jackets and trousers. These items are expensive on stowage space and two other assemblies are available. The lightest assembly comprises an electrically heated coverall (complete with electrically heated socks and gloves), string vest, long knitted drawers, action/working dress shirt and trousers, white jersey, Balaclava helmet, rubber goggles, one pair of seaboot stockings and oversized half Wellington leather boots with felt inner sole. Another assembly, which is not electrically heated, comprises wind and showerproof hooded jacket and trousers (made of polyurethane coated nylon), string vest, long knitted drawers, action/working dress shirt and trousers, two white jerseys, Balaclava helmet, rubber goggles, PVC mittens, fleece fabric inner gloves, two pairs of seaboot stockings and oversized half Wellington boots with felt inner sole.

The thick woollen clothing traditionally worn by seafarers gives some protection if the wearer falls in the water, but if the temperature is low and the period of immersion likely to last more than a few minutes, then special clothing is necessary. Moreover the accumulation of trapped air may result in a dangerous posture; air trapped near the feet, for example, may well result in the head being forced under the water and the survivor would find it very difficult or even impossible, to attain a safe posture.

Survival Suit

The simplest form of protective garment is the one-piece survival suit made from waterproof materials coloured fluorescent flame orange. It completely covers the feet, legs, trunk and arms and is fitted with a hood which gives protection to the head, leaving the hands and face exposed. Rubber wrist seals are fitted to the sleeves and there is a drawstring and non-slip rubber toggle at the neck, which is made wide to facilitate donning the garment.

The survivor normally dons his lifejacket as a first precaution; the suit is therefore made large enough to fit over the lifejacket. Such a garment unfortunately involves a large amount of entrapped air and to minimize the amount of air at the most dangerous position, namely the feet, tapes are provided for securing round the legs, below the knees and at the ankles. As an additional precaution, when abandoning ship or otherwise taking to the water, the survivor jumps feet first. This has the effect of forcing air up through the suit and out at the top, which does not make a watertight seal against the neck of the survivor. Water which has entered the suit is removed when the survivor is on a liferaft by unplugging a drain hole at the heel of each leg of the suit.

The suit is not suitable for wearing on shipboard for any length of time as it is impermeable to body vapours. It is supplied to RN personnel operating in cold waters as a 'once-only' suit for emergency use only. It is kept rolled and packed in a pouch attached to the lifejacket and is therefore immediately available with the lifejacket.

Survival Bag

The bag measures only 4 in. x 2 in. x 1 in. when packed, but opens out to 6 ft 6 in. x 3 ft and is thus capable of enveloping a man. Made from aluminized polyester film, about 0·005 in. thick, it reflects up to about 90% of the user's body heat. It is carried in the inflatable rafts of deep-sea fishing trawlers; undoing the bag and getting into it is difficult in a crowded, tossing raft. The bag is not suitable for use in the water.

Exposure Suit

The exposure suit consists of two layers of lightweight proofed material with air or gas at low pressure between the layers and is intended for survivors on open rafts or boats. The two layers are held together every few inches by spacer diaphragms which give the suit a quilted appearance.

For survival in cold climates it is advisable to have plenty of warm clothing under the exposure suit.

A special hooded suit of this type is the Submarine Escape and Immersion Suit, used in the Royal Navy, which enables a man to rise from a sunken submarine, float at a safe posture on the surface and protect him from exposure. The suit includes an inflatable stole, a gas cylinder for inflating the suit, oral inflation valve for topping-up, and hood with central viewing panel. Additional equipment are insulating mitts, goggles, nose clip and padded pants for absorbing urine. The wearer inflates the buoyancy stole, which is integral with the suit, from air in the escape tower. This clean air overflows via two relief valves into the hood and is breathed. Any excess air and carbon dioxide escapes from an opening in the bottom of the hood. On reaching the surface the wearer first unzips the hood to breathe from atmosphere; he then gags the relief valves in the stole and inflates the suit from the CO_2 cylinder. To urinate, he deflates the suit and turns over; the suit is reinflated through the oral inflation valve.

Immersion Suit

Aircraft of the fighting services may be involved in sudden emergency in which there would be no time for the crew to don special clothing. Aircrew who are at hazard over water must therefore wear clothing which permits ventilation when in normal use, but is sufficiently waterproof to keep the body dry when the wearer is immersed for the longest period expected. 'Ventile' water-resistant woven cotton fabric meets these requirements.

One type of Aircrew Immersion Suit is in two pieces consisting of blouse and trousers with half Wellington boots attached. Each garment is made from two layers of Ventile material. The blouse is fitted with neck, waist and wrist seals and the trousers with a waist seal. The two waist seals are rolled together to provide watertightness. A parka-type hood is temporarily attached to the blouse and may be arranged so as to clear the flying helmet. The trousers are fitted with a urinating sleeve which can be made watertight.

Another form of the Ventile suit is in one piece, with two slide fasteners to permit donning. This suit is also available in other materials—a lightweight version in impermeable fabric and a tough working suit in neoprene proofed core spun terylene fabric. The latter suit is used particularly by helicopter crewmen who may have to go into the water; the winchman opens the sliding fastener across the chest to provide ventilation when he is not actually engaged on a rescue operation.

Mitts

These are made from an outer layer of rubber proofed fabric, an inner layer of cotton fabric and insulating material between the two layers. They are fastened by the oral inflation of a bladder which encircles the wrist. They are not normally worn when flying, but are usually carried in the survival pack.

Wet Suit

The two-piece suit, as normally worn for water sports, consists of a tunic and trousers made from an expanded neoprene which is sometimes reinforced with a stretch nylon fabric; the thickness of the material is $\frac{3}{16}$ inch. The four-piece diving suit comprises a combined vest and hood $\frac{1}{8}$ inch thick, tunic and trousers $\frac{1}{4}$ inch thick and bootees $\frac{3}{16}$ inch thick. Materials of other thicknesses, for particular applications, are available.

The expanded neoprene is a closed-cell foam which acts as a thermal barrier between the water which has entered the suit and the surrounding sea. The suits are usually made a stretch fit, so that the water which enters forms a very thin layer; this is quickly warmed up from the body-heat, after which the rate of loss of body-heat is greatly reduced. The garments overlap one another so as to restrict the flow of water inside the suit.

The thicker the foamed neoprene the greater is its insulating value and buoyancy and, in consequence, the heavier are the weights needed for underwater swimming or diving. The deeper the dive the greater the compression of the foam and the less the insulating value and buoyancy.

Fire-Resistant Clothing

Protective clothing is available for use in fighting fires on ship-board. Early types of clothing are the fearnought smocks, trousers and gauntlets, all flame-proofed by the borax/boric acid method. Later types include reflecting surfaces (e.g. aluminized) to give protection from radiant heat, materials of high thermal resistance and non-combustibility, e.g. asbestos and glass fabrics, and cotton and other textiles treated chemically, e.g. with antimony oxide, for fire retardance. An air barrier in the clothing, such as that provided by a string vest, adds greatly to the insulation.

Headwear with visor, handwear and non-slip footwear giving protection from fire are also available.

ANTI-GAS EQUIPMENT

Explosimeter or Flammable Gas Detector

The explosimeter is a portable instrument used in a compartment for determining whether a flash or explosion is likely to occur therein. One form of the instrument comprises a chamber into which a sample of the atmosphere is drawn by means of a rubber bulb. In the chamber there is an electrically heated filament forming part of a Wheatstone Bridge circuit which measures the heat generated by the burning of the sample and activates a needle on a dial. If the needle moves to 100 on the dial the atmosphere is highly dangerous, for it would flash or explode on ignition. If the needle registers less than 100 then the atmosphere is either too lean or too rich to react. To determine whether the atmosphere is too lean or too rich a diluted sample is taken by the use of a dilution attachment provided with the instrument. A sample is taken at the same place in the compartment as the original sample. If a higher reading is obtained the original sample was too rich for flashing or exploding. Samples are taken at various levels and parts of the compartment.

Flammable/Toxic Gas Indicator

An improved type of instrument is a self-contained unit operating from internal dry cells and having a sensor mounted on a flexible probe. It has ranges of 0–100% and 0–10% of the Lower Explosive Limit and can be calibrated for individual gases or groups of gases as required. Compared with the instrument described above it has the advantages of immediate response, the sample at the sensor is the same as at the probe end (i.e. fuel vapours, etc., have not been absorbed or delayed in the sample pipe) and the lack of an aspirating hand pump eliminates any trouble due to perforation, etc.

Safety Lamp

The safety lamp is used to determine whether there is enough oxygen in a compartment to support life. It is essentially an oil-burning lamp the flame of which is enclosed in a wire gauze cylinder. The flame is watched for changes in appearance; if it becomes dim and unsteady, increases in size and draws to a fine point, if a cap is formed over the top of the flame or the flame is extinguished—then the compartment is dangerous and must be ventilated with clean air and be retested.

The gauze is inspected before the lamp is used and the wick adjusted to give a clear steady flame. The gauze is locked and the key is retained by a person who does not enter the compartment to be tested.

The lamp is protected from draughts whilst being taken into the compartment. It is firstly held at the entrance, then at arm's length at the entrance, then as high as possible (on a stave if necessary) and finally as low as possible (on a line if necessary). If the flame shows no changes the compartment is then entered, the operator maintaining communication with a person outside the compartment, and the lamp is held in upper and lower corners and in any recesses. If the flame still shows no changes the compartment is deemed safe to enter.

The flame safety lamp must not be used before making tests with the explosimeter and must not be used if the explosimeter shows flammable gases to be present.

Smoke Mask

The smoke mask enables a firefighter or rescuer to work in a space containing smoke, vitiated air, petrol vapour, etc. The apparatus comprises a facepiece with window and non-return air outlet valve; a breathing pipe incorporating an inlet valve; and a harness to prevent the breathing pipe dislodging the facepiece during movements of the wearer. The breathing pipe is supplied in lengths of 30 or 60 feet which can be joined together, but the overall length cannot exceed about 120 feet without seriously impeding the air flow, which is induced by

267

the wearer's respiratory effort. A strainer is fitted at the free end of the breathing pipe.

When the smoke mask is in use the strainer is kept in fresh air, free from smoke and water and is tended by a responsible person, who also tends the lifeline on the wearer.

There are some designs where air is pumped into the face mask by a bellows or air blower sited in a pure atmosphere.

Self-contained Breathing Apparatus

The use of a self-contained breathing apparatus by which the wearer carries his own atmosphere around with him permits of greater mobility than when wearing the smoke mask. There are various types of apparatus, but they all have a face mask with a window or eyepieces. One type includes an oxygen cylinder, breathing bag and soda-lime canister.

There are also a number of self-contained compressed-air designs which are approved by the DTI for use on merchant ships. One type consists of a compressed-air cylinder; face mask and demand valve assembly; an auxiliary air-line adaptor which enables a second airline to be plugged into the apparatus; a reducing valve; pressure constant flow valve and a pressure gauge with an auxiliary shut-off valve which shuts in the event of mechanical failure of the pressure gauge. The harness comprises a chest strap and 120 feet of hemp-covered wire lifeline. In another type of this apparatus there are two compressed air cylinders.

The Royal Navy uses a special Damage Control Breathing Apparatus which not only permits of operating in a smoke- or gas-filled compartment but can also be used underwater in a flooded compartment. Its use for diving in open water is limited to qualified divers only. The apparatus comprises two compressed-air cylinders and associated valves fitted to a light metal cradle which is hung on the operator's back; it is kept close to the body by a webbing harness and belt.

8

Treatment following rescue

First-aid treatment in the survival craft is described in Chapter 3. After rescue survivors may require treatment where no medical help is available and something other than simple first aid is necessary. The treatment for the more common conditions arising from exposure at sea is given below.

Medical advice and assistance may be obtained from shore agencies as stated in Chapter 6.

Burns

Swelling of the part often accompanies burns; if the first-aid dressings become tight loosen them. Only if sepsis is present need the dressing be changed. The signs of sepsis (infection) are described on page 272.

If there are signs of sepsis remove the dressing and clean the burn with antiseptic lotion or boiled water. The operator's hands should be scrubbed and he should not touch the burn, the dressings or the swabs. Use instruments sterilized by boiling for five minutes, or by heating in a flame. After cleaning the burn it can be re-dressed, using antiseptic ointment and sterile dressings.

If there is no surgical kit, and if there is gross sepsis of the burn, with pain and fever, improvised dressings will have to be used with a technique which is as clean as possible. This technique is described in the section on wounds on page 273.

Shock always accompanies burns; morphine will relieve pain, and frequent drinks should be given to replace fluid-loss.

Dehydration

Drink as much as possible, in frequent small amounts so as to avoid vomiting. The drinks should be hot if the survivor is cold.

Drowning

When a survivor is found to be not breathing, he must be given artificial respiration immediately (see page 119). Nothing should delay this measure. Artificial respiration must be applied to the victim where he is found, without waiting to move him. It is not possible to drain water out of his lungs, and it is a waste of valuable time to attempt to do this by tipping him. Commence artificial respiration immediately.

On recovery he must be placed in the 'Coma' position (see fig. on page 121), for he may vomit. In the coma position he will be safe, as his air passage will remain clear. Watch him carefully, for he may stop breathing again.

Exhaustion

Survivors who have been without food or sufficient water will be exhausted and debilitated. The stress for survival often keeps them alive long after the body is exhausted by dehydration, exposure, hunger and lack of sleep. After rescue they will need careful treatment and constant supervision.

The first priority is to replace the body fluids, but drinks must be given slowly at first or the survivor may overfill his stomach and vomit. Body fluid should be restored before any surgical treatment is undertaken, and before solid food can be given. Nourishment should be given in liquid form to begin with, firstly milk or sweetened drinks, then thin stews, soups, milk and cereals, etc. Overfeeding in the early stages may cause vomiting and diarrhoea, which could be fatal.

Fractures

The soft tissues around a fracture will swell; inspect frequently and slacken the bandages where necessary. If there is an open wound over the fracture take great care to keep the wound clean. Use only sterile dressings and give antibiotic tablets. Immobilize the part in the most comfortable and practicable way.

Frostbite

Do not forcibly remove any clothing over the affected part, but thaw in warm water and remove the clothing gently. Rapidly rewarm the frozen part in water of 38°–44.5°C (100°–112°F) for up to 20 minutes; if this is not possible apply heavy fabric and a heat pack. Then dry the part and expose it, with moderate elevation, to the warm air of the room. Do not give alcohol or tobacco.

Glare

Place the survivor in a shaded area, where even reflected ultra-violet radiation cannot reach him; alternatively an eye-shade can be improvised. Bathe the eyes with warm saline solution and apply antibiotic eye ointment. For a saline solution use one teaspoonful of salt to one pint of boiled water.

Hypothermia

When exposure to cold is only of short duration the central 'core' of the body is still warm. The best treatment is to rewarm the outer layers of the body as quickly as possible. Warm in a hot bath or wrap in hot towels, changing the towels frequently. Put on warm, dry clothing. Give hot drinks. Do not give alcohol.

When exposure to cold has been of long duration, even the deep 'core' of the body is chilled. (Rectal temperature may be lower than 35°C, 95°F.) Warming the surface of the body will only draw blood to the surface and cause even greater cooling of the inner core; and so will cause death. In this situation survivors should be re-warmed slowly. Cover with blankets to conserve natural body warmth, put in a warm sheltered place and give warm drinks. Give light food as soon as the survivor can swallow and digest it. Do not apply heat to the skin.

If there is any doubt about the temperature of the survivor, or the duration and degree of his exposure, re-warm slowly. Do not be misled by his appearance; his skin may be white or blue. Sometimes people suffering from severe hypothermia have a pink skin.

Immersion Foot or Hand

Handle the survivor very carefully. Remove his clothes and wrap him in warm blankets. Improve the general circulation by placing hot-water bottles near the body, but *never* on or near the affected limbs; wrap the hot-water bottles in fabric.

Oil Fuel Contamination

Smear the eyelids with paraffin jelly. Remove oil from the skin by use of rags moistened with oil of eucalyptus; diesel fuel oil or kerosene will do. Do not remove oil from open wounds; treat the wounds as advised below. Oil on the skin is not dangerous, but the survivor will feel more comfortable when the oil is removed. Give milk or warm sweet drinks.

Salt-water Boils

Bathe the affected parts with hot water, and clean the surrounding skin with surgical spirit, antiseptic lotion or boiled water. If the boils are discharging the removal of the discharge can be increased by applying Magnesium Sulphate paste and covering with dressings. If there are many boils and the patient is ill with the sepsis, give an antibiotic.

Starvation

Give light, easily digested food (milk, soup, etc.) in very small quantities at first, at well-spaced intervals.

Sunburn

Treat as for any form of burn.

Wounds

When survivors are rescued where medical aid is available, full surgical treatment will be given. In other circumstances dressings will have to be improvised and technique modified to fit the resources. The following points should be remembered:

Healing

The body possesses natural powers of healing; keep disturbance of wounds to a minimum. Interference with dressings is indicated only when healing is prevented or delayed by sepsis.

Clots

The clotting of blood stops bleeding, and the clots eventually become involved in the healing tissues. Do *not* disturb them.

Sepsis

Sepsis is indicated by pain, swelling, redness and tenderness of the surrounding area, a foul discharge, and the general effects of fever, loss of appetite, sickness, and eventually delirium. It is important to give antibiotic tablets as soon as sepsis is suspected.

Shock

All wounds will cause surgical shock, the degree of shock depending on the amount of blood loss.

If a wound is septic, and medical aid is not available, change the dressing in a way which is as close as possible to the aseptic technique. The principle is to avoid adding fresh infection from the hands of the operator or from unclean materials. The following rules give guidance on the technique:

Preparation
Do not disturb the first-aid dressings until preparations have been made to re-dress the wound, to treat the patient's shock and to relieve his pain.

The patient. If the wound is very painful, give an injection of morphine fifteen minutes before re-dressing. The effects of shock can be reduced by resting the patient before re-dressing, and by keeping him at rest for several hours afterwards. Give him frequent small drinks. Psychologically, the patient will be helped by the exercise of extreme gentleness, and by the cheerfulness and tact of his mates.

The dressings and instruments. The dressings should be sterile, and the sterile dressings in the first-aid kit are quite suitable. If no sterile dressings are available then the cleanest possible cloth can be used.

Avoid touching the dressings. If forceps are available sterilize them by boiling for five minutes, or by heating in a flame. If there are no forceps, or none can be improvised, then the operator will have to touch the dressing. He should only touch one corner or an edge, and ensure that this touched part is not put over the open wound.

The operator. The operator must avoid adding to infection of the wound; he should wash his hands thoroughly. Scrubbing with a brush, soap and hot water is best. He must not speak when bending over the wound, and he must not breathe on it. A single layer of cloth tied round his head, covering his nose and mouth, will act as a surgical mask.

Removal of the old dressing
The soiled dressing should be removed by someone else, who has first scrubbed his hands. Place it away from the clean dressings and burn it or bury it as soon as possible. The person who has touched the soiled dressings must not touch the clean

ones. If there is no one to help, the operator must clean his hands again, very thoroughly, before applying the new dressing.

Cleaning the wound
Discharge in the wound should be wiped away gently with cotton wool or small pieces of sterile or clean cloth soaked in antiseptic solution or cooled, boiled water. When wiping, use a fresh piece of cloth with each wipe, and each time wipe from the centre outwards. Finally, dry the wound by gently dabbing it with a dry sterile or clean cloth.

Re-dressing
Antiseptic ointment can be applied to the dressing before placing it on the wound. Cover the dressing with bandages, or strips of clean cloth. The bandages should extend beyond the edges of the dressing, to completely seal it off. Be prepared to slacken off the bandage if constriction occurs due to swelling around the wound.

Splints
Rest is important. If the wound is large and on a limb, splints may be used to keep the part still. When applying splints, whether for wounds or fractured bones, always place some soft material between the splint and the limb, to provide for padding and to prevent pressure sores. Inspect the bandages frequently, as swelling of the limb will cause tightening and constriction.

When applying splints for fractured bones, the splint must be extended and secured beyond the joints at each end of the broken bone in order to obtain sufficient immobilization.

Antibiotics
If antibiotic drugs are available give them as soon as signs of sepsis appear. Continue the treatment for the full course, even if improvement occurs in the first few days.

Acknowledgements

Grateful acknowledgement is made to the following authorities, and to the owners of copyright of the publications listed below, for permitting the reproduction of excerpts from reports and books, free of charge:

Public Record Office
United States Coast Guard
Lloyd's List and Shipping Gazette
The Times
The Sunday Times
Le Figaro
The Canberra Times
The Straits Times

AINSLIE, K., *Pacific Ordeal* (Hart-Davis: London, 1956)
ARNOLD, E., *Rescue* (McIntosh & Otis, 1956)
BOND, G., *'Lancastria'* (Oldbourne: London, 1959)
BULLEN, F., *The Cruise of the 'Cachalot'* (Murray: London, 1922)
BURDICK, E. L., *The Blue of Capricorn* (Houghton Mifflin: Boston)
CHEESMAN, EVELYN, *Things Worthwhile* (Hutchinson: London, 1957)
CHICHESTER, F., *'Gipsy Moth' Circles the World* (Coward McCann & Geoghegan: New York)
COPPLESON, V. W., *Shark Attack* (Angus and Robertson: London, 1958)
COWARD, R. V., *Sailors in Cages* (Macdonald: London, 1967)
DAVISON, ANN, *My Ship is so Small* (A. M. Heath (Peter Davies): London, 1956)
DAVISON, ANN, *Last Voyage* (A. M. Heath (Peter Davies): London, 1951)
ELLSBERG, E., *Hell on Ice* (Dodd, Mead & Co: New York, 1938)
EVANS, E. R. B. G., *The Desolate Antarctic* (Lutterworth Press: London, 1950)
GILBERT, P. W., *Sharks and Survival* (D. C. Heath & Co: Lexington, 1963)
GRETTON, P., *Convoy Escort Commander* (Cassell: London, 1964)
GRIMBLE, A., *We Chose the Islands* (Morrow: New York, 1952)
HAWKINS, DORIS M., *Atlantic Torpedo* (Gollancz: London, 1943)
HEYERDAHL, T., *The 'Kon-Tiki' Expedition* (Rand McNally: Chicago, 1950)
JENNINGS, C. O., *An Ocean without Shores* (Hodder & Stoughton: London, 1950)

KLESTADT, A., *The Sea was Kind* (David McKay: New York, 1959)

KNOX-JOHNSTON, R., *A World of My Own* (Morrow: New York, 1969)

LEWIS, D. H., *The Ship would not travel due West* (Hamlyn (Temple Press): London, 1961)

LEWIS, D. H., *Daughters of the Wind* (Gollancz: London, 1967)

LEWIS, D. H., *Children of Three Oceans* (Collins: London, 1969)

LINDEMANN, H., *Allein über den Ozean* (Scheffler: Frankfurt am Main, 1957)

LORD, W., *A Night to Remember* (Longmans: London, 1956)

McCORMICK, D., *Blood on the Sea* (Muller: London, 1962)

McKEE, A., *The Golden Wreck* (Souvenir Press: London, 1961)

DE MONFREID, H., *Sea Adventures* (Penguin: London, 1946)

NANSEN, F., *Farthest North* (Constable: London, 1897)

NAYDLER, M., *The Penance Way* (Morrow: New York)

NEWBY, E., *The Last Grain Race* (Secker & Warburg: London, 1956)

NEWCOMB, R. F., *Abandon Ship* (Holt, Rinehart and Winston: New York, 1960)

OGDEN, W. G., *My Sea Lady* (Curtis Brown (Hutchinson): London, 1963)

RIDGWAY, J. and BLYTH, C., *A Fighting Chance* (Hamlyn: London, 1966)

RIESENBERG, F., *Cape Horn* (Dodd, Mead & Co.: New York, 1941)

ROBERTSON, R. B., *Of Whales and Men* (Macmillan: London, 1956)

ROCKETT, S., *It's Cold in the Channel* (Winant, Towers)

ROSE, A., *My Lively Lady* (Nautical Pub. Co.: Lymington, 1968)

RUSSELL, LORD, *The Knights of Bushido* (Dutton: New York)

SAVIGNY, J. B., *Narrative of a Voyage to Senegal* [Dawsons of Pall Mall: London, 1818]

SCHOFIELD, B. B. and MARTIN, L. F., *The Rescue Ships* (Blackwood: Edinburgh, 1968)

SHACKLETON, E. H., *South* (Macmillan: New York)

SMEETON, M., *Once is Enough* (Norton: New York)

TABARLY, E., *Lonely Victory* (Souvenir Press: London, 1965)

THOMAS, L., *Sir Hubert Wilkins* (McGraw-Hill: New York)

LE TOUMELIN, J.-Y., *'Kurun' Around the World* (Flammarion: Paris; and Hart-Davis: London, 1954)

WARDROP, D., *Sunday at Sea* (Guideposts Magazine: Carmel, New York)

WATERS, CAPT. JOHN M., JR., *Rescue at Sea* (Litton Ed. Pub. Inc: New York, 1966)

WEST, F. L., *Lifeboat No. 7* (Kimber: London, 1960)

WILD, F., *Shackleton's Last Voyage* (Cassell: London, 1923)

WILLIS, W., *The Epic Voyage of the 'Seven Little Sisters'* (Hutchinson: London, 1956)

WORSLEY, F. W., *Shackleton's Boat Journey* (Hodder & Stoughton: London, 1940)

Acknowledgement is also made to copyright holders for permission to reproduce excerpts from the following books:

BARDIAUX, M., *Four Winds of Adventure* (Adlard Coles: London, 1961)

BERGE, V. and LANIER, H. W., *Pearl Diver* (Doubleday: New York)

DE BISSCHOP, E., *'Tahiti-Nui'* (Mr Carlos Garcia Palacios)

BOMBARD, A., *The Bombard Story* (Deutsch: London, 1953)

CALDWELL, J., *Desperate Voyage* (Collins-Knowlton-Wing (Little, Brown): Boston, 1949)

CHASE, O., *The Wreck of the Whaleship 'Essex'*: Edited by Iola Haverstick and Betty Shepard (Harcourt Brace Jovanovich: New York, 1965)

COOKE, K., *What Cares the Sea?* (McGraw Hill: New York, 1960)

FOSTER, C., *1,700 Miles in Open Boats* (Hart-Davis: London, 1924)

GORSKY, B., *'Moana'* (Elek Books: London, 1956)

GORSKY, B., *'Moana' Returns* (Elek Books: London, 1959)

SLOCUM, J., *Sailing Alone around the World* (Hart-Davis: London, 1948)

TIIRA, E., *Raft of Despair* (Hutchinson: London, 1954)

Index